The Library of Literature

Under the General Editorship of
JOHN HENRY RALEIGH & IAN WATT

POEMS
and
BALLADS

ATALANTA
in
CALYDON

The Library of Literature

Algernon Charles Swinburne

POEMS
and
BALLADS

ATALANTA
in
CALYDON

*Edited, with an Introduction
and Annotation, by
Morse Peckham*

THE BOBBS-MERRILL COMPANY, INC.
Indianapolis & New York

Algernon Charles Swinburne

1837–1909

Poems and Ballads was first published in 1866
Atalanta in Calydon was first published in 1865

Preface

This volume offers two books, *Poems and Ballads* (1866) and *Atalanta in Calydon* (1865). They are printed in reverse order of publication because most of the lyrics were composed before the play was written; the direction of Swinburne's thinking goes from the lyrics to the play, and the play is more meaningful if the lyrics are read first. Furthermore, *Poems and Ballads* is presented not in its original form but in the revised form proposed by Swinburne in 1876 but never published; he wished to omit the juvenilia but left the order of the original edition intact.

The text is that of the 1904 edition published by Chatto & Windus. The only differences between the 1904 edition and the 1865 are the correction of a few typographical errors, and the edition was carefully supervised by Swinburne himself. A few errors not discovered by Swinburne have been corrected and annotated.

The annotation is primarily of proper names; a few other unusual words have also been annotated, and several easily misunderstood passages have been clarified. The appendices are designed to provide some background for Swinburne's literary interests up to the publication of *William Blake* in 1867 and the shift into social poetry. They also include Swinburne's principal sources for *Atalanta* and significant fragments of Sappho, the latter to make it possible to observe how Swinburne incorporated many of these fragments, as well as one complete poem, into his own verse.

Contents

Introduction

On July 20, 1876, Swinburne wrote to Andrew Chatto, who had become his publisher in 1873.

Dear Sir

As you tell me that 'even now' many purchasers of Poems and Ballads seem to fancy that some of the contents of the first edition issued were afterwards suppressed, I think it would be advisable to take the opportunity of the appearance of a new edition altered in form to put forward in any fashion of advertisement you may think best an emphatic declaration that from the first day of publication to the present not one line, not one word, not one syllable has been changed or cancelled. The rumour may probably have been spread by the since convicted swindler who robbed me under cover of the name of Moxon, with a view to sell his stolen goods (the copies secretly filched and kept back from the stock transferred to Hotten) at a higher price under false pretences to clandestine purchasers. The advertisement might then I think proceed to this effect; that in the present edition some of the earlier poems will be transferred from this to a forthcoming volume of Early Poems which will contain all and more than all ever yet published. I see by your last account that the Songs of Two Nations were issued while there was yet a considerable stock on hand of the original edition of the Song of Italy; I suppose therefore there can be no reason against the adoption of a similar course in the present case by publishing at once or shortly after (if not simultaneously with) the new edition of P. and B. this companion volume of Early Poems, including The Queen-Mother and Rosamond (though as in the case of the Song of Italy there may be a separate stock on hand of these) together with all the poems removed from P. and B. to this their proper and natural place, and also with additions never before published. By adopting this course it seems to me that you might turn the disadvantage of the current suspicion of incompleteness in the later edition to a positive advantage, and make it actually further instead of injuring the sale of both books. I enclose the list of early poems which would be under these circumstances transferred from the one volume to the other. They would then have to appear in a different order of arrangement; but no change would need to be made in the order of contents of P. and B. beyond their withdrawal. Please keep and return this list when done with. . . .

> Yours Very truly,
> A. C. Swinburne[1]

The publishing history of the 1866 *Poems and Ballads*[2] had been filled with difficulty, confusion, and frustration, and the new proposal was to be no exception. The book had originally been published by the old and dignified firm of Moxon & Co., which had issued so much important nineteenth-century poetry; but James B. Payne, who then owned the publishing house, was frightened by the outcry in the press over Swinburne's book and withdrew it from publication.[3] Swinburne, furious, disregarded the advice of some of his friends to remove the more offensive matter and transferred publication to John Camden Hotten, a bookseller and publisher of dubious reputation, best known for his circulation of erotica. On Hotten's death in 1873 Andrew Chatto bought his firm and thus acquired Swinburne as his most important author. Although in 1876 Chatto & Windus issued yet another printing of *Poems and Ballads* and were to issue 31 more before Swinburne's death, this proposal of 1876 was never carried out. Another letter tells us why, this time to Theodore Watts, Swinburne's financial and legal adviser, and later his friend, house-companion, and guardian:

> October 15 [1876]

My dear Watts

I send by the first post I can manage one line of answer to your last. You know that my own wish was to issue in one volume of the proposed new edition of my books all the poems written as an under-

---

[1] This letter, now in the British Museum, was first printed in T. J. Wise, *A Swinburne Library* (London, 1925); the present text is from Cecil Y. Lang, *The Swinburne Letters* (New Haven: Yale University Press, 1960), III, 199; the letter has also been printed in Georges Lafourcade, *La Jeunesse de Swinburne* (Paris, 1928). The list of poems to be omitted is printed here in Appendix 3.

[2] There was a *Second Series* in 1868, and a *Third Series* in 1889.

[3] He withheld an unknown number of copies on transfer of the stock to Hotten and sold them clandestinely.

graduate at Oxford—viz. the two early plays and some dozen or more of the minor and less important 'Poems and Ballads'—with additions (if you should approve) from one or two remaining MSS of the same date—as Tennyson has done in his later editions. These of course will otherwise remain in MS. I certainly understood from Chatto that he thought this a good plan and likely to prove profitable to the book if duly advertised and explained—but if you are of one opinion with him that it would have the opposite effect, of course that must be the first consideration, and my *Juvenilia* must remain in dust or return to ashes.[4]

We do not know what reasons offered by Watts persuaded Swinburne to change his mind. Certainly in letters of October 2 and 9 to Watts, Swinburne writes as if the matter were settled: he talks about a chronological arrangement for the early poems. Yet it is not impossible to speculate why Watts objected to the plan. That the idea was an excellent one, Chatto, an astute publisher, certainly agreed; and anyone familiar with the original who examines the present edition, the first to follow Swinburne's wishes, will concur. The book —as a book, which is what Swinburne always claimed it was, rather than a collection of miscellaneous poems—is vastly improved by the omission of nearly a third of it, poems not in Swinburne's mature style, poems that weaken the impact of the volume.

But that, very probably, is precisely why Swinburne wanted to do it this way and why Watts advised against it. It was the erotic material that had proved most offensive on its original publication; it was the erotic material that still caused scandal, although, no doubt, it was also at least partly responsible for the continued and steady sale of the book, which, by 1876, had gone through eight printings in ten years. But when it is read without the atypical juvenilia, the erotic subject matter and the strangeness and perversity of so much of that subject matter is intensified; the very continuity of the style strengthens the book's effect. Now Watts was above all anxious to make Swinburne respectable, an increasingly difficult task. For years Swinburne's family and friends had been concerned about his growing alcoholism, and only three years later at the request and with the financial aid of Swinburne's mother, Watts took Swin-

[4] First published in full in Lang, II, 207.

burne in and made a home for him, a home of sobriety and hard work.

However, we also know that Watts repeatedly steered Swinburne away from contentious subjects. For instance, Swinburne wanted to write novels, and so fine a critic as Edmund Wilson thinks that his one completed work of fiction, *Love's Cross Currents: A Year's Letters*—written in 1862, published as a magazine serial in 1877, and finally appearing in book form in 1905—is a brilliant affair. It undoubtedly is; it shows that Swinburne could have written the kind of novel that George Meredith believed himself to be writing. But Watts discouraged him. Why? Watts, to be sure, was prudent, concerned over Swinburne's reputation, eager to make him respectable. But was this mere suburbanity, as Harold Nicolson has suggested? Perhaps, and perhaps not. Watts was by no means a stupid man; he was not incapable of thinking what every person concerned with such problems has observed, that for the alcoholic it is best to avoid the emotionally disturbing. Though as late as 1904 for an English boy to request Swinburne as a book-prize was an occasion for scandal, and though as late as the 1920's the editors of The Modern Library thought *Poems and Ballads* one of the important and liberating modern books, yet in spite of the scandal, by 1876 it had already become part of the literary scene. It would have been reasonable for Watts to have decided that even though publishing it in a new form might add to the sales, as Chatto evidently thought it would, the whole controversy might start up again, and the effect might very well lead to a further deterioration in Swinburne's already deeply distressing condition, a condition which justified the utmost concern. The revival of the scandal, and the effect of that revival on Swinburne—these were possibly the reasons that led Watts to discourage the 1876 proposal. Whatever we may think of him—and it is easy to make fun of him—Watts took care of Swinburne out of admiration and affection; there is no reason not to be generous in assessing his possible motives for preventing the publication of what would have been a book considerably improved over its original form.

For, Swinburne always insisted, it was a book. This edition offers in *Poems and Ballads* and *Atalanta in Calydon* two books, intimately and intricately related; moreover, it offers them in the proper order. *Atalanta in Calydon* was published in March 1865, *Poems and Ballads* in July 1866; yet most of the shorter poems were written before Atalanta. In Swinburne's development as a thinker, the poems explore a problem which is further explored and in part solved in *Atalanta*.[5]

Yet before the special problems in Swinburne's most important poetry can be explored, something needs to be said of the general problem of all of his work. There is an enormous advantage in getting interested in Swinburne at the present time. The whole literary world "knows" that Swinburne's poetry is bad; something, indeed, of a joke; something that no sensible man could possibly read for pleasure or instruction. Everyone knows that the faint signs of a Swinburne revival are but the consequences of the fact that scholars must publish, and that it does not make much difference what they publish about; that since little has been written of late about Swinburne, he makes an admirable subject for scholarship. In such a situation the man of independent and catholic taste is in a happy position; there is no official canon of what is good Swinburne and what is bad—it is all bad. Consequently it is not necessary for him to find out if the canonical judgments are to be relied upon; that trouble he can save himself. All he has to do is to read Swinburne's poetry, explore it, find out what is going in this work, find out for himself why for sixty years or so people of intelligence, learning, and exquisite taste thought Swinburne a great poet, and why a few people think so today.

But if such a reader undertakes to discover Swinburne for himself, he is immediately faced with an enormous difficulty, one which more than anything else has been responsible for the downfall of Swinburne's once great reputation. Swinburne is at once an extraordinarily seductive poet and an extraordinarily difficult one. Because of this his charm has been dismissed over and over again, an untold number of times, as simply a matter of "word-music": in Swinburne, it is alleged, there is nothing but a leaping rhythm that hurls you

[5] See Appendix 2 for Swinburne's publications through 1867, and Appendix 4 for what is known about dates of composition for the two volumes.

along and a completely irresponsible use of the various devices of euphony (or more precisely, phonic over-determination), particularly alliteration. He is recognized to be the greatest virtuoso of sound in English poetry, but that prodigious technique, it is asserted, is entirely without foundation or justification, for Swinburne *says* nothing.

It is not always recognized that the major Victorian poets are in fact difficult poets. To be sure, everyone knows that Gerard Manley Hopkins' work is difficult; so difficult that many think of him still as a "modern poet," though what of his technique he did not learn from Browning he learned from Swinburne. Arnold is admittedly quite transparent; Tennyson seems to be transparent to the point of simple-mindedness, but in fact is an exceedingly subtle, devious, and baffling writer. It is obvious that much of Browning is very difficult indeed, but the most difficult works of Browning are, for the most part, unread even by Victorian specialists, and are generally, though quite unjustifiably, dismissed. But the advantage of Browning over Tennyson is that he looks difficult, and over Swinburne that it is obvious that he is saying something. Swinburne, by contrast, seems to be almost contentless. Yet he is not. Quite the contrary . The difficulty of Browning, like the difficulty of Hopkins, is a difficulty of syntactic compression and distortion. Swinburne also offers a syntactic difficulty, but one of quite a different order. The effect of monotony comes not primarily from the unflagging splendor of the rhythm or the obviously beautiful sound, but rather from the fact that Swinburne constructs his sentences by building them up of long syntactic sub-units; the first sentence of *Atalanta*, for example, is sixteen lines long. What he exploits are the possibilities of parallel syntactic structure. The effect is that the unpracticed reader loses control over the syntax. In Hopkins and Browning the extreme use of elision and syntactic distortion confuses the reader. There is not, so to speak, enough syntactic redundancy to keep the reader oriented. But in Swinburne there is too much syntactic redundancy. In this he resembles to a certain extent Milton; but the difficulty of reading Milton comes from trying to follow a syntactic style of dependent syntactic units, while Swinburne exploits the possibilities of disorienting the reader by presenting him with parallel structures so far apart that it is difficult to remember and grasp their syntactical relationship. The consequence with all four of these poets is that the reader untrained in their syntactic styles loses semantic control. Yet he knows, at least, that Hopkins, Browning, and Milton are saying something; but Swinburne further confuses him by offering a continuum of beautiful sound which seems to have no relationship to anything at all. The result is that for the first three, the unpracticed reader, though baffled, is at least aware that he is not understanding what is before him, but with Swinburne he rapidly comes to the conclusion that there is nothing to understand.

To learn to read Swinburne it is necessary, therefore, to resist with all one's power both the seductiveness of the rhythm and the seductiveness of the phonic character. One must read him slowly, very slowly. The mind must always remain focused intensively on the task of comprehending the syntax, of grasping how the parallel syntactic sub-units fit into the larger sentence construction; and it must do this as they come along, in the order in which the poem offers them. It may be said that there is at every cultural level an upward limit to both the complexity and the length of the syntactic structure that may be comprehended. Obviously, the higher the cultural level, the greater the complexity and the length of the syntactical structure that can be grasped. But the fact is that today the general simplification and deterioration of the cultural milieu have meant that most people are not exposed even in prose to much opportunity for extending the range of their syntactic grasp. The power to extemporize extremely long and complex syntactic structures with an extensive use of parallelisms is rapidly disappearing, and has been for some time; and at the higher cultural levels the sentence fragment, which presents precisely the opposite difficulty from Swinburne's, has long been a standard device in both verse and prose. The first task, then, of the reader of Swinburne is to train himself by extending very far indeed the upward limit of his range of syntactic comprehension. The problem is analogous to that presented by Bruckner's symphonies, which seem too long for people who have trained themselves on shorter symphonies, but are not a

moment too long for those who have developed their capacity to
maintain their attention span during a symphonic movement that
lasts half an hour.

But when the reader who wishes to come to terms with Swinburne has conquered this difficulty—and it takes both time and a
great deal of rereading to do so—he is faced with still further
problems.

Swinburne was born on April 5, 1837. In January 1857 he entered
Balliol College at Oxford, but failed to take his degree and left for
good in the spring of 1860. In that year he published *The Queen-
Mother* and *Rosamond*, two plays in the Elizabethan manner, and
started on another, *Chastelard*, not published until 1865. More than
the other two, *Chastelard* shows the direction in which both his tem-
perament and his poetry were moving, and by 1862, at the latest,
under the pressure of this movement he had achieved a new and for
the first time a truly Swinburnian style, the style we think of as his,
so uniquely his that any attempt by another to use it results only in a
kind of parody. In that year he published six lyrics in *The Spectator*,
but of these only one, "Faustine," was to be retained in the abor-
tive 1876 proposal. However, that year saw also the composition of a number of other poems[6] that belong to what Swinburne
came to think of as the real *Poems and Ballads*. In addition we can
be sure that a number of others were also composed in that year and
in the next, and that probably most were completed before *Atalanta*
was begun in August or early autumn of 1863. "Faustine," then, is
the earliest poem we can be sure of which is in the fully Swinburnian
style, and since it is one of those that aroused and still arouse the
greatest distaste, anger, and contempt, the problem it presents is
crucial.

That problem can be stated in a simple and direct way. Swinburne
was an active masochist; he could achieve sexual pleasure only
through suffering, specifically through being beaten. His letters to
some of his more disreputable correspondents are full of references
to whips; indeed, he composed a long work on the subject, *The*

[6] See Appendix 4.

Whippingham Papers. He was constantly importuning some of his correspondents to tell him about real or imaginary boys being whipped or caned for school offenses. At the time—and to some extent still—it was a basic principle of the English philosophy of education, particularly in such schools as Eton, to which Swinburne went, that the aims of pedagogy, particularly for boys, could not possibly be achieved without the frequent and extremely painful application of the birch rod or similar instruments. It is unquestionable that at an unknown period in his life Swinburne began to experience sexual excitement and pleasure when he was beaten; and *Chastelard* makes it clear that when that feeling was translated into adult sexuality, the only type of woman Swinburne could respond to was masterful, domineering, and punishing, as well as intensely sensual.

As sexual perversions go, neither masochism nor sadism is particularly uncommon; and what little evidence we have seems to indicate that the kind of permanent impact schoolboy whipping had on Swinburne's erotic nature was by no means unusual. In the brothels of Paris sado-masochism was simply called the Engish vice. However, since it is also true that not all English schoolboys grew up to be practicing sadists or masochists, just as not all those who went to the English public schools grew to be practicing and permanent homosexuals in spite of the widespread, perhaps almost universal school practice of adolescent homosexuality, it is clear that his experiences with Etonian whipping could not have been the cause of the erotic tastes which Swinburne retained for the rest of his life, but at best only the catalyst. His Eton whipping teachers did not make him become masochistic; they merely encouraged him. Furthermore, Swinburne was not content to practice masochism; he insisted on writing poetry about it, and poetry about other sexual perversions, such as lesbianism and male homosexuality, though the latter is handled much less obviously. And further, he insisted on publishing that poetry, even though his friends advised him against it, and he insisted on republishing it, intact, after it had created a major literary and moral scandal. The first problem to be faced in trying to come to terms with Swinburne as a poet is whether or not these poems are to be considered as expressions of his sexual tastes or as analyses not merely of masochism and other perversions but also of the relation of such non-normal behavior to the rest of human behavior. Are they symptoms of a compulsion, or do they reveal comprehension? Is he defending his nature, or is he trying to understand it? Does Swinburne think that the comprehension of such aberrations is central to a comprehension of the problems of mankind, or that they are completely discontinuous from what most human beings think is really worth talking about?

Now the traditional interpretation is that they are symptoms of the compulsion of an immature and aberrant sexual personality. And the evidence for this is that *Atalanta*, generally thought of as his finest single work, was little affected by them, and that as soon as he got this material out of his system he turned to political and religious and social problems in his poetry, as indeed he did, beginning in 1867.[7] Nevertheless, rightly or wrongly, Swinburne did not think so. He clearly differentiated between his serious study of the problems of eroticism in *Poems and Ballads* as well as in the much later and altogether remarkable *Tristram of Lyonesse*,[8] on the one hand, and verses such as *The Whippingham Papers* which were verbal indulgences in his compulsions, usually in a joking tone. Put in another way, is the bulk of *Poems and Ballads* literature or is it merely neurotic fantasy?

To ask that question is already to have made a mistake. If the psychologist can examine any utterance for clues to the personality of an individual, he can examine all utterances. A work is, in the technical sense, fantasy or literature not because of the character of the work but because of the character of the investigation, the purposes of the inquiry. Thus even *The Whippingham Papers* are really literature, if one chooses to read them as such and if the purposes of the investigator are literary and not psychological. A psychologist will consider whether the obscene limericks a man chooses to tell exhibit a pattern of selection which is a clue to his personality, but to the ordinary listener whose attitude is a literary attitude, not a psychological one, they are either amusing limericks or they are not.

---

[7] See Appendix 2.
[8] Published in 1882, though begun much earlier; the Prelude was published as early as 1871.

The argument that Swinburne's erotic poems are symptoms of his neurotic disorder and not literary analyses of human emotions is ordinarily put in the following form: since Swinburne was a compulsive masochist, his poems about masochism and sadism must necessarily be merely symptoms of his compulsion. But such a line of argument incorporates a serious error. It depends upon the assumption that to understand a neurotic symptom means to be free of it. This is the claim of too many books of popular psychiatry, and of far too many professional psychiatrists as well: "Know ye the truth, and the truth shall make ye free." The unhappy fact is that the ability to provide an explanation, even an explanation acceptable to one's analyst, for what the neurotic himself regards as undesirable behavior does not entail the power to generate alternative and acceptable behavior. According to Philip Rieff, the author of what is probably the best book on Freud yet to have appeared, *Freud: The Mind of the Moralist*, only the healthy can benefit from psychoanalysis at all, and further, only a tiny fraction of human beings could benefit from analysis as Freud thought of it even if they could have a chance to experience it. Yet Freudian explanations, even explanations the great man might have himself accepted as adequate, are as common as leaves in a forest. An explanation, even a Freudian explanation, is after all only an explanation. Understanding is not ineluctably tied to behavior. It is possible for an individual to have a crystal-clear comprehension of his own undesirable behavior and yet be able to do nothing about it. There is no inherent reason why Swinburne should not simultaneously have had a profound understanding of the failure of masochism as a way of erotic life and at the same time have been quite unable to throw it off. The first two poems in *Poems and Ballads* are "A Ballad of Life" and "A Ballad of Death," both addressed to the same legendary voluptuous, cruel, and domineering woman, Lucrezia Borgia. Masochism leads to the desire for death. Eros, at least of that sort, and perhaps of all sorts, leads straight to the gates of Thanatos. Swinburne knew the longing for death more intimately and profoundly than did any English poet, even Keats, but he did not approve of it. What he approved of was the longing for life and freedom.

It takes, in fact, a considerably more sophisticated comprehen-

sion of eroticism than that offered by popular and literary Freudianism to understand Swinburne; and to do so it is necessary—since
such a vulgarized Freudianism is almost automatic in our culture
whenever sexual and erotic matters are up for discussion—to get
some of the worst Freudian commonplaces out of the way. It is
notorious, of course, that Freud asserted that every personality
disorder may be traced to a sexual disorder. What lay behind this
statement was a chain of reasoning more or less like this:

The consequence of sexual activity is the reproduction of the species, the creation of life. It is therefore meaningful to call activities
which contribute to the creation of life—that is, to the maintenance
of the species—sexual activity. Now the individual is necessary to
the maintenance of the species. All activities, then, that contribute
to the maintenance and enhancement of the individual's life may be
properly called sexual activities. But a neurotic activity may be defined as one that does not contribute to the individual's maintenance
of his own life, or, therefore, the life of the species. Therefore, all
neurosis may be identified as having its origins in psychological
malfunctions of sexual behavior. Further, as Freud ultimately asserted, since such activities do not contribute to life, they must contribute to the deterioration rather than the enhancement of life—
in short, to death. A universal death-wish, or Thanatos, as opposed
to the universal life-wish, or Eros, must be postulated, since all
human beings exhibit some behavior which cannot be considered in
any way life-enhancing or life-maintaining. Consequently, any failure of the life-enhancing and life–maintaining functions of sexuality
must be ascribed to a yearning for death.

Yet it is not so simple as that. To understand the full power of
Freud's thrust at humanity's self-respect, as well as Swinburne's
similar thrust, it is useful to recognize as a simple fact that the human mind is incurably insane, and that what human beings identify
as insane is only a slight exaggeration of what human beings identify as sane and normal. Freud was in the direct line of Kantian
thinking, and Kant asserted that the mind cannot know the true
nature of reality; rather, it can know reality only as phenomena
made meaningful by the constructions of its own understanding,
regulated by reason. For reason as the regulator of the mind, Freud

substituted instinct, the unconscious. The understanding, then, is not regulated by reason but by desire, by Eros, by sexuality. But to be divorced from reality is, of course, to be insane. This is more than mere wordmongering. It points to an unavoidable truth: that the mind's anticipations of what a situation will yield are necessarily different from what the situation actually does yield; and that, governed by the powers of sexual instinct to maintain itself and its own constructions, the mind will do everything it can to avoid correcting and abandoning its constructed anticipations. Culture, or civilization, is what man has managed to achieve which has a more effective relationship to reality than do the uncorrected fantasies of instinct. As Nietzsche put it, the will wants everything; not to have everything is to be frustrated; to be frustrated is to deny the will, the instinctual sexually derived drive to life; since it is impossible to have everything, to live is to desire, at least part of the time, death. Such desires for death reveal themselves as neurosis. Hence, all neurosis can be traced to a distortion of sexual functioning. The free expression of the sexual instinct necessarily results in incorrect fantasy, or insanity; the correction of those fantasies necessarily leads to the desire for death. Freud placed man in an incurable and irresolvable tension between instinct and culture, subject and object, self and world, biological drive and reality.

However, it is evident that something in Freud's reasoning is either specious or merely rhetorical. To say that whatever we categorize as life-enhancing and life-maintaining is identical with whatever we categorize as sexual behavior is merely to assert that one name may be substituted for another name; it is a purely tautological process, a mere verbalism. It is merely to assert that any adaptational strategy is a sexual strategy; the result is to deprive either one term or the other of all useful meaning. It means that either we forget about sexuality or that we forget about everything else in human behavior.

But as rhetoric it is superbly effective. What Freud was eager to get and force upon people is that in the Judeo-Christian cultural tradition, sexual behavior is relegated to a disapproved, private, and concealed area of life, and so is precisely the place in which the fundamental human insanity shows up most uncompromisingly

—the area of behavior in which the failures of adaptation, and therefore in which the clues to adaptational failure are most easily discovered. That Freud's interest was rhetorical, and his purpose to shock people into an awareness of their failures, is demonstrated by the proposition, *supposed* to be derived from him, that a proper sexual life means happiness for the individual and success for the culture, or that if the individual and the culture could achieve an unfrustrated expression of the sexual instincts, there would be no disparity between the instinct and the requirements of the situation in which humans find themselves. Nothing could be farther from the lessons that Freud himself drew from his investigations: that civilization is necessary for human survival and is necessarily at odds with instinct; that the price of civilization is frustration, discontent, and neurosis; and that in our culture that price shows up most clearly in the sexual area of human behavior.

This rhetorical aspect of Freud's terminology comes out in his insistence that his language was morally neutral. Thus, narcissism is "the state or stage of development in which there is a heavy investment of libido in one's own ego and which in abnormal forms persists through fixation or reappears through regression." Now ultimately, libido is, presumably, instinctual; the word simply means the desire to live. A person so grossly fat that his adaptive ability and life expectancy are seriously impaired may be said to be either excessively narcissistic or deficient in narcissism. It is obvious that, as defined, narcissism is essential to any human being. Too much narcissism or too little damages the effectiveness of the individual's adaptational strategies. "Libido," then, is simply a sensational substitution for the old word "will"; the advantage of the substitution is that the new word removes the concept from its traditional metaphysical and above all its religious and moral context which has compromised the force of its meaning. It is not for nothing that Freud read Schopenhauer as a young man, and that he was in the direct tradition of the German idealistic philosophy of the early nineteenth century.

Moving a little closer to the Swinburnian problem, consider sadism, the personality characteristic of the individual who can achieve sexual gratification only by forcing his sexual partner to experience extreme suffering. Surely here is a perversion that is totally disconnected from normal human behavior; but it is actually no more disconnected than overeating is from eating. The sadist dominates his partner; masculinity is the ability to dominate the social and physical environment, the attitude of demand toward one's circumstances, the power to adjust one's strategies so that the environment contributes to one's desire to live. So sadism is then an intensified mode of an attitude essential to life. And so with masochism. A strategy as important as the power to impose one's will upon the environment, it is the power to recognize the limitations of that will, to accept those elements that cannot be changed, to cooperate, as it were, with conditions of the environment, particularly the social conditions. It is, then, the attitude we call femininity, and an intensified mode of that strategy of acceptance, manifested in the sexual sphere of behavior, is masochism. Thus the male masochist demands that the woman he loves be domineering and brutal. To be whipped in sexual circumstances is to have one's strategy of acceptance confirmed. The gratification comes from the reinforcement of what might as well be called a faith. It is difficult to "cure" people of such aberrations because every such experience, real or fantasied, permits and encourages the individual to say, triumphantly, "I'm right!" On the other hand, it is obvious that the confirmation of a strategy by isolating and exaggerating it can occur in any area of human behavior. And once this is realized it is evident that sexual masochism is an *instance* of intensified acceptance, not a *cause* for such intensification in some other area of behavior. It is, for example, hotly argued—and this is most pertinent to Swinburne— whether the cause of alcoholism is psychological or physiological. The argument is probably pointless and meaningless; there may be reason to believe that the physiologies of some people are abnormally sensitive to alcohol, but there is also reason to believe that some people will use that sensitivity for whatever purposes they may have. Like sex, the consumption of alcohol tends to belong to the private sphere of life. Certainly excessive consumption is separated from situations in which the environment must be dealt with; it is protected by banquets, parties, and bars. The reason of course is that too much alcohol makes one at first psychologically and then physically defenseless. Probably, then, Swinburne's alcoholism was linked to his masochism. The surrender to alcohol had the same attribute of confirming a strategy of acceptance by offering the experience of helplessness towards an external and superior force. That may be why he could accept so readily having his life ruled by Watts.

Perhaps it is impossible to understand why strategies of extreme acceptance should have had such an appeal to Swinburne. But we do know that some of his behavior was surprisingly demanding for a masochist. As a boy he was a daring horseman, a superb swimmer —as he remained all his life—a bold climber of dangerous cliffs; more than anything else he desired passionately to be what his diminutive stature made impossible: a soldier. Furthermore, as a young man in London his behavior in social groups was extraordinarily dominating and demanding; his masochism was connected not to a weakness of will but to a very powerful will, of which his determination not to withdraw or censor his poems is another instance. He exhibited a vitality so astounding that men less alive were half frightened by it and defended themselves by calling it hysterical. Was the masochistic and perhaps alcoholic reinforcement of the strategy of acceptance or submission a way he developed to handle a sense of demand so powerful that it threatened to run away with him, so strong that it frightened him, so beyond his physiological resources that it threatened to damage him? At any rate, a contemporary school of psychiatry is beginning to entertain the possibility that what a culture defines as neuroses are in fact strategies necessary to keep the individual going, strategies that pay the price of a deterioration in one area of life in order to keep the other areas successful, flexible, and adaptive. Does the human mind find it necessary to anchor itself in an insane fantasy in order to deal with reality with any success at all? Be that as it may, from all this we may derive one vital clue to Swinburne's poetry, the word "necessary."

To feel compelled to do something absurd, or ugly, or shameful, or pointless—as Dr. Johnson had to touch lampposts—is to adopt a psychological strategy that, no matter how successful it may be, is a psychological bondage. Even though it may be a strategy for survival, it is experienced as a failure; indeed, it is a failure, for it is a limitation of the possible range of experience. And thus it is humiliating. To rationalize is to persuade oneself that it is none of these but is in fact a triumph. Swinburne, however, was too intelligent to rationalize, and too civilized and cultured. So he set out, in 1860 or shortly thereafter, to ask himself, What is the nature of this psychological bondage from which I suffer? What is its immediate source? Its ultimate source? His literary career was the search for those answers.

The crucial year seems to have been 1861. Perhaps Swinburne was already acquainted with the poetry of Baudelaire. The augmented edition of *Les Fleurs du Mal* was published in January 1861, four years after the book's first appearance; Swinburne's review of it did not appear until September 1862, but his knowledge of French literature was so intimate that it seems more than probable that if he had not known the great poet's work before 1861, he certainly became acquainted with it not long after.[9] From Baudelaire Swinburne either learned or was confirmed in an attitude of the utmost importance to him; and when soon after he began to work on an essay on Blake not published until 1867,[10] that attitude either was reinforced by the study of Blake or else helped to understand Blake in a way which, though now outdated, was pioneering at the time. That attitude was that the task of poetry is neither to inculcate morals (and certainly not religion), nor to present moral-opposites and judge between them, but rather to explore the emotional significance of moral problems. Poetry, therefore, was beyond and above the moral realm in the sense that no emotion or moral problem could properly be forbidden it, for morals exist for man and not man for morals. Consequently, if there is a morally forbidden area, it is above all the task of poetry to explore what human significance is concealed there. It comes down to asking what problems of human existence and of the human situation are concealed behind the respectable facade of public morality.

That is why Swinburne eventually discovered that in composing

[9] See Appendix 5.
[10] Though dated 1868; see Appendix 6 and Appendix 2.

a series of poems he was in fact writing a book, as he insisted in his defense of his work in the brash and defiant *Notes on Poems and Reviews*.[11] But he had asserted this before, in a letter to Lord Lytton, the aging Bulwer-Lytton, still known for *The Last Days of Pompeii*. Lytton was as experienced an author, especially in dealing with publishers, as one could find in England, and Swinburne asked him for advice and help when Payne withdrew the *Poems and Ballads* from publication.

> As to the suppression of separate passages or poems, it could not be done without injuring the whole structure of the book, where every part has been as carefully considered and arranged as I could manage.[12]

This does not mean that he had intended to write a book of inter-related poems from the very beginning, any more than Balzac had, when he discovered he was writing *The Human Comedy* after he had been writing it for ten years. And so, it seems, with Swinburne. The discovery may have come in the early fall of 1863, shortly before he began to work on *Atalanta*. At any rate the themes of *Poems and Ballads* are all present in that work, and to them had been added a still further understanding, a comprehension of the source of psychological bondage.

The most respectable institutions in Swinburne's England, in which the mores of the old aristocracy, of which Swinburne was a member, had been abandoned in favor of those of the middle classes, were religion and marriage; the link between the two was the family. Now Swinburne had not only discovered the humiliation of psychological bondage to a distorted eroticism; he had also discovered precisely how that eroticism limited sharply the availability to him of the means whereby most men solved the problem of sex and the interpretation of sex, or eroticism—namely, marriage. "The Triumph of Time" may or may not be autobiographical; if he did propose to a young woman and was rejected, it was probably his cousin Mary Gordon. On the other hand, he may have had and indeed probably already did have the insight to know that any attempt

---

[11] See Appendix 7.
[12] Lang, I, 172. Dated August 13 [1866].

for him to live an ordinary married life would be a failure. It seems probable that he wrote the poem in lieu of proposing.

> Your lithe hands draw me, your face burns through me,
> I am swift to follow you, keen to see;
> But love lacks might to redeem or undo me,
> As I have been, I know I shall surely be;
> "What should such fellows as I do?" Nay,
> My part were worse if I chose to play;
> For the worst is this after all; if they knew me,
> Not a soul upon earth would pity me.

"Such fellows as I"—it is a phrase that may be condemned for its self-pity, and it has been, but such a judgment lacks discernment as well as generosity.[13] These are the words of a man who knows what it is to be humiliated by one's own personality.

Yet to recognize the fact of that humiliation is the first step on the way to learning to live with it, if one is unable to change it. For it entails the recognition that one's personality—and this Swinburne could well have learned from Baudelaire—is simply something one is given, or that one discovers as one grows up; that one's personality is, in a strange but true sense, entirely alien to oneself; that it has been, in a strange but true sense, foisted on one. By whom? One's responsibility, one perceives, is not for what one is, but for what one does about it. And the first thing to be done is to understand this strange collection of possible modes of behavior—called personality—which one has been burdened with. Swinburne's immediate response was to withdraw to the great sweet mother, the sea, whom he implores to "set free my soul as thy soul is free." The sea, then, is like a loving mother; it accepts everything her child does, without judgment, without rejection. The sea, "born without sister, born without brother," is, moreover, better than a mother, or is the ideal mother—it is free from social relations; it is without a family.

"The Triumph of Time" is preceded by "Laus Veneris," the story of a man enslaved by the erotic perception of femininity, and by

---

[13] The usual tone for the criticism of Swinburne's erotic poems is to condemn him, or to revile him, or to be shocked, or to make fun of him, or to patronize him. I can remember no critic who has even tried to understand that an intelligent and sensitive man was suffering.

"Phaedra," a parallel instance of a woman enslaved by the erotic perception of masculinity. In understanding these and so many other poems in the book, it is always useful to remember Freud's assertion that erotic love is the model psychosis. That men have made a goddess of it, or have asserted that it is an instrument of Satan, is proof without parallel of the incurable insanity of the human mind. It must not be imagined that Swinburne saw in "true love" and marriage a way out of his dilemma and a way for redemption from the psychosis of eroticism. "Love lacks might to redeem or undo me." That is, if ordinary eroticism had the power to rescue him from his masochistic eroticism, he would still be in the trap of eroticism. If there is any uncertainty here, there is none in the great chorus from *Atalanta*, "We have seen thee, O love, thou art fair." Behind the respectable facade of marriage, then, lies half concealed, but revealed to those, such as Swinburne, whose personalities have forced them into it, the terrible emotional and moral swamp and madness of eroticism. The proof is that in marriage religion has blessed eroticism.

The savage attacks on *Poems and Ballads* were prompted as much by what Swinburne had to say about religion as what he had to say about sex. That he saw a link between them comes out forcefully in "Anactoria," the monologue of Sappho the Lesbian addressed to a young woman with whom she is madly in love. It was not enough that Swinburne should have introduced publicly the forbidden subject of homosexuality; he also had Sappho revile God. In Swinburne's classical poems two levels, as it were, of divinity are present. The one, nearer to man, is that of the classical deities, projections of man's superficial desires; but above and beyond them stands a high God. "God knows," Anactoria cries, "I might be crueller than God," and she hurls at him the dreadful accusation that the suffering of man feeds "the mute melancholy lust of heaven."

To explain this it is not enough to fall back on Swinburne's interest in the Marquis de Sade, whom he thought of as a very poor pornographer but a very profound theologian. De Sade's point was that it is vain effort to try to create a theodicy that reconciles the wisdom, goodness, and power of God with what he has done to man, or with the kind of humanity he has created: suffering is the charac-

ter of experience, pain is what is natural; to follow the God of
Christianity or the Deist God of nature is to cooperate with him and
with the active force in nature by inflicting pain. But Swinburne
went farther.

> Which is most worthy the rod
> That justice wields when she can;
> Man, the creator of God,
> Or God, the creator of man?[14]

In short, man is as cruel as God, for God is the projection of man's
deepest will, and the suffering of man feeds the mute melancholy
lust of man. The only rational recourse is "The Garden of Proserpine," where there will be "only the sleep eternal in an eternal
night." Some unbearable humiliation inflicted upon oneself by a
personality for which one cannot be responsible—this, then, is the
common lot of man, proved by the projection of the deepest drives
of that personality into the figure of God. Hell is personality, Baudelaire implies, and behind the public facade of religion lurks that
hell. And further, as we understand when we read "Ilicet," behind
the facade of the religious assertion of the immortality of the soul
lurks the desire for death.

The *Poems and Ballads*, then, should be read as a long monologue
of a single voice which, however, assumes many personae in order
to explore the intricate interrelationship of the themes of suffering,
and the shameful pleasure of suffering; humiliation, and the shameful escape from humiliation into the longing for death; the madness
of Eros, and the madness of Thanatos—with only a glimpse or two
of a world in which freedom and self-respect might be possible.

This was the point Swinburne had reached when he began *Atalanta*; and that work was to extend his thinking to new and more
complete dimensions. The lyrics in *Poems and Ballads*—including
those written after *Atalanta*, evidently to fill out his scheme for a
book—were concerned with the individual alone or in situations,
almost always erotic, which range from the frustrating to the
shattering. Yet the last poem in the book before the "Dedication,"
which is really a postlude complementary to the first two poems,

[14] Lang, I, xvi.

is a border ballad about the terrors of family relationships. In *Atalanta* he turns directly to the first level of social organization, the family, and behind it, scarcely seen, society itself, in the form of the huntsmen come together from all Greece to kill the boar sent by a goddess because she had not received what she conceived to be her proper sacrifices. Although the play is named *Atalanta* it is in fact about Althea, the mother who kills her son out of loyalty to her family. Her son has killed her brothers; since she can get no more brothers but can get more sons, she kills her son. But that, to Swinburne, is not her prime motive. Her son was in love with a strange woman, strange in two senses: first, she was an unnatural woman, dedicated to the hunt and to virginity, modeling herself on man and denying the responsibilities of a woman—children, the hearth, spinning, and weaving; and second, because she was simply a stranger, not an Aetolian, a woman from Arcadia, an outsider, too far from the family and social system of Calydon. The intricacies of Swinburne's scheme and how he works it out are properly left to the reader. The situation is so rich, so meaningful, and so close to every human being's experience as Swinburne presents it that each reader will find something of his own to be horrified at. Nevertheless several points that might be easily overlooked need to be pointed out.

Two utterances of Meleager provide one key to the play.

> For there is nothing terribler to men
> Than the sweet face of mothers, and the might.

> Mother, I dying with unforgetful tongue
> Hail thee as holy and worship thee as just
> Who art unjust and unholy;[15]

It has often been said that the shock Freud gave the world came from his tracing everything to sex; but it is probable that an even profounder shock was administered. In the western tradition, as in many others, the family is sacred, the source of all good. But Freud pointed out that in the familial relationship is rooted all that is most terrible in human nature; that the cognitive corruption of

---

[15] *Atalanta in Calydon*, lines 710–711, 2220–2222.

man, from which his emotional and moral corruption stem, emerges from the infant's and growing child's relation to his parents and siblings. It is on this sore and diseased spot in the human situation that Swinburne puts his finger in this play and particularly in these two speeches. It is possible to understand the enthusiasm generated by the publication of *Atalanta* only by assuming that nobody understood it or could even follow its argument, by reason of the stylistic difficulties already discussed.

A second point is also easily overlooked. Althea and Meleager represent two antithetical theologies and two antithetical moralities. For Althaea the gods are not to be trusted; they must be served, and only the traditional ways of serving them are—not the good ways— but the safe ones. Meleager insists that the gods are to be trusted and that they will approve new ways to achieve the human satisfactions they want us to achieve. These may be called the Christian and the Enlightenment positions. Althea insists that safety lies in not trusting life—and kills her son; Meleager insists that life is to be trusted—and is killed by his mother.

The final point is equally important. At line 1037, not long before the midpoint of the play, the chorus begins a vast lyric cry which ends not long after the midpoint. The chorus is now alone on the stage; Althea has withdrawn into the palace; everyone else has gone to the hunt. And the chorus begins, "Who hath given man speech?" The climax comes with, "The supreme evil, God." And the end comes with: "For words divide and rend; / But silence is most noble till the end." Language is the instrument by which man visits his insanity on his fellow man. But language is not merely the instrument of society; without it, society would not be possible. In the most meaningful possible sense, language is society.

One of the problems of Swinburne criticism has always been the sudden shift from the erotic poems to the political poems which he began to write in 1867. And this is all the more puzzling because *Atalanta* was published before *Poems and Ballads*, although, as we have seen, it presents a later stage of thinking and the transcendence of the attitudes explored and analyzed in the lyrics. But it should be evident from what has been said that the political poems were not a break from the direction Swinburne had been following but the log-

ical and necessary development of it.[16] Of course it was noticed that
two poems, discarded from the 1876 proposal, were clearly political, "A Song in Time of Order: 1852," and "A Song in Time of
Revolution: 1860." These were sandwiched between two poems to
be retained, those to Hugo and to Landor. It is easy to say, then, that
after getting his eroticism out of his system (though this leaves
Atalanta unaccounted for), Swinburne turned back to his youthful
republicanism. And there is just enough truth in this to make it
entirely misleading. In 1876 Swinburne discarded the two youthful
"Songs" but kept the poems to Landor and Hugo, his two heroes,
men who had fought publicly and privately for freedom. The poems
to them, therefore, were links to his later political poems. But to
call these new works political poems is to miss the point, and to read
them as such is to be confused by them and to find them pointless.
The younger Swinburne, the Swinburne of the 1850's, had simply
seen republicanism as superior to monarchy, and religion as the instrument of monarchy. It was a typical Enlightenment and liberal
attitude, nor unusual at the time. There were a good many republi-
cans in monarchical England, and Victorian politics was busy in
further dismantling the monarchy as a politically meaningful in-
stitution. Rather, the poems Swinburne began to write in 1867 are
poems about the character and structure of society. The psychological bondage and the humiliation which he had experienced in the
erotic realm of experience he had traced to religion and to the family. Now he traced it farther back to the social relation itself. In language—the instrument and the very being of society—is to be
found the ultimate source of that insanity which is so humiliating
to mankind. The ultimate source, then, of human failure is in the
very nature and character and structure of society itself. There,
and there only, in the social nexus itself, is the ultimate prison in
which are forged the humiliating manacles of the psychological
bondage from which all men suffer.

Is there a way out of that prison? For a while, at least, Swinburne thought so, and he thought he knew the key that would turn

[16] Many of these poems were published in magazines and were collected
with hitherto unpublished poems in two volumes, *Songs before Sunrise* (1871),
and *Songs of Two Nations* (1875).

the lock. But even he could see only a visionary possibility. No one has been able to see anything more. If Freud was right, there is no way out. The humiliating psychological bondage of men to themselves and to each other is the inescapable and eternal condition of human existence. This is the bitter illumination of Swinburne's *Poems and Ballads* and his *Atalanta in Calydon.*

Chronology

April 5, 1837   Born at No. 7 Chester Street, Grosvenor Place, London, the eldest child of Captain (later Admiral) Charles Henry Swinburne (1797–1877) and his wife, Lady Jane Henriette Ashburnham, daughter of the Earl of Ashburnham.

1837–1849   Grows up in Bonchurch, Isle of Wight, with frequent visits to his grandfather's home, Capheaton, Northumbria, the family seat of the Swinburnes, baronets since shortly after 1660.

1849–1853   Schooling at Eton.

1853–1856   Private tutoring at Bonchurch and for a time at Kempsford, Gloucestershire.

December 1854   Father's decision that he is not to enter the army.

Summer 1855   Trip to Germany with his maternal uncle.

January 23, 1856   Enters Balliol College, Oxford.

November 1856   Joins with a group of brilliant and unorthodox undergraduates to found "Old Mortality," an intellectual society. The most important member was John Nichol, of republican convictions and a follower of J. S. Mill.

November 1, 1857   Meets D. G. Rossetti, William Morris, Edward Burne-Jones, and other members of the Pre-Raphaelite group, in Oxford to decorate the Union Debating Hall.

1858   First essays and poetry published in *Undergraduate Papers*, organ of "Old Mortality."

November 1859   Fails examination in classics. His tutor, Benjamin Jowett, translator of Plato, advises him to read in the country with William Stubbs, future constitutional historian.

April–June 1860   Returns to Oxford. Passes classics examination but either withdraws from or fails Honors examination in law and history. Leaves Oxford.

1860   *The Queen-Mother* and *Rosamond*, two verse plays.

Winter 1861   Visits French Riviera and Italy.

Spring 1861   Settles in London to pursue a literary career, having been granted a small personal allowance by his father. Renews friendship with Rossetti and his circle.

May 5, 1861   Meets Richard Monckton Milnes, who gives him access to the works of the Marquis de Sade and other pornographic writers.

1862   Achieves his mature style in poetry and begins his literary career with publication of verse and prose in *The Spectator*.

March 1863   Visits Paris with J. M. Whistler.

1863–February 1864   Shares house with Rossetti, but is not often in residence.

February–May 1864   Travels in Italy; meets W. S. Landor.

1864   *The Pilgrimage of Pleasure*, a medieval morality play in verse, published in *The Children of the Chapel*, a novel by his cousin Mary Gordon.

February 1865   First edition of *Atalanta in Calydon: A Tragedy*. Great success requires second edition in July.

November 1865   *Chastelard: A Tragedy* (the first verse play in the Mary Stuart trilogy, to Swinburne more an epic in dramatic form than drama). Family moves to Holmwood, Oxfordshire.

1866   *Poems and Ballads* published and withdrawn by Moxon, then republished by Hotten; *Notes on Poems and Reviews*; first signs of alcoholism.

1867   *A Song of Italy* (beginning of series of political poems).

1868   *William Blake: A Critical Essay*.

Summer 1869   Long visit to France.

1870   *Ode on the Proclamation of the French Republic*.

1871   *Songs before Sunrise*.

Autumn 1871   First serious alcoholic breakdown. His father takes him to Holmwood and requires him to give up London residence.

March 1872   Re-establishes residence in London.

1872   *Under the Microscope* (reply to "The Fleshly School of Poetry," an attack made on himself and Rossetti by Robert Buchanan in *The Contemporary Review*, October 1871).

1873   Mostly at Holmwood.

1874–1877   Alternates between London and Holmwood.

1874   *Bothwell: A Tragedy* (the second part of the Mary Stuart trilogy).

1875   *George Chapman: A Critical Essay* (introduction to the complete works of Chapman, edited by R. H. Shepherd) ; *Songs of Two Nations* (political poems published 1867–1873) ; *Essays and Studies* (periodical essays from 1866 to 1872, and introductions to his selections from Byron [1866] and Coleridge [1869]) ; *The Devil's Due* (another pamphlet attacking Buchanan).

1876   *Erechtheus: A Tragedy* (like *Atalanta*, on the Greek model).

1877   *A Note on Charlotte Brontë.*

March 5, 1877   Death of his father leaves Swinburne temporarily out of debt and financially independent. Lives mostly in London; alcoholism becomes severe, 1877–1879.

1877   *A Year's Letters* (novel published serially in *The Tatler*) ; unfinished novel, *Lesbia Brandon*, is partly set up in galleys.

1878   *Poems and Ballads. Second Series* (miscellaneous poems, mostly printed in periodicals between 1867 and 1878).

June 1879   Theodore Watts, later Watts-Dunton, removes a critically ill Swinburne from his lodgings and takes him to Watts' sister's home at Putney; in a few days Swinburne goes to Holmwood, which is about to be sold.

September 27, 1879   Moves in with Watts at The Pines, Putney Hill. Within a year is entirely recovered, and under Watts' care maintains his health.

1879–1909   Lives with Watts, who wisely permits few visits or travel excursions without his company, except to Swinburne's mother's home.

1880   *A Study of Shakespeare* (mostly previously printed, 1875–
1876) ; *Songs of the Springtides* (miscellaneous poems) ; *Studies
in Song* (miscellaneous poems) ; *Specimens of Modern Poets. The
Heptalogia, or The Seven Against Sense, A Cap with Seven Bells*
(parodies of Tennyson, Browning, Elizabeth Browning, Coventry
Patmore, Robert, Lord Lytton ["Owen Meredith"], D. G. Rossetti, and Swinburne himself ["Nephelidia"]).

1881   *Mary Stuart: A Tragedy* (the conclusion of the Mary Stuart
trilogy).

1882   *Tristram of Lyonesse and Other Poems* (his principal narrative poem plus miscellaneous poems).

1882   With Watts visits Hugo in Paris.

1883   *A Century of Roundels* (100 poems in rondeau form).

1884   *A Midsummer Holiday* (miscellaneous poems).

1885   *Marino Faliero. A Tragedy* (verse play).

1886   *Miscellanies* (periodical esasys, 1876–1882, some for the
Encyclopaedia Brittanica, 9th edition); *A Study of Victor Hugo*
(previously published in periodicals, 1877–1885).

1887   *Locrine: A Tragedy* (verse play) ; *A Selection from the Poet-
ical Works of A. C. Swinburne.*

1888   *The Whippingham Papers* (mild sado-masochistic pornog-
raphy, published anonymously).

1889   *A Study of Ben Jonson* (previous periodical publication,
1888) ; *Poems and Ballads, Third Series* (mostly previously published miscellaneous poems, 1885–1889, and poems from the uncompleted *Lesbia Brandon*).

1892   *The Sisters: A Tragedy* (verse play).

1894   *Astrophel and Other Poems* (miscellaneous poems, mostly
previously published, 1889–1894) ; *Studies in Prose and Poetry*
(previously published periodical essays, 1889–1893).

1896   *The Tale of Balen* (a narrative poem). Death of his mother.

1904   *A Channel Passage and Other Poems.*

1899   *Rosamund, Queen of the Lombards: A Tragedy* (verse play).

1904   *A Channel Passage and Other Poems* (miscellaneous poems, mostly previously published, 1886–1904) ; *The Poems of Algernon Charles Swinburne* (the only collected edition published by Swinburne).

1904   *Love's Cross-Currents* (publication as a book of *A Year's Letters*) ; *The Tragedies of Algernon Charles Swinburne* (the only collected edition published by Swinburne).

1908   *The Duke of Gandia* (verse tragedy) ; *The Age of Shakespeare* (essays from the *Encyclopaedia Brittanica,* 9th edition, and several periodicals, 1883–1907).

1909   *Three Plays of Shakespeare* (essays from *Harper's,* 1902–1904) ; *Shakespeare.*

April 10, 1909   Dies at The Pines. His will leaves everything he possessed to Watts-Dunton. Buried April 15 in Bonchurch churchyard.

1917   *Posthumous Poems,* edited by Gosse and Wise (mostly from manuscript, some previously published in periodicals).

1925   *Ballads of the English Border.*

1926–1927   *The Complete Works of Algernon Charles Swinburne,* Bonchurch Edition.

1927   *Swinburne's Hyperion and Other Poems,* with an essay on Swinburne by Georges Lafourcade.

1952   *Lesbia Brandon,* edited by Randolph Hughes.

1959–1962   *The Letters of A. C. Swinburne,* edited by Cecil Y. Lang.

1962   *The Novels of A. C. Swinburne. Love's Cross-Currents. Lesbia Brandon.* With an introduction by Edmund Wilson.

1964   *New Writings by Swinburne; or, Miscellanea nova et curiosa. Being a medley of poems, critical essays, hoaxes, and burlesques,* edited by Cecil Y. Lang.

Bibliography

EDITIONS

Atalanta in Calydon: A Tragedy. London: Edward Moxon & Co., 1865.

Poems and Ballads. London: Edward Moxon & Co., 1866.

————. London: John Camden Hotten, 1866.

Poems. 6 vols. London: Chatto & Windus, 1904; New York: Harper & Brothers, 1904. (This includes *Atalanta in Calydon*).

The Complete Works of Algernon Charles Swinburne. The Bonchurch Edition. Edited by Sir Edmund Gosse and Thomas James Wise, 20 vols. London, 1925–1927. (This edition is highly unreliable, particularly for the poems).

BOOKS ABOUT SWINBURNE

Not very much written about Swinburne is worth the trouble it takes to read it; most readers can do as well or better by reading Swinburne's poetry, plays, and prose with care, something not all the writers listed below give one the impression of having done. Lafourcade's work is the most valuable, but the most satisfactory introduction to Swinburne's life, personality, and writings is to be found in his letters, edited by Cecil Y. Lang (Yale University Press, 1959–1962).

Gosse, Edmund W. *The Life of Algernon Charles Swinburne.* London and New York, 1917.

Beerbohm, Max. "No. 2, The Pines." *And Even Now,* London, 1926.

Nicolson, Harold G. *Swinburne.* London and New York, 1926.

Welby, T. Earle. *A Study of Swinburne.* London and New York, 1926.

Lafourcade, Georges. *La Jeunesse de Swinburne (1837–1867).* Paris, London, and New York, 1928.

————. *Swinburne: A Literary Biography.* London, 1932.

Chew, Samuel C. *Swinburne.* Boston, 1929.

Rutland, William R. *Swinburne: A Nineteenth Century Hellene.* Oxford, 1931.

Hyder, Clyde K. *Swinburne's Literary Career and Fame.* Durham, N.C., 1933.

Hare, Humphrey. *Swinburne: A Biographical Approach.* London, 1949.

Cassidy, John A. *Swinburne.* New York, 1964.

Connally, Thomas E. *Swinburne's Theory of Poetry.* Albany, N.Y., 1964.

Peters, Robert L. *The Crowns of Apollo: Swinburne's Principles of Literature and Art.* Detroit, 1965.

POEMS
and
BALLADS

The 1876 Proposal

Edward Burne-Jones (1833–1898) was one of the leading painters of the later or second Pre-Raphaelite school, to which Swinburne was allied both in friendship and taste. Burne-Jones was a friend of Rossetti and a friend and business partner of William Morris, as well as fellow-worker in the decorative arts.

Contents

A Ballad of Life

IN HONOREM D. LUCRETIAE ESTENSIS BORGIAE

I FOUND in dreams a place of wind and flowers,
    Full of sweet trees and colour of glad grass,
      In midst whereof there was
A lady clothed like summer with sweet hours.
Her beauty, fervent as a fiery moon,   5
    Made my blood burn and swoon
      Like a flame rained upon.
Sorrow had filled her shaken eyelids' blue,
And her mouth's sad red heavy rose all through
    Seemed sad with glad things gone.   10

She held a little cithern by the strings,
    Shaped heartwise, strung with subtle-coloured hair
    Of some dead lute-player

Epigraph: "In honor of Lucrezia of Este and Borgia." In his letter of July 20, 1876, to Andrew Chatto, proposing the new edition of *Poems and Ballads*, Swinburne requested that this epigraph be added, and a similar one to the next poem, "A Ballad of Death." Lucrezia Borgia (1480–1519) was the daughter of Rodrigo de Borgia, Pope Alexander VI (1431–1503), and was born before her father became pope in 1492. She was used as a political pawn by her father and by her brother Cesare (1476–1507) and was married three times, the last time to Alfonso of Este, the ruler of Ferrara. In her later years she was known for her piety and her patronage of arts and letters; but in her earlier life she is reputed to have been guilty of sexual license and even incest with her father and her two brothers. That the Borgias were unscrupulous in their efforts to found an Italian principality for their family is unquestionable. That they committed as many criminal poisonings as legend has it is doubtful. Swinburne, of course, is here referring to the legendary Lucrezia of vice and crime.

11. *cithern:* A small fig-shaped musical instrument, usually of the guitar family, popular in Europe from the end of the fifteenth century into the eighteenth. Swinburne perhaps confused it with the Greek cithara, an instrument of the lyre family.

13. *lute:* A pear-shaped instrument with six to thirteen pairs of strings; the most popular musical instrument in Europe in the Middle Ages and the Renaissance, particularly the sixteenth century.

That in dead years had done delicious things.
15   The seven strings were named accordingly;
            The first string charity,
                The second tenderness,
        The rest were pleasure, sorrow, sleep, and sin,
        And loving-kindness, that is pity's kin
20   And is most pitiless.

        There were three men with her, each garmented
            With gold and shod with gold upon the feet;
            And with plucked ears of wheat
        The first man's hair was wound upon his head.
25   His face was red, and his mouth curled and sad;
            All his gold garment had
                Pale stains of dust and rust.
        A riven hood was pulled across his eyes;
        The token of him being upon this wise
30   Made for a sign of Lust.

        The next was Shame, with hollow heavy face
            Coloured like green wood when flame kindles it.
            He hath such feeble feet
        They may not well endure in any place.
35   His face was full of grey old miseries,
            And all his blood's increase
                Was even increase of pain.
        The last was Fear, that is akin to Death;
        He is Shame's friend, and always as Shame saith
40   Fear answers him again.

        My soul said in me; This is marvellous,
            Seeing the air's face is not so delicate
                Nor the sun's grace so great,
        If sin and she be kin or amorous.

24. head. 1904] head:
28. *riven:* Torn.

And seeing where maidens served her on their knees,   45
  I bade one crave of these
    To know the cause thereof.
Then Fear said: I am Pity that was dead.
And Shame said: I am Sorrow comforted.
    And Lust said: I am Love.   50

Thereat her hands began a lute-playing
  And her sweet mouth a song in a strange tongue;
    And all the while she sung
There was no sound but long tears following
Long tears upon men's faces, waxen white   55
    With extreme sad delight.
    But those three following men
Became as men raised up among the dead;
Great glad mouths open and fair cheeks made red
    With child's blood come again.   60

Then I said: Now assuredly I see
  My lady is perfect, and transfigureth
    All sin and sorrow and death,
Making them fair as her own eyelids be,
Or lips wherein my whole soul's life abides;   65
    Or as her sweet white sides
    And bosom carved to kiss.
Now therefore, if her pity further me,
Doubtless for her sake all my days shall be
    As righteous as she is.   70

Forth, ballad, and take roses in both arms,
  Even till the top rose touch thee in the throat
    Where the least thornprick harms;
  And girdled in thy golden singing-coat,
Come thou before my lady and say this;   75
    Borgia, thy gold hair's colour burns in me,
      Thy mouth makes beat my blood in feverish rhymes;

> Therefore so many as these roses be,
>   Kiss me so many times.
> Then it may be, seeing how sweet she is,
>   That she will stoop herself none otherwise
>   Than a blown vine-branch doth,
> And kiss thee with soft laughter on thine eyes,
>   Ballad, and on thy mouth.

80

A Ballad of Death

IN OBITUM D. LUCRETIAE ESTENSIS BORGIAE

KNEEL down, fair Love, and fill thyself with tears,
Girdle thyself with sighing for a girth
Upon the sides of mirth,
Cover thy lips and eyelids, let thine ears
Be filled with rumour of people sorrowing;   5
Make thee soft raiment out of woven sighs
Upon the flesh to cleave,
Set pains therein and many a grievous thing,
And many sorrows after each his wise
For armlet and for gorget and for sleeve.   10

O Love's lute heard about the lands of death,
Left hanged upon the trees that were therein;
O Love and Time and Sin,
Three singing mouths that mourn now underbreath,
Three lovers, each one evil spoken of;   15
O smitten lips wherethrough this voice of mine
Came softer with her praise;
Abide a little for our lady's love.
The kisses of her mouth were more than wine,
And more than peace the passage of her days.   20

O Love, thou knowest if she were good to see.
O Time, thou shalt not find in any land

Epigraph: "On the death of Lucrezia of Este and Borgia." See preceding poem.

10. *armlet:* A band of cloth covering the upper arm. *gorget:* A covering
for the throat. Both are used also in armor.
11. *lute:* See note, "A Ballad of Life," line 11.

9

Till, cast out of thine hand,
The sunlight and the moonlight fail from thee,
25   Another woman fashioned like as this.
O Sin, thou knowest that all thy shame in her
Was made a goodly thing;
Yea, she caught Shame and shamed him with her kiss,
With her fair kiss, and lips much lovelier
30   Than lips of amorous roses in late spring.

By night there stood over against my bed
Queen Venus with a hood striped gold and black,
Both sides drawn fully back
From brows wherein the sad blood failed of red,
35   And temples drained of purple and full of death.
Her curled hair had the wave of sea-water
And the sea's gold in it.
Her eyes were as a dove's that sickeneth.
Strewn dust of gold she had shed over her,
40   And pearl and purple and amber on her feet.

Upon her raiment of dyed sendaline
Were painted all the secret ways of love
And covered things thereof,
That hold delight as grape-flowers hold their wine;
45   Red mouths of maidens and red feet of doves,
And brides that kept within the bride-chamber
Their garment of soft shame,
And weeping faces of the wearied loves
That swoon in sleep and awake wearier,
50   With heat of lips and hair shed out like flame.

The tears that through her eyelids fell on me
Made mine own bitter where they ran between

32. *Queen Venus:* Swinburne calls the goddess of love "Queen" to fit the medieval atmosphere of the poem.
36. hair 1904] air
41. *sendaline:* A very thick medieval silk cloth, usually called "sendal"; the suffix is probably Swinburne's.

As blood had fallen therein,
She saying; Arise, lift up thine eyes and see
If any glad thing be or any good   55
Now the best thing is taken forth of us;
Even she to whom all praise
Was as one flower in a great multitude,
One glorious flower of many and glorious,
One day found gracious among many days: 60

Even she whose handmaiden was Love—to whom
At kissing times across her stateliest bed
Kings bowed themselves and shed
Pale wine, and honey with the honeycomb,
And spikenard bruised for a burnt-offering;   65
Even she between whose lips the kiss became
As fire and frankincense;
Whose hair was as gold raiment on a king,
Whose eyes were as the morning purged with flame,
Whose eyelids as sweet savour issuing thence.   70

Then I beheld, and lo on the other side
My lady's likeness crowned and robed and dead.
Sweet still, but now not red,
Was the shut mouth whereby men lived and died.
And sweet, but emptied of the blood's blue shade,   75
The great curled eyelids that withheld her eyes.
And sweet, but like spoilt gold,
The weight of colour in her tresses weighed.
And sweet, but as a vesture with new dyes,
The body that was clothed with love of old.   80

65. *spikenard:* An expensive ointment of ancient times valued for its musky
odor. *burnt-offering:* Old Testament term, referring to offerings of food
burned on the altar of Jehovah.
    67. *frankincense:* A precious incense from Arabia and East Africa, used in
both ancient and modern times.
    68. *gold:* Gold, frankincense, and myrrh, another anciently valued source
of perfume and incense, were the gifts brought by the three wise men to the
infant Christ.

Ah! that my tears filled all her woven hair
And all the hollow bosom of her gown—
Ah! that my tears ran down
Even to the place where many kisses were,
85   Even where her parted breast-flowers have place,
Even where they are cloven apart—who knows not this?
Ah! the flowers cleave apart
And their sweet fills the tender interspace;
Ah! the leaves grown thereof were things to kiss
90   Ere their fine gold was tarnished at the heart.

Ah! in the days when God did good to me,
Each part about her was a righteous thing;
Her mouth an almsgiving,
The glory of her garments charity,
95   The beauty of her bosom a good deed,
In the good days when God kept sight of us;
Love lay upon her eyes,
And on that hair whereof the world takes heed;
And all her body was more virtuous
100   Than souls of women fashioned otherwise.

Now, ballad, gather poppies in thine hands
And sheaves of brier and many rusted sheaves
Rain-rotten in rank lands,
Waste marigold and late unhappy leaves
105   And grass that fades ere any of it be mown;
And when thy bosom is filled full thereof
Seek out Death's face ere the light altereth,
And say "My master that was thrall to Love
Is become thrall to Death."
110   Bow down before him, ballad, sigh and groan,
But make no sojourn in thy outgoing;
For haply it may be
That when thy feet return at evening
Death shall come in with thee.

Laus Veneris

Lors dit en plourant; Hélas trop malheureux homme et
mauldict pescheur, oncques ne verrai-je clémence et miséri-
corde de Dieu. Ores m'en irai-je d'icy et me cacherai dedans
le mont Horsel, en requérant de faveur et d'amoureuse
merci ma doulce dame Vénus, car pour son amour serai-je
bien à tout jamais damné en enfer. Voicy la fin de tous mes
faicts d'armes et de toutes mes belles chansons. Hélas, trop
belle estoyt la face de ma dame et ses yeulx, et en mauvais
jour je vis ces chouses-là. Lors s'en alla tout en gémissant et
se retourna chez elle, et là vescut tristement en grand amour
près de sa dame. Puis après advint que le pape vit un jour
esclater sur son baston force belles fleurs rouges et blanches
et maints boutons de feuilles, et ainsi vit-il reverdir toute
l'escorce. Ce dont il eut grande crainte et moult s'en esmut,
et grande pitié lui prit de ce chevalier qui s'en estoyt
départi sans espoir comme un homme misérable et damné.
Doncques envoya force messaigers devers luy pour le rame-
ner, disant qu'il aurait de Dieu grace et bonne absolution de
son grand pesché d'amour. Mais oncques plus ne le virent;
car toujours demeura ce pauvre chevalier auprès de Vénus
la haulte et forte déesse ès flancs de la montagne amoureuse.

*Livre des grandes merveilles d'amour, escript en latin
et en françoys par Maistre Antoine Gaget.* 1530.

Title: "Praise of Venus," or possibly "A Glorious Deed of Venus."
Introduction: There was no Antoine Gaget; he is an invention of Swinburne's. The passage he wrote in more or less Renaissance French can be
translated as follows: "Then he said, weeping, Alas, miserable man and cursed
sinner that I am, I shall never see the mercy and pity of God. Now I shall go
from here and hide myself within Mount Horsel, begging again the favor and
the loving mercy of my sweet lady Venus, because for her love I shall be forever damned to hell. Here is the end of all my deeds of arms and my lovely
songs. Alas, too beautiful were the face of my lady and her eyes, and it was an
evil day when I saw them. Then he departed groaning and returned to her, and
there lived sadly in great love with his lady. Then afterwards it came about
that one day the pope saw beautiful red and white flowers and many buds of

1   ASLEEP or waking is it? for her neck,
           Kissed over close, wears yet a purple speck
               Wherein the pained blood falters and goes out;
           Soft, and stung softly—fairer for a fleck.

5   But though my lips shut sucking on the place,
           There is no vein at work upon her face;
               Her eyelids are so peaceable, no doubt
           Deep sleep has warmed her blood through all its ways.

9   Lo, this is she that was the world's delight;
           The old grey years were parcels of her might;
               The strewings of the ways wherein she trod
           Were the twain seasons of the day and night.

13   Lo, she was thus when her clear limbs enticed

---

leaves break forth on his staff, and thus he saw the dead wood become green
again. Then he was much afraid and greatly moved, and a great pity took for
that knight who had departed without hope like a man miserable and damned.
Then he sent eagerly messengers to him to bring him back, saying that God
had given him grace and good absolution for his great sin of love. But they saw
him no more; for this poor knight lived forever with the high and powerful
goddess Venus within the flanks of the mountain of love.—*Book of the great
marvels of love, written in Latin and French by Master Antoine Gaget. 1530.*"
The legend of Tannhäuser had been published several times in nineteenth-
century Germany. Originally a medieval legend, it was retold by Ludwig Tieck
(1799); by Achim von Arnim and Clemens Brentano (1804); by Ludwig
Bechstein, in a collection of folktales of Thuringia (Central Germany), the
site of Mount Horsel, the legendary mountain of Venus; and by Heine, in a
satirical poem published in 1837. Wagner's opera, first produced in 1849, made
the story famous throughout Europe. A scandalous production at Paris in 1861
attracted European attention; there were pictures of the splendid production in
The Illustrated London News. Charles Baudelaire, the greatest French poet
of the times, defended Wagner in a pamphlet published the same year, which
he mentioned in a letter to Swinburne in 1863. Swinburne was stimulated by
Wagner's music, and later said that his own *Tristram of Lyonesse* (1882) was
inspired by Wagner's *Tristan und Isolde.*

       1–4. The stanza is taken from Edward Fitzgerald's *The Rubáiyát of Omar
Khayyám,* first published in 1859 and as yet little known. Swinburne learned of
it from Rossetti and other members of the Pre-Raphaelite group. However,
Swinburne's stanza differs from Fitzgerald's in that the stanzas are paired by
a rhyming third line.

All lips that now grow sad with kissing Christ,
　　Stained with blood fallen from the feet of God,
　　The feet and hands whereat our souls were priced.

Alas, Lord, surely thou art great and fair. 17
But lo her wonderfully woven hair!
　　And thou didst heal us with thy piteous kiss;
　　But see now, Lord; her mouth is lovelier.

She is right fair; what hath she done to thee? 21
Nay, fair Lord Christ, lift up thine eyes and see;
　　Had now thy mother such a lip—like this?
　　Thou knowest how sweet a thing it is to me.

Inside the Horsel here the air is hot; 25
Right little peace one hath for it, God wot;
　　The scented dusty daylight burns the air,
　　And my heart chokes me till I hear it not.

Behold, my Venus, my soul's body, lies 29
With my love laid upon her garment-wise,
　　Feeling my love in all her limbs and hair
　　And shed between her eyelids through her eyes.

She holds my heart in her sweet open hands 33
Hanging asleep; hard by her head there stands,
　　Crowned with gilt thorns and clothed with flesh like fire,
　　Love, wan as foam blown up the salt burnt sands—

Hot as the brackish waifs of yellow spume 37
That shift and steam—loose clots of arid fume
　　From the sea's panting mouth of dry desire;
　　There stands he, like one labouring at a loom.

The warp holds fast across; and every thread 41

36. *Love:* Cupid, still represented in the Middle Ages as a beautiful youth.

That makes the woof up has dry specks of red;
   Always the shuttle cleaves clean through, and he
Weaves with the hair of many a ruined head.

45   Love is not glad nor sorry, as I deem;
   Labouring he dreams, and labours in the dream,
     Till when the spool is finished, lo I see
His web, reeled off, curls and goes out like steam.

49   Night falls like fire; the heavy lights run low,
   And as they drop, my blood and body so
     Shake as the flame shakes, full of days and hours
That sleep not neither weep they as they go.

53   Ah yet would God this flesh of mine might be
   Where air might wash and long leaves cover me,
     Where tides of grass break into foam of flowers,
Or where the wind's feet shine along the sea.

57   Ah yet would God that stems and roots were bred
   Out of my weary body and my head,
     That sleep were sealed upon me with a seal,
And I were as the least of all his dead.

61   Would God my blood were dew to feed the grass,
   Mine ears made deaf and mine eyes blind as glass,
     My body broken as a turning wheel,
And my mouth stricken ere it saith Alas!

65   Ah God, that love were as a flower or flame,
   That life were as the naming of a name,
     That death were not more pitiful than desire,
That these things were not one thing and the same!

69   Behold now, surely somewhere there is death:
   For each man hath some space of years, he saith,
     A little space of time ere time expire,
A little day, a little way of breath.

And lo, between the sundawn and the sun,   73
His day's work and his night's work are undone;
    And lo, between the nightfall and the night,
He is not, and none knoweth of such an one.

Ah God, that I were as all souls that be,   77
As any herb or leaf of any tree,
    As men that toil through hours of labouring night,
As bones of men under the deep sharp sea.

Outside it must be winter among men;   81
For at the gold bars of the gates again
    I heard all night and all the hours of it
The wind's wet wings and fingers drip with rain.

Knights gather, riding sharp for cold; I know   85
The ways and woods are strangled with the snow;
    And with short song the maidens spin and sit
Until Christ's birthnight, lily-like, arow.

The scent and shadow shed about me make   89
The very soul in all my senses ache;
    The hot hard night is fed upon my breath,
And sleep beholds me from afar awake.

Alas, but surely where the hills grow deep,   93
Or where the wild ways of the sea are steep,
    Or in strange places somewhere there is death,
And on death's face the scattered hair of sleep.

There lover-like with lips and limbs that meet   97
They lie, they pluck sweet fruit of life and eat;
    But me the hot and hungry days devour,
And in my mouth no fruit of theirs is sweet.

No fruit of theirs, but fruit of my desire,   101

75. night 1904] light,

For her love's sake whose lips through mine respire;
Her eyelids on her eyes like flower on flower,
Mine eyelids on mine eyes like fire on fire.

105   So lie we, not as sleep that lies by death,
With heavy kisses and with happy breath;
Not as man lies by woman, when the bride
Laughs low for love's sake and the words he saith.

109   For she lies, laughing low with love; she lies
And turns his kisses on her lips to sighs,
To sighing sound of lips unsatisfied,
And the sweet tears are tender with her eyes.

113   Ah, not as they, but as the souls that were
Slain in the old time, having found her fair;
Who, sleeping with her lips upon their eyes,
Heard sudden serpents hiss across her hair.

117   Their blood runs round the roots of time like rain:
She casts them forth and gathers them again;
With nerve and bone she weaves and multiplies
Exceeding pleasure out of extreme pain.

121   Her little chambers drip with flower-like red,
Her girdles, and the chaplets of her head,
Her armlets and her anklets; with her feet
She tramples all that winepress of the dead.

125   Her gateways smoke with fume of flowers and fires,
With loves burnt out and unassuaged desires;
Between her lips the steam of them is sweet,
The languor in her ears of many lyres.

129   Her beds are full of perfume and sad sound,

122. *chaplets:* Wreaths worn on the head.

Her doors are made with music, and barred round
  With sighing and with laughter and with tears,
With tears whereby strong souls of men are bound.

There is the knight Adonis that was slain;   133
With flesh and blood she chains him for a chain;
  The body and the spirit in her ears
Cry, for her lips divide him vein by vein.

Yea, all she slayeth; yea, every man save me;   137
Me, love, thy lover that must cleave to thee
  Till the ending of the days and ways of earth,
The shaking of the sources of the sea.

Me, most forsaken of all souls that fell;   141
Me, satiated with things insatiable;
  Me, for whose sake the extreme hell makes mirth,
Yea, laughter kindles at the heart of hell.

Alas thy beauty! for thy mouth's sweet sake   145
My soul is bitter to me, my limbs quake
  As water, as the flesh of men that weep,
As their heart's vein whose heart goes nigh to break.

Ah God, that sleep with flower-sweet finger-tips   149
Would crush the fruit of death upon my lips;
  Ah God, that death would tread the grapes of sleep
And wring their juice upon me as it drips.

There is no change of cheer for many days,   153
But change of chimes high up in the air, that sways
  Rung by the running fingers of the wind;
And singing sorrows heard on hidden ways.

133. *Adonis:* Calling an ancient Greek figure a knight is part of the medieval atmosphere of the poem. The beautiful youth Adonis, offspring of an incestuous union between his mother, Myrrha, and her father, was out hunting
when Aphrodite (Venus) fell in love with him. He preferred hunting to dal-
liance and was killed by a boar.

157   Day smiteth day in twain, night sundereth night,
And on mine eyes the dark sits as the light;
     Yea, Lord, thou knowest I know not, having sinned,
If heaven be clean or unclean in thy sight.

161   Yea, as if earth were sprinkled over me,
Such chafed harsh earth as chokes a sandy sea,
     Each pore doth yearn, and the dried blood thereof
Gasps by sick fits, my heart swims heavily,

165   There is a feverish famine in my veins;
Below her bosom, where a crushed grape stains
     The white and blue, there my lips caught and clove
An hour since, and what mark of me remains?

169   I dare not always touch her, lest the kiss
Leave my lips charred. Yea, Lord, a little bliss,
     Brief bitter bliss, one hath for a great sin;
Nathless thou knowest how sweet a thing it is.

173   Sin, is it sin whereby men's souls are thrust
Into the pit? yet had I a good trust
     To save my soul before it slipped therein,
Trod under by the fire-shod feet of lust.

177   For if mine eyes fail and my soul takes breath,
I look between the iron sides of death
     Into sad hell where all sweet love hath end,
All but the pain that never finisheth.

181   There are the naked faces of great kings,
The singing folk with all their lute-playings;
     There when one cometh he shall have to friend
The grave that covets and the worm that clings.

185   There sit the knights that were so great of hand,

---

182. *lute:* See note to "A Ballad of Life," line 13.

The ladies that were queens of fair green land,
  Grown grey and black now, brought unto the dust,
Soiled, without raiment, clad about with sand.

There is one end for all of them; they sit   189
Naked and sad, they drink the dregs of it,
  Trodden as grapes in the wine-press of lust,
Trampled and trodden by the fiery feet.

I see the marvellous mouth whereby there fell   193
Cities and people whom the gods loved well,
  Yet for her sake on them the fire gat hold,
And for their sakes on her the fire of hell.

And softer than the Egyptian lote-leaf is,   197
The queen whose face was worth the world to kiss,
  Wearing at breast a suckling snake of gold;
And large pale lips of strong Semiramis,

Curled like a tiger's that curl back to feed;   201
Red only where the last kiss made them bleed;
  Her hair most thick with many a carven gem,
Deep in the mane, great-chested, like a steed.

Yea, with red sin the faces of them shine;   205
But in all these there was no sin like mine;
  No, not in all the strange great sins of them
That made the wine-press froth and foam with wine.

193–196. Probably an allusion to Helen of Troy.
197–199. Cleopatra.
200. *Semiramis:* A lengendary queen and founder of the Assyrian city of
Nineveh (ninth century B.C.). At this time Nineveh was very much in the news.
Henry Austin Layard (1817–1894) had discovered its ruins in the 1840's, and
in the 1850's the magnificent sculptures he found were brought to England and
installed in the British Museum. Rossetti had mentioned Semiramis in a poem
on this installation, "The Burden of Nineveh"; although it was not published
until 1870, Swinburne probably was familiar with it. These lines (193–204)
are most meaningfully read with a knowledge of Tennyson's "A Dream of Fair
Women" (1832), for Swinburne frequently derided Tennyson and his other
predecessors for their pallid presentation of eroticism.

209 For I was of Christ's choosing, I God's knight,
   No blinkard heathen stumbling for scant light;
    I can well see, for all the dusty days
   Gone past, the clean great time of goodly fight.

213 I smell the breathing battle sharp with blows,
   With shriek of shafts and snapping short of bows;
    The fair pure sword smites out in subtle ways,
   Sounds and long lights are shed between the rows

   Of beautiful mailed men; the edged light slips,
   Most like a snake that takes short breath and dips
    Sharp from the beautifully bending head,
   With all its gracious body lithe as lips

221 That curl in touching you; right in this wise
   My sword doth, seeming fire in mine own eyes,
    Leaving all colours in them brown and red
   And flecked with death; then the keen breaths like sighs,

225 The caught-up choked dry laughters following them,
   When all the fighting face is grown a flame
    For pleasure, and the pulse that stuns the ears,
   And the heart's gladness of the goodly game.

229 Let me think yet a little; I do know
   These things were sweet, but sweet such years ago,
    Their savour is all turned now into tears;
   Yea, ten years since, where the blue ripples blow,

233 The blue curled eddies of the blowing Rhine,
   I felt the sharp wind shaking grass and vine
    Touch my blood too, and sting me with delight
   Through all this waste and weary body of mine

237 That never feels clear air; right gladly then
   I rode alone, a great way off my men,

210. *blinkard:* Weak-eyed.
217. *edged light:* The light on sword edges.

And heard the chiming bridle smite and smite,
And gave each rhyme thereof some rhyme again,

Till my song shifted to that iron one;   241
Seeing there rode up between me and the sun
    Some certain of my foe's men, for his three
White wolves across their painted coats did run.

The first red-bearded, with square cheeks—alack,   245
I made my knave's blood turn his beard to black;
    The slaying of him was a joy to see:
Perchance too, when at night he came not back,

Some woman fell a-weeping, whom this thief   249
Would beat when he had drunken; yet small grief
    Hath any for the ridding of such knaves;
Yea, if one wept, I doubt her teen was brief.

This bitter love is sorrow in all lands,   253
Draining of eyelids, wringing of drenched hands,
    Sighing of hearts and filling up of graves;
A sign across the head of the world he stands,

An one that hath a plague-mark on his brows;   257
Dust and spilt blood do track him to his house
    Down under earth; sweet smells of lip and cheek,
Like a sweet snake's breath made more poisonous

With chewing of some perfumed deadly grass,   261
Are shed all round his passage if he pass,
    And their quenched savour leaves the whole soul weak,
Sick with keen guessing whence the perfume was.

239. *chiming bridle:* Medieval bridles were often hung with little bells.
244. *painted coats:* "Painted" here means "decorated," or "having a design." In late medieval times knights frequently wore a surcoat, or long sleeve-
less tunic, over their armor. Frequently across the chest was depicted the
coat of arms or heraldic device.
252. *teen:* Grief.

265   As one who hidden in deep sedge and reeds
         Smells the rare scent made where a panther feeds,
             And tracking ever slotwise the warm smell
         Is snapped upon by the sweet mouth and bleeds,

269   His head far down the hot sweet throat of her—
         So one tracks love, whose breath is deadlier,
             And lo, one springe and you are fast in hell,
         Fast as the gin's grip of a wayfarer.

273   I think now, as the heavy hours decease
         One after one, and bitter thoughts increase
             One upon one, of all sweet finished things;
         The breaking of the battle; the long peace

277   Wherein we sat clothed softly, each man's hair
         Crowned with green leaves beneath white hoods of vair;
             The sounds of sharp spears at great tourneyings,
         And noise of singing in the late sweet air.

281   I sang of love too, knowing nought thereof;
         "Sweeter," I said, "the little laugh of love
             Than tears out of the eyes of Magdalen,
         Or any fallen feather of the Dove.

267. *slotwise:* Following the track of an animal.
271. *springe:* Animal trap, specifically one made with a noose.
272. *gin:* Animal snare; also, in England, as here, a man-trap, or trap set off by a trigger and spring, large enough to catch and hold a man and even break a leg, and used to discourage poachers. They were outlawed only in the nineteenth century.
278. *vair:* In the Middle Ages, a valued fur of squirrel skin.
283. *Magdalen:* Mary Magdalene, one of the three Marys at the foot of the crucified Christ. She is traditionally represented as a repentant sinner, specifically a prostitute. She is said to have come to Marseilles, France, and converted many people, and afterwards to have retired into a nearby deserted country, where she remained in solitude for thirty years eating and drinking no human food but ministered to by angels. She is traditionally represented as weeping.
284. *Dove:* The traditional representation of the Holy Ghost.

"The broken little laugh that spoils a kiss,   285
The ache of purple pulses, and the bliss
    Of blinded eyelids that expand again—
Love draws them open with those lips of his,

"Lips that cling hard till the kissed face has grown   289
Of one same fire and colour with their own;
    Then ere one sleep, appeased with sacrifice,
Where his lips wounded, there his lips atone."

I sang these things long since and knew them not;   293
"Lo, here is love, or there is love, God wot,
    This man and that finds favour in his eyes,"
I said, "but I, what guerdon have I got?

"The dust of praise that is blown everywhere   297
In all men's faces with the common air;
    The bay-leaf that wants chafing to be sweet
Before they wind it in a singer's hair."

So that one dawn I rode forth sorrowing;   301
I had no hope but of some evil thing,
    And so rode slowly past the windy wheat
And past the vineyard and the water-spring,

Up to the Horsel. A great elder-tree   305
Held back its heaps of flowers to let me see
    The ripe tall grass, and one that walked therein,
Naked, with hair shed over to the knee.

She walked between the blossom and the grass;   309
I knew the beauty of her, what she was,
    The beauty of her body and her sin,
And in my flesh the sin of hers, alas!

296. *guerdon:* Recompense, or earned reward.
299. *bay-leaf:* The crown of bay, or laurel, leaf was traditionally placed on the head of a victor in ancient Greece, particularly at the Pythian games, held in honor of Apollo, who among other attributes was the god of poetry.
305. *Horsel:* See note to Introduction.

313   Alas! for sorrow is all the end of this.
         O sad kissed mouth, how sorrowful it is!
            O breast whereat some suckling sorrow clings,
         Red with the bitter blossom of a kiss!

317   Ah, with blind lips I felt for you, and found
         About my neck your hands and hair enwound,
            The hands that stifle and the hair that stings,
         I felt them fasten sharply without sound.

321   Yea, for my sin I had great store of bliss:
         Rise up, make answer for me, let thy kiss
            Seal my lips hard from speaking of my sin,
         Lest one go mad to hear how sweet it is.

325   Yet I waxed faint with fume of barren bowers,
         And murmuring of the heavy-headed hours;
            And let the dove's beak fret and peck within
         My lips in vain, and Love shed fruitless flowers.

329   So that God looked upon me when your hands
         Were hot about me; yea, God brake my bands
            To save my soul alive, and I came forth
         Like a man blind and naked in strange lands

333   That hears men laugh and weep, and knows not whence
         Nor wherefore, but is broken in his sense;
            Howbeit I met folk riding from the north
         Towards Rome, to purge them of their souls' offence,

337   And rode with them, and spake to none; the day
         Stunned me like lights upon some wizard way,
            And ate like fire mine eyes and mine eyesight;
         So rode I, hearing all these chant and pray,

336. *Rome:* One of the principal goals for medieval pilgrims, second only to Jerusalem.
338. *wizard:* Enchanted by magic.

And marvelled; till before us rose and fell   341
White cursed hills, like outer skirts of hell
   Seen where men's eyes look through the day to night,
Like a jagged shell's lips, harsh, untunable,

Blown in between by devils' wrangling breath;   345
Nathless we won well past that hell and death,
   Down to the sweet land where all airs are good,
Even unto Rome where God's grace tarrieth.

Then came each man and worshipped at his knees   349
Who in the Lord God's likeness bears the keys
   To bind or loose, and called on Christ's shed blood,
And so the sweet-souled father gave him ease.

But when I came I fell down at his feet,   353
Saying, "Father, though the Lord's blood be right sweet,
   The spot it takes not off the panther's skin,
Nor shall an Ethiop's stain be bleached with it.

"Lo, I have sinned and have spat out at God,   357
Wherefore his hand is heavier and his rod
   More sharp because of mine exceeding sin,
And all his raiment redder than bright blood

"Before mine eyes; yea, for my sake I wot   361
The heat of hell is waxen seven times hot
   Through my great sin." Then spake he some sweet word,
Giving me cheer; which thing availed me not;

---

342. *White cursed hills:* The Alps.
347. *the sweet land:* Italy.
350. *keys:* Christ said to the Apostle Peter, "I will give unto thee the keys of the kingdom of heaven." Peter is traditionally believed to have founded the papacy, and hence the popes are also presented as having inherited these keys, which are displayed on the papal arms.
352. *the sweet-souled father:* The pope in the Tannhäuser legend was traditionally one of the Popes Urban, of whom there were six in the Middle Ages.
356. *Ethiop:* Generic term for Negro.

365   Yea, scarce I wist if such indeed were said;
           For when I ceased—lo, as one newly dead
               Who hears a great cry out of hell, I heard
           The crying of his voice across my head.

369   "Until this dry shred staff, that hath no whit
           Of leaf nor bark, bear blossom and smell sweet,
               Seek thou not any mercy in God's sight,
           For so long shalt thou be cast out from it."

373   Yea, what if dried-up stems wax red and green,
           Shall that thing be which is not nor has been?
               Yea, what if sapless bark wax green and white,
           Shall any good fruit grow upon my sin?

377   Nay, though sweet fruit were plucked of a dry tree,
           And though men drew sweet waters of the sea,
               There should not grow sweet leaves on this dead stem,
           This waste wan body and shaken soul of me.

381   Yea, though God search it warily enough,
           There is not one sound thing in all thereof;
               Though he search all my veins through, searching them
           He shall find nothing whole therein but love.

385   For I came home right heavy, with small cheer,
           And lo my love, mine own soul's heart, more dear
               Than mine own soul, more beautiful than God,
           Who hath my being between the hands of her—

389   Fair still, but fair for no man saving me,
           As when she came out of the naked sea
               Making the foam as fire whereon she trod,
           And as the inner flower of fire was she.

393   Yea, she laid hold upon me, and her mouth

369. *shred:* Stripped of all vegetation and bark.
390–391. See note to "Anactoria," lines 48–49.

Clove unto mine as soul to body doth,
    And, laughing, made her lips luxurious;
Her hair had smells of all the sunburnt south,

Strange spice and flower, strange savour of crushed fruit,   397
And perfume the swart kings tread underfoot
    For pleasure when their minds wax amorous,
Charred frankincense and grated sandal-root.

And I forgot fear and all weary things,   401
All ended prayers and perished thanksgivings,
    Feeling her face with all her eager hair
Cleave to me, clinging as a fire that clings

To the body and to the raiment, burning them;   405
As after death I know that such-like flame
    Shall cleave to me for ever; yea, what care,
Albeit I burn then, having felt the same?

Ah love, there is no better life than this;   409
To have known love, how bitter a thing it is,
    And afterward be cast out of God's sight;
Yea, these that know not, shall they have such bliss

High up in barren heaven before his face   413
As we twain in the heavy-hearted place,
    Remembering love and all the dead delight,
And all that time was sweet with for a space?

For till the thunder in the trumpet be,   417

398. *swart:* Black, or Negro; or Asiatic Indian.

400. *frankincense:* See note to "A Ballad of Death," line 67. One of the three kings—the Wise Men, or Magi—who came to the nativity of Christ is traditionally presented as black, or dark-skinned. Of their three gifts, gold, myrrh, and frankincense, the last is the emblem of death and of self-sacrifice. *sandal-root:* Anciently, and today, a source for perfume.

417–424. *thunder in the trumpet:* The sound of the last trumpet, announcing the day of judgment, at which time souls shall rejoin their bodies for the final assignment to heaven or hell.

Soul may divide from body, but not we
    One from another; I hold thee with my hand,
I let mine eyes have all their will of thee,

421   I seal myself upon thee with my might,
        Abiding alway out of all men's sight
            Until God loosen over sea and land
        The thunder of the trumpets of the night.

EXPLICIT LAUS VENERIS.

Explicit: "Here ends," a formula for indicating the end; found in medieval manuscripts.

421. *seal:* See Song of Solomon, 8:6. "Set me as a seal upon thine heart, as a seal upon thine arm; for love is strong as death; jealousy is cruel as the grave: the coals thereof are coals of fire, which hath a most vehement flame." This book of the Bible, now widely considered a love poem, has traditionally been taken as an allegory of the love of Christ for his bride, the Church.

Phœdra

HIPPOLYTUS; PHÆDRA;
CHORUS OF TRŒZENIAN WOMEN

HIPPOLYTUS.

Lay not thine hand upon me; let me go;
Take off thine eyes that put the gods to shame;
What, wilt thou turn my loathing to thy death?

PHÆDRA.

Nay, I will never loosen hold nor breathe
Till thou have slain me; godlike for great brows   5
Thou art, and thewed as gods are, with clear hair:
Draw now thy sword and smite me as thou are god,
For verily I am smitten of other gods,
Why not of thee?

Title: The story of Phaedra, Theseus, and Hippolytus is complex, and Swinburne uses most of it. On his way home from the Delphic oracle Aegeus, King
of Athens, was tricked by Pittheus, King of Troezen, into lying with Aithra,
Pittheus' daughter. Their child was Theseus, brought up by his grandfather in
Troezen. On reaching manhood he went to Athens and proved he was Aegeus'
son. The Athenians were required by Minos, King of Crete, to send youths and
maidens every year to be sacrificed to the Minotaur, half man and half bull,
the offspring of Pasiphae, wife of Minos and mother also of Ariadne and
Phaedra. Pasiphae had fallen in love with a splendid bull sent by the gods to
Minos and persuaded Dedalus, the great craftsman, to build for her an artificial cow in which she might conceal herself and couple with the bull. The offspring was the Minotaur. With the aid of Ariadne, Theseus slew the Minotaur
at the heart of the labyrinth constructed by Dedalus. He fled with Ariadne and
subsequently abandoned her on Naxos, where she was found by Dionysos. On
his return to Athens, his father having died through his carelessness in changing black sails for white, Theseus became King of Athens. He battled the
Amazons, the tribe of warrior women, and seduced their queen Hippolyta. The

CHORUS.

O queen, take heed of words;
10   Why wilt thou eat the husk of evil speech?
Wear wisdom for that veil about thy head
And goodness for the binding of thy brows.

PHÆDRA.

Nay, but this god hath cause enow to smite;
If he will slay me, baring breast and throat,
15   I lean toward the stroke with silent mouth
And a great heart.   Come, take thy sword and slay;
Let me not starve between desire and death,
But send me on my way with glad wet lips;
For in the vein-drawn ashen-coloured palm
20   Death's hollow hand holds water of sweet draught
To dip and slake dried mouths at, as a deer
Specked red from thorns laps deep and loses pain.
Yea, if mine own blood ran upon my mouth,
I would drink that.   Nay, but be swift with me;

---

child was Hippolytus. Subsequently Theseus married Phædra. Since Hippolytus was illegitimate, though loved, Theseus sent him to his grandfather at
Trœzen to be brought up there and inherit the rule of Trœzen, while his legiti-
mate sons should rule Athens. Subsequently losing control of Athens, Theseus
fled with Phædra to Trœzen. There Phædra fell in love with Hippolytus and in
the absence of Theseus attempted to seduce him. Repulsed, she cursed him,
hanged herself, and left behind a letter accusing him of having raped her and
asserting that she had committed suicide out of shame. Theseus exiled Hippolytus and cursed him. Poseidon, the god of the sea, had granted Theseus three
wishes, and one of these was used to fulfill Theseus' curse: as Hippolytus drove
along the shores of the Saronic Gulf, a sea-monster, sent by Poseidon, rose out of
the sea and so frightened Hippolytus' horses that they bolted. He was thrown
from his chariot and killed. The principal works for the story of Hippolytus
are the play of that name by Euripides, the *Phædra* (or *Hippolytus*) of Seneca,
Ovid's *Metamorphoses* XV, and Racine's seventeenth-century French tragedy,
Phèdre. According to Euripides, Aphrodite hated Hippolytus because he reviled her as the worst of the divinities and devoted his worship to her enemy
Artemis, the goddess of hunting and virginity. His play begins with a speech
by Aphrodite outlining her punishment of Hippolytus; but he does not present
Phædra in direct confrontation with Hippolytus. In another play, now lost—
Hippolytus Veiled—Euripides does present Phædra making advances. This
probably led Swinburne to create such a scene.

Set thy sword here between the girdle and breast,　　25
For I shall grow a poison if I live
Are not my cheeks as grass, my body pale,
And my breath like a dying poisoned man's?
O whatsoever of godlike names thou be,
By thy chief name I charge thee, thou strong god,　　30
And bid thee slay me.　Strike, up to the gold,
Up to the hand-grip of the hilt; strike here;
For I am Cretan of my birth; strike now;
For I am Theseus' wife; stab up to the rims,
I am born daughter to Pasiphæ.　　35
See thou spare not for greatness of my blood,
Nor for the shining letters of my name:
Make thy sword sure inside thine hand and smite,
For the bright writing of my name is black,
And I am sick with hating the sweet sun.　　40

HIPPOLYTUS.

Let not this woman wail and cleave to me,
That am no part of the gods' wrath with her;
Loose ye her hands from me lest she take hurt.

CHORUS.

Lady, this speech and majesty are twain;
Pure shame is of one counsel with the gods.　　45

HIPPOLYTUS.

Man is as beast when shame stands off from him.

PHÆDRA.

Man, what have I to do with shame or thee?
I am not of one counsel with the gods.
I am their kin, I have strange blood in me,
I am not of their likeness nor of thine:　　50
My veins are mixed, and therefore am I mad,

Yea therefore chafe and turn on mine own flesh,
Half of a woman made with half a god.
But thou wast hewn out of an iron womb
55   And fed with molten mother-snow for milk.
A sword was nurse of thine; Hippolyta,
That had the spear to father, and the axe
To bridesman, and wet blood of sword-slain men
For wedding-water out of a noble well,
60   Even she did bear thee, thinking of a sword,
And thou wast made a man mistakingly.
Nay, for I love thee, I will have thy hands,
Nay, for I will not loose thee, thou art sweet,
Thou art my son, I am thy father's wife,
65   I ache toward thee with a bridal blood,
The pulse is heavy in all my married veins,
My whole face beats, I will feed full of thee,
My body is empty of ease, I will be fed,
I am burnt to the bone with love, thou shalt not go,
70   I am heartsick, and mine eyelids prick mine eyes,
Thou shalt not sleep nor eat nor say a word
Till thou hast slain me.   I am not good to live.

CHORUS.

This is an evil born with all its teeth,
When love is cast out of the bound of love.

HIPPOLYTUS.

75   There is no hate that is so hateworthy.

PHÆDRA.

I pray thee turn that hate of thine my way,
I hate not it nor anything of thine.
Lo, maidens, how he burns about the brow,
And draws the chafing sword-strap down his hand.
80   What wilt thou do? wilt thou be worse than death?

Be but as sweet as is the bitterest,
The most dispiteous out of all the gods,
I am well pleased. Lo, do I crave so much?
I do but bid thee be unmerciful,
Even the one thing thou art. Pity me not: 85
Thou wert not quick to pity. Think of me
As of a thing thy hounds are keen upon
In the wet woods between the windy ways,
And slay me for a spoil. This body of mine
Is worth a wild beast's fell or hide of hair,   90
And spotted deeper than a panther's grain.
I were but dead if thou wert pure indeed;
I pray thee by thy cold green holy crown
And by the fillet-leaves of Artemis.
Nay, but thou wilt not. Death is not like thee,   95
Albeit men hold him worst of all the gods.
For of all gods Death only loves not gifts,*
Nor with burnt-offering nor blood-sacrifice
Shalt thou do aught to get thee grace of him;
He will have nought of altar and altar-song,   100
And from him only of all the lords in heaven
Persuasion turns a sweet averted mouth.
But thou art worse: from thee with baffled breath
Back on my lips my prayer falls like a blow,
And beats upon them, dumb.   What shall I say?   105
There is no word I can compel thee with
To do me good and slay me.   But take heed;
I say, be wary; look between thy feet,
Lest a snare take them though the ground be good.

HIPPOLYTUS.

Shame may do most where fear is found most weak;   110
That which for shame's sake yet I have not done,

---

* Æsch. Fr. Niobe:—μόνος θεῶν γὰρ Θάνατος οὐ δώρων ἐρᾷ, κ.τ.λ.

94. *fillet-leaves:* In Euripides' play Hippolytus lays a garland on the altar
of Artemis.

Shall it be done for fear's?   Take thine own way;
Better the foot slip than the whole soul swerve.

PHÆDRA.

The man is choice and exquisite of mouth;
115   Yet in the end a curse shall curdle it.

CHORUS.

He goes with cloak upgathered to the lip,
Holding his eye as with some ill in sight.

PHÆDRA.

A bitter ill he hath i' the way thereof,
And it shall burn the sight out as with fire.

CHORUS.

120   Speak no such word whereto mischance is kin.

PHÆDRA.

Out of my heart and by fate's leave I speak.

CHORUS.

Set not thy heart to follow after fate.

PHÆDRA.

O women, O sweet people of this land,
O goodly city and pleasant ways thereof,
125   And woods with pasturing grass and great well-heads,
And hills with light and night between your leaves,
And winds with sound and silence in your lips,
And earth and water and all immortal things,
I take you to my witness what I am.
130   There is a god about me like as fire,

Sprung whence, who knoweth, or who hath heart to say?
A god more strong than whom slain beasts can soothe,
Or honey, or any spilth of blood-like wine,
Nor shall one please him with a whitened brow
Nor wheat nor wool nor aught of plaited leaf.   135
For like my mother am I stung and slain,
And round my cheeks have such red malady
And on my lips such fire and foam as hers.
This is that Ate out of Amathus
That breeds up death and gives it one for love.   140
She hath slain mercy, and for dead mercy's sake
(Being frighted with this sister that was slain)
Flees from before her fearful-footed shame,
And will not bear the bending of her brows
And long soft arrows flown from under them   145
As from bows bent.   Desire flows out of her
As out of lips doth speech: and over her
Shines fire, and round her and beneath her fire.
She hath sown pain and plague in all our house,
Love loathed of love, and mates unmatchable,   150
Wild wedlock, and the lusts that bleat or low,
And marriage-fodder snuffed about of kine.
Lo how the heifer runs with leaping flank
Sleek under shaggy and speckled lies of hair,
And chews a horrible lip, and with harsh tongue   155
Laps alien froth and licks a loathlier mouth.
Alas, a foul first steam of trodden tares,
And fouler of these late grapes underfoot.
A bitter way of waves and clean-cut foam
Over the sad road of sonorous sea   160
The high gods gave king Theseus for no love,
Nay, but for love, yet to no loving end.
Alas the long thwarts and the fervent oars,
And blown hard sails that straightened the scant rope!

---

139. *Ate:* Goddess of the blind folly that ruins men. *Amathus:* City on
the south shore of Cyprus, site of a famous shrine to Aphrodite.

165   There were no strong pools in the hollow sea
To drag at them and suck down side and beak,
No wind to catch them in the teeth and hair,
No shoal, no shallow among the roaring reefs,
No gulf whereout the straining tides throw spars,
170   No surf where white bones twist like whirled white fire.
But like to death he came with death, and sought
And slew and spoiled and gat him that he would.
For death, for marriage, and for child-getting,
I set my curse against him as a sword;
175   Yea, and the severed half thereof I leave
Pittheus, because he slew not (when that face
Was tender, and the life still soft in it)
The small swathed child, but bred him for my fate.
I would I had been the first that took her death
180   Out from between wet hoofs and reddened teeth,
Splashed horns, fierce fetlocks of the brother bull!
For now shall I take death a deadlier way,
Gathering it up between the feet of love
Or off the knees of murder reaching it.

The Triumph of Time

BEFORE our lives divide for ever,   1
    While time is with us and hands are free,
(Time, swift to fasten and swift to sever
    Hand from hand, as we stand by the sea)
I will say no word that a man might say
Whose whole life's love goes down in a day;
For this could never have been; and never,
    Though the gods and the years relent, shall be.

Is it worth a tear, is it worth an hour,   9
    To think of things that are well outworn?
Of fruitless husk and fugitive flower,
    The dream foregone and the deed forborne?
Though joy be done with and grief be vain,
Time shall not sever us wholly in twain;
Earth is not spoilt for a single shower;
    But the rain has ruined the ungrown corn.

It will grow not again, this fruit of my heart,   17
    Smitten with sunbeams, ruined with rain.
The singing seasons divide and depart,
    Winter and summer depart in twain.
It will grow not again, it is ruined at root,
The bloodlike blossom, the dull red fruit;
Though the heart yet sickens, the lips yet smart,
    With sullen savour of poisonous pain.

I have given no man of my fruit to eat;   25
    I trod the grapes, I have drunken the wine.
Had you eaten and drunken and found it sweet,
    This wild new growth of the corn and vine,

This wine and bread without lees or leaven,
We had grown as gods, as the gods in heaven,
Souls fair to look upon, goodly to greet,
    One splendid spirit, your soul and mine.

33   In the change of years, in the coil of things,
                In the clamour and rumour of life to be,
            We, drinking love at the furthest springs,
                Covered with love as a covering tree,
            We had grown as gods, as the gods above,
            Filled from the heart to the lips with love,
            Held fast in his hands, clothed warm with his wings,
                O love, my love, had you loved but me!

41   We had stood as the sure stars stand, and moved
                As the moon moves, loving the world; and seen
            Grief collapse as a thing disproved,
                Death consume as a thing unclean.
            Twain halves of a perfect heart, made fast
            Soul to soul while the years fell past;
            Had you loved me once, as you have not loved;
                Had the chance been with us that has not been.

49   I have put my days and dreams out of mind,
                Days that are over, dreams that are done.
            Though we seek life through, we shall surely find
                There is none of them clear to us now, not one.
            But clear are these things; the grass and the sand,
            Where, sure as the eyes reach, ever at hand,
            With lips wide open and face burnt blind,
                The strong sea-daisies feast on the sun.

57   The low downs lean to the sea; the stream,
                One loose thin pulseless tremulous vein,

57. *downs:* Treeless chalk uplands on the south and southeast coasts of
England.

Rapid and vivid and dumb as a dream,
  Works downward, sick of the sun and the rain;
No wind is rough with the rank rare flowers;
The sweet sea, mother of loves and hours,
Shudders and shines as the grey winds gleam,
  Turning her smile to a fugitive pain.

Mother of loves that are swift to fade,   65
  Mother of mutable winds and hours.
A barren mother, a mother-maid,
  Cold and clean as her faint salt flowers.
I would we twain were even as she,
Lost in the night and the light of the sea,
Where faint sounds falter and wan beams wade,
  Break, and are broken, and shed into showers.

The loves and hours of the life of a man,   73
  They are swift and sad, being born of the sea.
Hours that rejoice and regret for a span,
  Born with a man's breath, mortal as he;
Loves that are lost ere they come to birth,
Weeds of the wave, without fruit upon earth.
I lose what I long for, save what I can,
  My love, my love, and no love for me!

It is not much that a man can save   81
  On the sands of life, in the straits of time,
Who swims in sight of the great third wave
  That never a swimmer shall cross or climb.
Some waif washed up with the strays and spars
That ebb-tide shows to the shore and the stars;
Weed from the water, grass from a grave,
  A broken blossom, a ruined rhyme.

There will no man do for your sake, I think,   89
  What I would have done for the least word said.

I had wrung life dry for your lips to drink,
    Broken it up for your daily bread:
Body for body and blood for blood,
As the flow of the full sea risen to flood
That yearns and trembles before it sink,
    I had given, and lain down for you, glad and dead.

97   Yea, hope at highest and all her fruit,
    And time at fullest and all his dower,
I had given you surely, and life to boot,
    Were we once made one for a single hour.
But now, you are twain, you are cloven apart,
Flesh of his flesh, but heart of my heart;
And deep in one is the bitter root,
    And sweet for one is the lifelong flower.

105   To have died if you cared I should die for you, clung
    To my life if you bade me, played my part
As it pleased you—these were the thoughts that stung,
    The dreams that smote with a keener dart
Than shafts of love or arrows of death;
These were but as fire is, dust, or breath,
Or poisonous foam on the tender tongue
    Of the little snakes that eat my heart.

113   I wish we were dead together to-day,
    Lost sight of, hidden away out of sight,
Clasped and clothed in the cloven clay,
    Out of the world's way, out of the light,
Out of the ages of worldly weather,
Forgotten of all men altogether,
As the world's first dead, taken wholly away,
    Made one with death, filled full of the night.

121   How we should slumber, how we should sleep,
    Far in the dark with the dreams and the dews!
And dreaming, grow to each other, and weep,

Laugh low, live softly, murmur and muse;
Yea, and it may be, struck through by the dream,
Feel the dust quicken and quiver, and seem
Alive as of old to the lips, and leap
   Spirit to spirit as lovers use.

Sick dreams and sad of a dull delight;   129
   For what shall it profit when men are dead
To have dreamed, to have loved with the whole soul's might,
   To have looked for day when the day was fled?
Let come what will, there is one thing worth,
To have had fair love in the life upon earth:
To have held love safe till the day grew night,
   While skies had colour and lips were red.

Would I lose you now? would I take you then,   137
   If I lose you now that my heart has need?
And come what may after death to men,
   What thing worth this will the dead years breed?
Lose life, lose all; but at least I know,
O sweet life's love, having loved you so,
Had I reached you on earth, I should lose not again,
   In death nor life, nor in dream or deed.

Yea, I know this well: were you once sealed mine,   145
   Mine in the blood's beat, mine in the breath,
Mixed into me as honey in wine,
   Not time, that sayeth and gainsayeth,
Nor all strong things had severed us then;
Not wrath of gods, nor wisdom of men,
Nor all things earthly, nor all divine,
   Nor joy nor sorrow, nor life nor death.

I had grown pure as the dawn and the dew,   153
   You had grown strong as the sun or the sea.
But none shall triumph a whole life through:
   For death is one, and the fates are three.

At the door of life, by the gate of breath,
There are worse things waiting for men than death;
Death could not sever my soul and you,
    As these have severed your soul from me.

161   You have chosen and clung to the chance they sent you,
            Life sweet as perfume and pure as prayer.
        But will it not one day in heaven repent you?
            Will they solace you wholly, the days that were?
        Will you lift up your eyes between sadness and bliss,
        Meet mine, and see where the great love is,
        And tremble and turn and be changed?   Content you;
            The gate is strait; I shall not be there.

169   But you, had you chosen, had you stretched hand,
            Had you seen good such a thing were done,
        I too might have stood with the souls that stand
            In the sun's sight, clothed with the light of the sun;
        But who now on earth need care how I live?
        Have the high gods anything left to give,
        Save dust and laurels and gold and sand?
            Which gifts are goodly; but I will none.

177   O all fair lovers about the world,
            There is none of you, none, that shall comfort me.
        My thoughts are as dead things, wrecked and whirled
            Round and round in a gulf of the sea;
        And still, through the sound and the straining stream,
        Through the coil and chafe, they gleam in a dream,
        The bright fine lips so cruelly curled,
            And strange swift eyes where the soul sits free.

185   Free, without pity, withheld from woe,
            Ignorant; fair as the eyes are fair.

175. *dust and laurels and gold and sand:* The dust and heat of the contest,
the laurels of victory, the gold of success, and the running sands of time.

Would I have you change now, change at a blow,
  Startled and stricken, awake and aware?
Yea, if I could, would I have you see
My very love of you filling me,
And know my soul to the quick, as I know
  The likeness and look of your throat and hair?

I shall not change you.   Nay, though I might,   193
  Would I change my sweet one love with a word?
I had rather your hair should change in a night,
  Clear now as the plume of a black bright bird;
Your face fail suddenly, cease, turn grey,
Die as a leaf that dies in a day.
I will keep my soul in a place out of sight,
  Far off, where the pulse of it is not heard.

Far off it walks, in a bleak blown space,   201
  Full of the sound of the sorrow of years.
I have woven a veil for the weeping face,
  Whose lips have drunken the wine of tears;
I have found a way for the failing feet,
A place for slumber and sorrow to meet;
There is no rumour about the place,
  Nor light, nor any that sees or hears.

I have hidden my soul out of sight, and said   209
  "Let none take pity upon thee, none
Comfort thy crying: for lo, thou art dead,
  Lie still now, safe out of sight of the sun.
Have I not built thee a grave, and wrought
Thy grave-clothes on thee of grievous thought,
With soft spun verses and tears unshed,
  And sweet light visions of things undone?

"I have given thee garments and balm and myrrh,   217
  And gold, and beautiful burial things.

But thou, be at peace now, make no stir;
    Is not thy grave as a royal king's?
Fret not thyself though the end were sore;
Sleep, be patient, vex me no more.
Sleep; what hast thou to do with her?
    The eyes that weep, with the mouth that sings?"

225   Where the dead red leaves of the years lie rotten,
    The cold old crimes and the deeds thrown by,
The misconceived and the misbegotten,
    I would find a sin to do ere I die,
Sure to dissolve and destroy me all through,
That would set you higher in heaven, serve you
And leave you happy, when clean forgotten,
    As a dead man out of mind, am I.

233   Your lithe hands draw me, your face burns through me,
    I am swift to follow you, keen to see;
But love lacks might to redeem or undo me;
    As I have been, I know I shall surely be;
"What should such fellows as I do?"   Nay,
My part were worse if I chose to play;
For the worst is this after all; if they knew me,
    Not a soul upon earth would pity me.

241   And I play not for pity of these; but you,
    If you saw with your soul what man am I,
You would praise me at least that my soul all through
    Clove to you, loathing the lives that lie;
The souls and lips that are bought and sold,
The smiles of silver and kisses of gold,
The lapdog loves that whine as they chew,
    The little lovers that curse and cry.

249   There are fairer women, I hear; that may be;
    But I, that I love you and find you fair,
Who are more than fair in my eyes if they be,
    Do the high gods know or the great gods care?

Though the swords in my heart for one were seven,
Should the iron hollow of doubtful heaven,
That knows not itself whether night-time or day be,
    Reverberate words and a foolish prayer?

I will go back to the great sweet mother, 257
    Mother and lover of men, the sea.
I will go down to her, I and none other,
    Close with her, kiss her and mix her with me;
Cling to her, strive with her, hold her fast:
O fair white mother, in days long past
Born without sister, born without brother,
    Set free my soul as thy soul is free.

O fair green-girdled mother of mine, 265
    Sea, that art clothed with the sun and the rain,
Thy sweet hard kisses are strong like wine,
    Thy large embraces are keen like pain.
Save me and hide me with all thy waves,
Find me one grave of thy thousand graves,
Those pure cold populous graves of thine
    Wrought without hand in a world without stain.

I shall sleep, and move with the moving ships, 273
    Change as the winds change, veer in the tide;
My lips will feast on the foam of thy lips,
    I shall rise with thy rising, with thee subside;
Sleep, and not know if she be, if she were,
Filled full with life to the eyes and hair,
As a rose is fulfilled to the roseleaf tips
    With splendid summer and perfume and pride.

This woven raiment of nights and days, 281
    Were it once cast off and unwound from me,
Naked and glad would I walk in thy ways,
    Alive and aware of thy ways and thee;

254. *Would*: 1904] *Should*.

Clear of the whole world, hidden at home,
Clothed with the green and crowned with the foam,
A pulse of the life of thy straits and bays,
    A vein in the heart of the streams of the sea.

289   Fair mother, fed with the lives of men,
                Thou art subtle and cruel of heart, men say.
            Thou hast taken, and shalt not render again;
                Thou art full of thy dead, and cold as they.
            But death is the worst that comes of thee;
            Thou art fed with our dead, O mother, O sea,
            But when hast thou fed on our hearts? or when,
                Having given us love, hast thou taken away?

297   O tender-hearted, O perfect lover,
                Thy lips are bitter, and sweet thine heart.
            The hopes that hurt and the dreams that hover,
                Shall they not vanish away and apart?
            But thou, thou art sure, thou art older than earth;
            Thou art strong for death and fruitful of birth;
            Thy depths conceal and thy gulfs discover;
                From the first thou wert; in the end thou art.

305   And grief shall endure not for ever, I know.
                As things that are not shall these things be;
            We shall live through seasons of sun and of snow,
                And none be grievous as this to me.
            We shall hear, as one in a trance that hears,
            The sound of time, the rhyme of the years;
            Wrecked hope and passionate pain will grow
                As tender things of a spring-tide sea.

313   Sea-fruit that swings in the waves that hiss,
                Drowned gold and purple and royal rings.
            And all time past, was it all for this?
                Times unforgotten, and treasures of things?
            Swift years of liking and sweet long laughter,

That wist not well of the years thereafter
Till love woke, smitten at heart by a kiss,
   With lips that trembled and trailing wings?

There lived a singer in France of old   321
   By the tideless dolorous midland sea.
In a land of sand and ruin and gold
   There shone one woman, and none but she.
And finding life for her love's sake fail,
Being fain to see her, he bade set sail,
Touched land, and saw her as life grew cold,
   And praised God, seeing; and so died he.

Died, praising God for his gift and grace: 329
   For she bowed down to him weeping, and said
"Live;" and her tears were shed on his face
   Or ever the life in his face was shed.
The sharp tears fell through her hair, and stung
Once, and her close lips touched him and clung
Once, and grew one with his lips for a space;
   And so drew back, and the man was dead.

O brother, the gods were good to you.   337
   Sleep, and be glad while the world endures.
Be well content as the years wear through;
   Give thanks for life, and the loves and lures;
Give thanks for life, O brother, and death,
For the sweet last sound of her feet, her breath,
For gifts she gave you, gracious and few,
   Tears and kisses, that lady of yours.

321–346. *There lived a singer:* Jaufré Rudel, a troubador of Provence, who heard such accounts of the princess of Tripoli, a small Crusader duchy in Syria on the Mediterranean, that he fell in love with her. In 1162 he set out, became mysteriously ill on the voyage, and apparently died. When the ship reached Tripoli, his body was brought ashore, and the princess, touched by the story, came to see it and took it by the hand. At her touch, Rudel revived for a few moments and then died.

345   Rest, and be glad of the gods; but I,
            How shall I praise them, or how take rest?
        There is not room under all the sky
            For me that know not of worst or best,
        Dream or desire of the days before,
        Sweet things or bitterness, any more.
        Love will not come to me now though I die,
            As love came close to you, breast to breast.

353   I shall never be friends again with roses;
            I shall loathe sweet tunes, where a note grown strong
        Relents and recoils, and climbs and closes,
            As a wave of the sea turned back by song.
        There are sounds where the soul's delight takes fire,
        Face to face with its own desire;
        A delight that rebels, a desire that reposes;
            I shall hate sweet music my whole life long.

361   The pulse of war and passion of wonder,
            The heavens that murmur, the sounds that shine,
        The stars that sing and the loves that thunder,
            The music burning at heart like wine,
        An armed archangel whose hands raise up
        All senses mixed in the spirit's cup
        Till flesh and spirit are molten in sunder—
            These things are over, and no more mine.

369   These were a part of the playing I heard
            Once, ere my love and my heart were at strife;
        Love that sings and hath wings as a bird,
            Balm of the wound and heft of the knife.
        Fairer than earth is the sea, and sleep
        Than overwatching of eyes that weep,
        Now time has done with his one sweet word,
            The wine and leaven of lovely life.

377   I shall go my ways, tread out my measure,
            Fill the days of my daily breath

With fugitive things not good to treasure,
   Do as the world doth, say as it saith;
But if we had loved each other—O sweet,
Had you felt, lying under the palms of your feet,
The heart of my heart, beating harder with pleasure
   To feel you tread it to dust and death—

Ah, had I not taken my life up and given   385
   All that life gives and the years let go,
The wine and honey, the balm and leaven,
   The dreams reared high and the hopes brought low?
   Come life, come death, not a word be said;
Should I lose you living, and vex you dead?
I never shall tell you on earth; and in heaven,
   If I cry to you then, will you hear or know?

Les Noyades

1 Whatever a man of the sons of men
  Shall say to his heart of the lords above,
 They have shown man verily, once and again,
  Marvellous mercies and infinite love.

5 In the wild fifth year of the change of things,
  When France was glorious and blood-red, fair
 With dust of battle and death of kings,
  A queen of men, with helmeted hair,

9 Carrier came down to the Loire and slew,
  Till all the ways and the waves waxed red:
 Bound and drowned, slaying two by two,
  Maidens and young men, naked and wed.

13 They brought on a day to his judgment-place
  One rough with labour and red with fight,
 And a lady noble by name and face,
  Faultless, a maiden, wonderful, white.

17 She knew not, being for shame's sake blind,

Les Noyades: The Drowned.

 5. *The wild fifth year:* 1794 in the French Revolution.
 9. *Carrier:* Jean Baptiste Carrier (1756–1794), French revolutionist, was sent in October 1793 to Nantes, in west France on the River Loire, to suppress the revolt against the revolutionists. In his effort to dispose of the great number of prisoners filling the jails, he had numbers placed on board vessels in the Loire and the vessels sunk. "By degrees, daylight itself witnesses Noyades: women and men are tied together, feet and feet, hands and hands; and flung in: this they call Mariage Republicain, Republican Marriage." Carlyle, *The French Revolution* (1837), Vol. III, Bk. I, Ch. III, a work with which Swinburne was thoroughly familiar.

If his eyes were hot on her face hard by.
And the judge bade strip and ship them, and bind
    Bosom to bosom, to drown and die.

The white girl winced and whitened; but he   21
    Caught fire, waxed bright as a great bright flame
Seen with thunder far out on the sea,
    Laughed hard as the glad blood went and came.

Twice his lips quailed with delight, then said,   25
    "I have but a word to you all, one word;
Bear with me; surely I am but dead;"
    And all they laughed and mocked him and heard.

"Judge, when they open the judgment-roll,   29
    I will stand upright before God and pray:
'Lord God, have mercy on one man's soul,
    For his mercy was great upon earth, I say.

" 'Lord, if I loved thee—Lord, if I served—   33
    If these who darkened thy fair Son's face
I fought with, sparing not one, nor swerved
    A hand's-breadth, Lord, in the perilous place—

" 'I pray thee say to this man, O Lord,   37
    Sit thou for him at my feet on a throne.
I will face thy wrath, though it bite as a sword,
    And my soul shall burn for his soul, and atone.

" 'For, Lord, thou knowest, O God most wise,   41
    How gracious on earth were his deeds towards me.
Shall this be a small thing in thine eyes,
    That is greater in mine than the whole great sea?

"I have loved this woman my whole life long,   45
    And even for love's sake when have I said

'I love you'? when have I done you wrong,
　　Living? but now I shall have you dead.

"Yea, now, do I bid you love me, love?
　　Love me or loathe, we are one not twain.
But God be praised in his heaven above
　　For this my pleasure and that my pain!

53　　"For never a man, being mean like me,
　　　Shall die like me till the whole world dies.
　　I shall drown with her, laughing for love; and she
　　　Mix with me, touching me, lips and eyes.

57　　"Shall she not know me and see me all through,
　　　Me, on whose heart as a worm she trod?
　　You have given me, God requite it you,
　　　What man yet never was given of God."

61　　O sweet one love, O my life's delight,
　　　Dear, though the days have divided us,
　　Lost beyond hope, taken far out of sight,
　　　Not twice in the world shall the gods do thus.

65　　Had it been so hard for my love? but I,
　　　Though the gods gave all that a god can give,
　　I had chosen rather the gift to die,
　　　Cease, and be glad above all that live.

69　　For the Loire would have driven us down to the sea,
　　　And the sea would have pitched us from shoal to shoal;
　　And I should have held you, and you held me,
　　　As flesh holds flesh, and the soul the soul.

73　　Could I change you, help you to love me, sweet,
　　　Could I give you the love that would sweeten death,

55. I 1904] *I*

We should yield, go down, locked hands and feet,
   Die, drown together, and breath catch breath;

But you would have felt my soul in a kiss,   77
   And known that once if I loved you well;
And I would have given my soul for this
   To burn for ever in burning hell.

A Leave-Taking

1   LET us go hence, my songs; she will not hear.
Let us go hence together without fear;
Keep silence now, for singing-time is over,
And over all old things and all things dear.
She loves not you nor me as all we love her.
Yea, though we sang as angels in her ear,
    She would not hear.

8   Let us rise up and part; she will not know.
Let us go seaward as the great winds go,
Full of blown sand and foam; what help is here?
There is no help, for all these things are so,
And all the world is bitter as a tear.
And how these things are, though ye strove to show,
    She would not know.

15   Let us go home and hence; she will not weep.
We gave love many dreams and days to keep,
Flowers without scent, and fruits that would not grow,
Saying 'If thou wilt, thrust in thy sickle and reap.'
All is reaped now; no grass is left to mow;
And we that sowed, though all we fell on sleep,
    She would not weep.

22   Let us go hence and rest; she will not love.
She shall not hear us if we sing hereof,
Nor see love's ways, how sore they are and steep.
Come hence, let be, lie still; it is enough.
Love is a barren sea, bitter and deep;
And though she saw all heaven in flower above,
    She would not love.

Let us give up, go down; she will not care.
Though all the stars made gold of all the air,
And the sea moving saw before it move
One moon-flower making all the foam-flowers fair;
Though all those waves went over us, and drove
Deep down the stifling lips and drowning hair,
    She would not care.

Let us go hence, go hence; she will not see. 36
Sing all once more together; surely she,
She too, remembering days and words that were,
Will turn a little toward us, sighing; but we,
We are hence, we are gone, as though we had not been there.
Nay, and though all men seeing had pity on me,
    She would not see.

Itylus

1   SWALLOW, my sister, O sister swallow,
      How can thine heart be full of the spring?
       A thousand summers are over and dead.
    What hast thou found in the spring to follow?
      What hast thou found in thine heart to sing?
       What wilt thou do when the summer is shed?

7   O swallow, sister, O fair swift swallow,
      Why wilt thou fly after spring to the south,
       The soft south whither thine heart is set?
    Shall not the grief of the old time follow?
      Shall not the song thereof cleave to thy mouth?
       Hast thou forgotten ere I forget?

13   Sister, my sister, O fleet sweet swallow,
      Thy way is long to the sun and the south;
       But I, fulfilled of my heart's desire,
    Shedding my song upon height, upon hollow,
      From tawny body and sweet small mouth
       Feed the heart of the night with fire.

19   I the nightingale all spring through,

Title: Pandion, king of Athens, had two daughters, Philomela and Procne. Procne married Tereus, king of Thrace, who, however, fell in love with her sister Philomela, raped her, cut out her tongue so that Procne should not know, and concealed her. Philomela, however, embroidered her story and sent it to her sister. Procne, in revenge, killed her own son Itys or Itylus, and served him in a banquet to Tereus. On discovering the truth, Tereus pursued the sisters to kill them; but Procne was turned into a nightingale and Philomela into a swallow, while Tereus was turned into a hoopoe. Thus the nightingale always sings mournfully for her child, and the swallow, being tongueless, chatters. In the poem Procne, the nightingale, sings and tells her story. (Latin versions reverse the roles of the two sisters.)

O swallow, sister, O changing swallow,
    All spring through till the spring be done,
Clothed with the light of the night on the dew,
    Sing, while the hours and the wild birds follow,
        Take flight and follow and find the sun.

Sister, my sister, O soft light swallow,   25
    Though all things feast in the spring's guest-chamber,
        How hast thou heart to be glad thereof yet?
For where thou fliest I shall not follow,
    Till life forget and death remember,
        Till thou remember and I forget.

Swallow, my sister, O singing swallow,   31
    I know not how thou hast heart to sing.
        Hast thou the heart? is it all past over?
Thy lord the summer is good to follow,
    And fair the feet of thy lover the spring:
        But what wilt thou say to the spring thy lover?

O swallow, sister, O fleeting swallow,   37
    My heart in me is a molten ember
        And over my head the waves have met.
But thou wouldst tarry or I would follow,
    Could I forget or thou remember,
        Couldst thou remember and I forget.

O sweet stray sister, O shifting swallow,   43
    The heart's division divideth us.
        Thy heart is light as a leaf of a tree;
But mine goes forth among sea-gulfs hollow
    To the place of the slaying of Itylus,
        The feast of Daulis, the Thracian sea.

48. *Daulis:* City in Phocis, Greece, at the foot of Mt. Parnassus, inhabited
by Thracians at the time of the Procne-Philomela story. Swinburne, however,
seems forgetfully or in ignorance to place the story in Thrace proper, which
borders the Aegean sea on the north.

49   O swallow, sister, O rapid swallow,
            I pray thee sing not a little space.
               Are not the roofs and the lintels wet?
        The woven web that was plain to follow,
            The small slain body, the flowerlike face,
              Can I remember if thou forget?

55   O sister, sister, thy first-begotten!
            The hands that cling and the feet that follow,
             The voice of the child's blood crying yet
      Who hath remembered me? who hath forgotten?
           Thou hast forgotten, O summer swallow,
             But the world shall end when I forget.

Anactoria

τίνος αὖ τὺ πειθοῖ
μὰψ σαγηνεύσας φιλότατα;
SAPPHO.

My life is bitter with thy love; thine eyes
Blind me, thy tresses burn me, thy sharp sighs
Divide my flesh and spirit with soft sound,
And my blood strengthens, and my veins abound.
I pray thee sigh not, speak not, draw not breath;   5
Let life burn down, and dream it is not death.
I would the sea had hidden us, the fire
(Wilt thou fear that, and fear not my desire?)
Severed the bones that bleach, the flesh that cleaves,
And let our sifted ashes drop like leaves.   10
I feel thy blood against my blood: my pain
Pains thee, and lips bruise lips, and vein stings vein.
Let fruit be crushed on fruit, let flower on flower,
Breast kindle breast, and either burn one hour.
Why wilt thou follow lesser loves? are thine   15
Too weak to bear these hands and lips of mine?
I charge thee for my life's sake, O too sweet

Title: Sappho of Lesbos, who lived in the seventh century B.C., was one of the greatest lyric poets of antiquity, and according to some, including Swinburne, one of the greatest lyric poets ever to have lived. She was as famous for loving women as Socrates was for loving men, as the common term for female homosexuality, lesbianism," indicates. Anactoria was one of the young women she was passionately in love with; others were Erinna and Atthis. She is also said to have committed suicide for the love of a young man, Phaon. See Appendices 7 and 8.

Epigraph: "Of whom by persuasion hast thou vainly caught love?"—a corrupt version of lines 18–19 of the *Ode to Aphrodite;* properly, "Whom shall I make to give thee room in her heart's love?"

To crush love with thy cruel faultless feet,
I charge thee keep thy lips from hers or his,
20   Sweetest, till theirs be sweeter than my kiss:
Lest I too lure, a swallow for a dove,
Erotion or Erinna to my love.
I would my love could kill thee; I am satiated
With seeing thee live, and fain would have thee dead.
25   I would earth had thy body as fruit to eat,
And no mouth but some serpent's found thee sweet.
I would find grievous ways to have thee slain,
Intense device, and superflux of pain;
Vex thee with amorous agonies, and shake
30   Life at thy lips, and leave it there to ache;
Strain out thy soul with pangs too soft to kill,
Intolerable interludes, and infinite ill;
Relapse and reluctation of the breath,
Dumb tunes and shuddering semitones of death.
35   I am weary of all thy words and soft strange ways,
Of all love's fiery nights and all his days,
And all the broken kisses salt as brine
That shuddering lips make moist with waterish wine,
And eyes the bluer for all those hidden hours
40   That pleasure fills with tears and feeds from flowers,
Fierce at the heart with fire that half comes through,
But all the flowerlike white stained round with blue;
The fervent underlid, and that above
Lifted with laughter or abashed with love;
45   Thine amorous girdle, full of thee and fair,
And leavings of the lilies in thine hair.
Yea, all sweet words of thine and all thy ways,
And all the fruit of nights and flower of days,
And stinging lips wherein the hot sweet brine
50   That Love was born of burns and foams like wine,

22. *Erotion:* Greek male name.   *Erinna:* See note to title.
49–50. *hot sweet brine / That Love was born of:* Uranos (Heaven) and his
consort, the goddess Gaia (Earth), had numerous children, among them
Kronos. Jealous of his children, Uranos hid them all in the body of Gaia. In

And eyes insatiable of amorous hours,
Fervent as fire and delicate as flowers,
Coloured like night at heart, but cloven through
Like night with flame, dyed round like night with blue,
Clothed with deep eyelids under and above—   55
Yea, all thy beauty sickens me with love;
Thy girdle empty of thee and now not fair,
And ruinous lilies in thy languid hair.
Ah, take no thought for Love's sake; shall this be,
And she who loves thy lover not love thee?   60
Sweet soul, sweet mouth of all that laughs and lives,
Mine is she, very mine; and she forgives.
For I beheld in sleep the light that is
In her high place in Paphos, heard the kiss
Of body and soul that mix with eager tears   65
And laughter stinging through the eyes and ears;
Saw Love, as burning flame from crown to feet,
Imperishable, upon her storied seat;
Clear eyelids lifted toward the north and south,
A mind of many colours, and a mouth   70
Of many tunes and kisses; and she bowed,
With all her subtle face laughing aloud,
Bowed down upon me, saying, "Who doth thee wrong,
Sappho?" but thou—thy body is the song,
Thy mouth the music; thou art more than I,   75
Though my voice die not till the whole world die;
Though men that hear it madden; though love weep,
Though nature change, though shame be charmed to sleep.
Ah, wilt thou slay me lest I kiss thee dead?
Yet the queen laughed from her sweet heart and said: 80
"Even she that flies shall follow for thy sake,
And she shall give thee gifts that would not take,

---

her suffering she begged her children to avenge her. Kronos cut off the genitals
of Uranos as he approached Gaia and flung them into the sea. From the phallus
was born the goddess Aphrodite, who came to shore on the island of Cythera
(or Cyprus, another island).
    64. *Paphos:* Cyprus, a center for the worship of Aphrodite.

Shall kiss that would not kiss thee" (yea, kiss me)
"When thou wouldst not"—when I would not kiss thee!
85   Ah, more to me than all men as thou art,
Shall not my songs assuage her at the heart?
Ah, sweet to me as life seems sweet to death,
Why should her wrath fill thee with fearful breath?
Nay, sweet, for is she God alone? hath she
90   Made earth and all the centuries of the sea,
Taught the sun ways to travel, woven most fine
The moonbeams, shed the starbeams forth as wine,
Bound with her myrtles, beaten with her rods,
The young men and the maidens and the gods?
95   Have we not lips to love with, eyes for tears,
And summer and flower of women and of years?
Stars for the foot of morning, and for noon
Sunlight, and exaltation of the moon;
Waters that answer waters, fields that wear
100   Lilies, and languor of the Lesbian air?
Beyond those flying feet of fluttered doves,
Are there not other gods for other loves?
Yea, though she scourge thee, sweetest, for my sake,
Blossom not thorns and flowers not blood should break.
105   Ah that my lips were tuneless lips, but pressed
To the bruised blossom of thy scourged white breast!
Ah that my mouth for Muses' milk were fed
On the sweet blood thy sweet small wounds had bled!
That with my tongue I felt them, and could taste
110   The faint flakes from thy bosom to the waist!
That I could drink thy veins as wine, and eat
Thy breasts like honey! that from face to feet
Thy body were abolished and consumed,
And in my flesh thy very flesh entombed!
115   Ah, ah, thy beauty! like a beast it bites,
Stings like an adder, like an arrow smites.

101. *doves:* The dove was the bird of Aphrodite, and sacred to her.
107. *Muses:* Goddesses of poetry, dance, etc.; here a generic term for
poetry.

Ah sweet, and sweet again, and seven times sweet,
The paces and the pauses of thy feet!
Ah sweeter than all sleep or summer air
The fallen fillets fragrant from thine hair!   120
Yea, though their alien kisses do me wrong,
Sweeter thy lips than mine with all their song;
Thy shoulders whiter than a fleece of white,
And flower-sweet fingers, good to bruise or bite
As honeycomb of the inmost honey-cells,   125
With almond-shaped and roseleaf-coloured shells
And blood like purple blossom at the tips
Quivering; and pain made perfect in thy lips
For my sake when I hurt thee; O that I
Durst crush thee out of life with love, and die,   130
Die of thy pain and my delight, and be
Mixed with thy blood and molten into thee!
Would I not plague thee dying overmuch?
Would I not hurt thee perfectly? not touch
Thy pores of sense with torture, and make bright   135
Thine eyes with bloodlike tears and grievous light?
Strike pang from pang as note is struck from note,
Catch the sob's middle music in thy throat,
Take thy limbs living, and new-mould with these
A lyre of many faultless agonies?   140
Feed thee with fever and famine and fine drouth,
With perfect pangs convulse thy perfect mouth,
Make thy life shudder in thee and burn afresh,
And wring thy very spirit through the flesh?
Cruel? but love makes all that love him well   145
As wise as heaven and crueller than hell.
Me hath love made more bitter toward thee
Than death toward man; but were I made as he
Who hath made all things to break them one by one,
If my feet trod upon the stars and sun   150
And souls of men as his have alway trod,

120. *fillets:* wreaths; here, of flowers.

God knows I might be crueller than God.
For who shall change with prayers or thanksgivings
The mystery of the cruelty of things?
155   Or say what God above all gods and years
With offering and blood-sacrifice of tears,
With lamentation from strange lands, from graves
Where the snake pastures, from scarred mouths of slaves,
From prison, and from plunging prows of ships
160   Through flamelike foam of the sea's closing lips—
With thwartings of strange signs, and wind-blown hair
Of comets, desolating the dim air,
When darkness is made fast with seals and bars,
And fierce reluctance of disastrous stars,
165   Eclipse, and sound of shaken hills, and wings
Darkening, and blind inexpiable things—
With sorrow of labouring moons, and altering light
And travail of the planets of the night,
And weeping of the weary Pleiads seven,
170   Feeds the mute melancholy lust of heaven?
Is not his incense bitterness, his meat
Murder? his hidden face and iron feet
Hath not man known, and felt them on their way
Threaten and trample all things and every day?
175   Hath he not sent us hunger? who hath cursed
Spirit and flesh with longing? filled with thirst
Their lips who cried unto him? who bade exceed
The fervid will, fall short the feeble deed,
Bade sink the spirit and the flesh aspire,
180   Pain animate the dust of dead desire,
And life yield up her flower to violent fate?
Him would I reach, him smite, him desecrate,
Pierce the cold lips of God with human breath,

161–169. *Strange signs . . . comets . . . stars . . . eclipse . . . moons . . . planets
. . . Pleiads:* Reference to the ancient belief that divine powers govern our
lives and that the strange behavior of these things indicates that the future is
threatening. *Sounds of shaken hills:* Rumblings of earthquakes. *Pleiads:*
Orion, a gigantic child of earth, pursued seven sisters; he and they were transported to heaven and placed among the stars.

And mix his immortality with death.
Why hath he made us? what had all we done 185
That we should live and loathe the sterile sun,
And with the moon wax paler as she wanes,
And pulse by pulse feel time grow through our veins?
Thee too the years shall cover; thou shalt be
As the rose born of one same blood with thee, 190
As a song sung, as a word said, and fall
Flower-wise, and be not any more at all,
Nor any memory of thee anywhere;
For never Muse has bound above thine hair
The high Pierian flower whose graft outgrows 195
All summer kinship of the mortal rose
And colour of deciduous days, nor shed
Reflex and flush of heaven about thine head,
Nor reddened brows made pale by floral grief
With splendid shadow from that lordlier leaf. 200
Yea, thou shalt be forgotten like spilt wine,
Except these kisses of my lips on thine
Brand them with immortality; but me—
Men shall not see bright fire nor hear the sea,
Nor mix their hearts with music, nor behold 205
Cast forth of heaven, with feet of awful gold
And plumeless wings that make the bright air blind,
Lightning, with thunder for a hound behind
Hunting through fields unfurrowed and unsown,
But in the light and laughter, in the moan 210
And music, and in grasp of lip and hand
And shudder of water that makes felt on land
The immeasurable tremor of all the sea,
Memories shall mix and metaphors of me.
Like me shall be the shuddering calm of night, 215
When all the winds of the world for pure delight
Close lips that quiver and fold up wings that ache;
When nightingales are louder for love's sake,

195. *Pierian flower:* Pieria was a district on the slopes of Olympus where
the cult of the Muses (see line 107) originated. Here a term for "poem."

And leaves tremble like lute-strings or like fire;
220   Like me the one star swooning with desire
Even at the cold lips of the sleepless moon,
As I at thine; like me the waste white noon,
Burnt through with barren sunlight; and like me
The land-stream and the tide-stream in the sea.
225   I am sick with time as these with ebb and flow,
And by the yearning in my veins I know
The yearning sound of waters; and mine eyes
Burn as that beamless fire which fills the skies
With troubled stars and travailing things of flame;
230   And in my heart the grief consuming them
Labours, and in my veins the thirst of these,
And all the summer travail of the trees
And all the winter sickness; and the earth,
Filled full with deadly works of death and birth,
235   Sore spent with hungry lusts of birth and death,
Has pain like mine in her divided breath;
Her spring of leaves is barren, and her fruit
Ashes; her boughs are burdened, and her root
Fibrous and gnarled with poison; underneath
240   Serpents have gnawn it through with tortuous teeth
Made sharp upon the bones of all the dead,
And wild birds rend her branches overhead.
These, woven as raiment for his word and thought,
These hath God made, and me as these, and wrought
245   Song, and hath lit it at my lips; and me
Earth shall not gather though she feed on thee.
As a shed tear shalt thou be shed; but I—
Lo, earth may labour, men live long and die,
Years change and stars, and the high God devise
250   New things, and old things wane before his eyes
Who wields and wrecks them, being more strong than they—
But, having made me, me he shall not slay.
Nor slay nor satiate, like those herds of his
Who laugh and live a little, and their kiss
255   Contents them, and their loves are swift and sweet,

And sure death grasps and gains them with slow feet,
Love they or hate they, strive or bow their knees—
And all these end; he hath his will of these.
Yea, but albeit he slay me, hating me—
Albeit he hide me in the deep dear sea   260
And cover me with cool wan foam, and ease
This soul of mine as any soul of these,
And give me water and great sweet waves, and make
The very sea's name lordlier for my sake,
The whole sea sweeter—albeit I die indeed   265
And hide myself and sleep and no man heed,
Of me the high God hath not all his will.
Blossom of branches, and on each high hill
Clear air and wind, and under in clamorous vales
Fierce noises of the fiery nightingales,   270
Buds burning in the sudden spring like fire,
The wan washed sand and the waves' vain desire,
Sails seen like blown white flowers at sea, and words
That bring tears swiftest, and long notes of birds
Violently singing till the whole world sings—   275
I Sappho shall be one with all these things,
With all high things for ever; and my face
Seen once, my songs once heard in a strange place,
Cleave to men's lives, and waste the days thereof
With gladness and much sadness and long love.   280
Yea, they shall say, earth's womb has borne in vain
New things, and never this best thing again;
Borne days and men, borne fruits and wars and wine,
Seasons and songs, but no song more like mine.
And they shall know me as ye who have known me here,   285
Last year when I loved Atthis, and this year
When I love thee; and they shall praise me, and say
"She hath all time as all we have our day,
Shall she not live and have her will"—even I?
Yea, though thou diest, I say I shall not die.   290
For these shall give me of their souls, shall give

286. *Atthis:* See note to title.

Life, and the days and loves wherewith I live,
Shall quicken me with loving, fill with breath,
Save me and serve me, strive for me with death.
295   Alas, that neither moon nor snow nor dew
Nor all cold things can purge me wholly through,
Assuage me nor allay me nor appease,
Till supreme sleep shall bring me bloodless ease;
Till time wax faint in all his periods;
300   Till fate undo the bondage of the gods,
And lay, to slake and satiate me all through,
Lotus and Lethe on my lips like dew,
And shed around and over and under me
Thick darkness and the insuperable sea.

302. *Lotus:* Flower of forgetfulness. *Lethe:* The river of forgetfulness in
Hades.

Hymn to Proserpine

(AFTER THE PROCLAMATION IN ROME
OF THE CHRISTIAN FAITH)

Vicisti, Galilæe.

I HAVE lived long enough, having seen one thing, that love hath an
    end;
Goddess and maiden and queen, be near me now and befriend.
Thou art more than the day or the morrow, the seasons that laugh
    or that weep;
For these give joy and sorrow; but thou, Proserpina, sleep.
Sweet is the treading of wine, and sweet the feet of the dove;   5
But a goodlier gift is thine than foam of the grapes or love.
Yea, is not even Apollo, with hair and harpstring of gold,
A bitter God to follow, a beautiful God to behold?
I am sick of singing: the bays burn deep and chafe: I am fain

Proclamation: Swinburne could be referring to the edict of toleration of the
emperor Galerius, in 311, or the edict of Milan, issued in 313 by the emperors
Constantine and Lactantius. Or he could be referring to the official establish-
ment of Christianity as the religion of the Roman Empire by Theodosius the
Great (379–385). Perhaps the latter is meant, since Theodosius established the
principle of persecuting the unorthodox, heretics, and pagans.

    Epigraph: "Thou hast conquered, Galilean," i.e., Christ. The emperor Julian
(361–363) attempted to re-establish paganism; according to legend he was
murdered by a Christian, and these were his dying words.

    2. *Goddess and maiden and queen:* Proserpine (or Persephone) was both
the goddess and queen of Hades—thus of forgetfulness—and goddess and
maiden of fertility, particularly of wheat.

    5. *wine:* Sacred to Dionysius, or Bacchus. *dove:* Sacred to Aphrodite, or
Venus.

    7. *Apollo:* God of the sun, and also of poetry (hence "bitter to follow"),
and intellectual illumination.

    9. *bays:* The laurel crown of recognized poets. This and the reference to
Apollo identified the speaker as a poet, particularly a poet of the celebration
and praise of the gods.

10   To rest a little from praise and grievous pleasure and pain.
      For the Gods we know not of, who give us our daily breath,
      We know they are cruel as love or life, and lovely as death.
      O Gods dethroned and deceased, cast forth, wiped out in a day!
      From your wrath is the world released, redeemed from your chains,
            men say.
15   New Gods are crowned in the city; their flowers have broken your
            rods;
      They are merciful, clothed with pity, the young compassionate
            Gods.
      But for me their new device is barren, the days are bare;
      Things long past over suffice, and men forgotten that were.
      Time and the Gods are at strife; ye dwell in the midst thereof,
20   Draining a little life from the barren breasts of love.
      I say to you, cease, take rest; yea, I say to you all, be at peace,
      Till the bitter milk of her breast and the barren bosom shall cease.
      Wilt thou yet take all, Galilean? but these thou shalt not take,
      The laurel, the palms and the pæan, the breasts of the nymphs in
            the brake;
25   Breasts more soft than a dove's, that tremble with tenderer breath;
      And all the wings of the Loves, and all the joy before death;
      All the feet of the hours that sound as a single lyre,
      Dropped and deep in the flowers, with strings that flicker like fire.
      More than these wilt thou give, things fairer than all these things?
30   Nay, for a little we live, and life hath mutable wings.
      A little while and we die; shall life not thrive as it may?
      For no man under the sky lives twice, outliving his day.
      And grief is a grievous thing, and a man hath enough of his tears:
      Why should he labour, and bring fresh grief to blacken his years?
35   Thou hast conquered, O pale Galilean; the world has grown grey
            from thy breath;
      We have drunken of things Lethean, and fed on the fullness of
            death.

   15. *New Gods:* The Christian saints.
   24. *laurels:* The rewards of victory as poet.   *palms:* The rewards of mili-
tary victory.   *pæan:* Hymn of triumph.
   26. *Loves:* Amoretti, winged infants who traditionally accompany and are
emblematic of Venus.
   36. *Lethean:* See note to "Anactoria," line 302.

Laurel is green for a season, and love is sweet for a day;
But love grows bitter with treason, and laurel outlives not May.
Sleep, shall we sleep after all? for the world is not sweet in the
    end;
For the old faiths loosen and fall, the new years ruin and rend.   40
Fate is a sea without shore, and the soul is a rock that abides;
But her ears are vexed with the roar and her face with the foam of
    the tides.
O lips that the live blood faints in, the leavings of racks and rods!
O ghastly glories of saints, dead limbs of gibbeted Gods!
Though all men abase them before you in spirit, and all knees   45
    bend,
I kneel not neither adore you, but standing, look to the end.
All delicate days and pleasant, all spirits and sorrows are cast
Far out with the foam of the present that sweeps to the surf of the
    past:
Where beyond the extreme sea-wall, and between the remote sea-
    gates,
Waste water washes, and tall ships founder, and deep death waits: 50
Where, mighty with deepening sides, clad about with the seas as
    with wings,
And impelled of invisible tides, and fulfilled of unspeakable things,
White-eyed and poisonous-finned, shark-toothed and serpentine-
    curled,
Rolls, under the whitening wind of the future, the wave of the
    world.
The depths stand naked in sunder behind it, the storms flee away;   55
In the hollow before it the thunder is taken and snared as a prey;
In its sides is the north-wind bound; and its salt is of all men's
    tears;
With light of ruin, and sound of changes, and pulse of years:
With travail of day after day, and with trouble of hour upon hour;
And bitter as blood is the spray; and the crests are as fangs that   60
    devour:
And its vapour and storm of its steam as the sighing of spirits to
    be;
And its noise as the noise in a dream; and its depth as the roots of
    the sea:

And the height of its heads as the height of the utmost stars of the
  air:

And the ends of the earth at the might thereof tremble, and time
  is made bare.

65 Will ye bridle the deep sea with reins, will ye chasten the high sea
  with rods?

Will ye take her to chain her with chains, who is older than all ye
  Gods?

All ye as a wind shall go by, as a fire shall ye pass and be past;

Ye are Gods, and behold, ye shall die, and the waves be upon you
  at last.

In the darkness of time, in the deeps of the years, in the changes
  of things,

70 Ye shall sleep as a slain man sleeps, and the world shall forget you
  for kings.

Though the feet of thine high priests tread where thy lords and our
  forefathers trod,

Though these that were Gods are dead, and thou being dead art a
  God,

Though before thee the throned Cytherean be fallen, and hidden
  her head,

Yet thy kingdom shall pass, Galilean, thy dead shall go down to
  thee dead.

75 Of the maiden thy mother men sing as a goddess with grace clad
  around;

Thou art throned where another was king; where another was
  queen she is crowned.

Yea, once we had sight of another: but now she is queen, say these.

Not as thine, not as thine was our mother, a blossom of flowering
  seas,

Clothed round with the world's desire as with raiment, and fair as
  the foam,

65–66. Compare the Lord's answer to Job out of the whirlwind (Job, 38–
41).

66. *her:* Venus, or Aphrodite.

73. *Cytherean:* The island of Cythera is where Aphrodite came to shore after
her birth in the sea. See "Anactoria," line 57.

And fleeter than kindled fire, and a goddess, and mother of Rome.   80
For thine came pale and a maiden, and sister to sorrow; but ours,
Her deep hair heavily laden with odour and colour of flowers,
White rose of the rose-white water, a silver splendour, a flame,
Bent down unto us that besought her, and earth grew sweet with
 her name.
For thine came weeping, a slave among slaves, and rejected; but   85
 she
Came flushed from the full-flushed wave, and imperial, her foot on
 the sea.
And the wonderful waters knew her, the winds and the viewless
 ways,
And the roses grew rosier, and bluer the sea-blue stream of the
 bays.
Ye are fallen, our lords, by what token? we wist that ye should
 not fall.
Ye were all so fair that are broken; and one more fair than ye   90
 all.
But I turn to her still, having seen she shall surely abide in the
 end;
Goddess and maiden and queen, be near me now and befriend.
O daughter of earth, of my mother, her crown and blossom of
 birth,
I am also, I also, thy brother; I go as I came unto earth.
In the night where thine eyes are as moons are in heaven, the night   95
 where thou art,
Where the silence is more than all tunes, where sleep overflows
 from the heart,
Where the poppies are sweet as the rose in our world, and the red
 rose is white,
And the wind falls faint as it blows with the fume of the flowers of
 the night,

---

 80. *Mother of Rome:* Aeneas, the founder of Rome, was under the protec-
tion of his mother Venus. *Venus Genetrix* was worshipped as the mother of
the Roman people.
 97. *poppies:* The traditional flowers of Proserpine, flowers of sleep, the
source of opium.

And the murmur of spirits that sleep in the shadow of Gods from
    afar
100 Grows dim in thine ears and deep as the deep dim soul of a star,
In the sweet low light of thy face, under heavens untrod by the
    sun,
Let my soul with their souls find place, and forget what is done
    and undone.
Thou art more than the Gods who number the days of our tem-
    poral breath;
For these give labour and slumber; but thou, Proserpina, death.
105 Therefore now at thy feet I abide for a season in silence.   I know
I shall die as my fathers died, and sleep as they sleep; even so.
For the glass of the years is brittle wherein we gaze for a span;
A little soul for a little bears up this corpse which is man. *
So long I endure, no longer; and laugh not again, neither weep.
110 For there is no God found stronger than death; and death is a
    sleep.

---

* ψυχάριον εἶ βαστάζον νεκρόν.—EPICTETUS.

108. *Epictetus:* Stoic philosopher, A.D. 60–140.

Ilicet

THERE is an end of joy and sorrow;   1
Peace all day long, all night, all morrow,
   But never a time to laugh or weep.
The end is come of pleasant places,
The end of tender words and faces,
   The end of all, the poppied sleep.

No place for sound within their hearing,   7
No room to hope, no time for fearing,
   No lips to laugh, no lids for tears.
The old years have run out all their measure;
No chance of pain, no chance of pleasure,
   No fragment of the broken years.

Outside of all the worlds and ages,   13
There where the fool is as the sage is,
   There where the slayer is clean of blood,
No end, no passage, no beginning,
There where the sinner leaves off sinning,
   There where the good man is not good.

There is not one thing with another,   19
But Evil saith to Good: My brother,
   My brother, I am one with thee:
They shall not strive nor cry for ever:
No man shall choose between them: never
   Shall this thing end and that thing be.

Wind wherein seas and stars are shaken   25
Shall shake them, and they shall not waken;

Ilicet: "All is over."

None that has lain down shall arise;
The stones are sealed across their places;
    One shadow is shed on all their faces,
    One blindness cast on all their eyes.

31   Sleep, is it sleep perchance that covers
Each face, as each face were his lover's?
    Farewell; as men that sleep fare well.
The grave's mouth laughs unto derision
Desire and dread and dream and vision,
    Delight of heaven and sorrow of hell.

37   No soul shall tell nor lip shall number
The names and tribes of you that slumber;
    No memory, no memorial.
"Thou knowest"—who shall say thou knowest?
There is none highest and none lowest:
    An end, an end, an end of all.

43   Good night, good sleep, good rest from sorrow
To these that shall not have good morrow;
    The gods be gentle to all these.
Nay, if death be not, how shall they be?
Nay, is there help in heaven? it may be
    All things and lords of things shall cease.

49   The stooped urn, filling, dips and flashes;
The bronzèd brims are deep in ashes;
    The pale old lips of death are fed.
Shall this dust gather flesh hereafter?
Shall one shed tears or fall to laughter,
    At sight of all these poor old dead?

55   Nay, as thou wilt; these know not of it;
Thine eyes' strong weeping shall not profit,
    Thy laughter shall not give thee ease;

49. *urn:* Here, a bronze vase in which are placed the ashes of the dead.

Cry aloud, spare not, cease not crying,
Sigh, till thou cleave thy sides with sighing,
　　Thou shalt not raise up one of these.

Burnt spices flash, and burnt wine hisses,　　　　　61
The breathing flame's mouth curls and kisses
　　The small dried rows of frankincense;
All round the sad red blossoms smoulder,
Flowers coloured like the fire, but colder,
　　In sign of sweet things taken hence;

Yea, for their sake and in death's favour　　　　　67
Things of sweet shape and of sweet savour
　　We yield them, spice and flower and wine;
Yea, costlier things than wine or spices,
Whereof none knoweth how great the price is,
　　And fruit that comes not of the vine.

From boy's pierced throat and girl's pierced bosom　　73
Drips, reddening round the blood-red blossom,
　　The slow delicious bright soft blood,
Bathing the spices and the pyre,
Bathing the flowers and fallen fire,
　　Bathing the blossoms by the bud.

Roses whose lips the flame has deadened　　　　　79
Drink till the lapping leaves are reddened
　　And warm wet inner petals weep;
The flower whereof sick sleep gets leisure,
Barren of balm and purple pleasure,
　　Fumes with no native steam of sleep.

Why will ye weep? what do ye weeping?　　　　　85
For waking folk and people sleeping,
　　And sands that fill and sands that fall,
The days rose-red, the poppied hours,
Blood, wine, and spice and fire and flowers,
　　There is one end of one and all.

91   Shall such an one lend love or borrow?
                         Shall these be sorry for thy sorrow?
                            Shall these give thanks for words or breath?
                         Their hate is as their loving-kindness;
                         The frontlet of their brows is blindness,
                            The armlet of their arms is death.

97   Lo, for no noise or light of thunder
                         Shall these grave-clothes be rent in sunder;
                            He that hath taken, shall he give?
                         He hath rent them: shall he bind together?
                         He hath bound them: shall he break the tether?
                            He hath slain them: shall he bid them live?

103   A little sorrow, a little pleasure,
                         Fate metes us from the dusty measure
                            That holds the date of all of us;
                         We are born with travail and strong crying,
                         And from the birth-day to the dying
                            The likeness of our life is thus.

109   One girds himself to serve another,
                         Whose father was the dust, whose mother
                            The little dead red worm therein;
                         They find no fruit of things they cherish;
                         The goodness of a man shall perish,
                            It shall be one thing with his sin.

115   In deep wet ways by grey old gardens
                         Fed with sharp spring the sweet fruit hardens;
                            They know not what fruits wane or grow;
                         Red summer burns to the utmost ember;
                         They know not, neither can remember,
                            The old years and flowers they used to know.

95–96. *frontlet . . . armlet:* Pieces of armor protecting the forehead and the
upper arm.

Ah, for their sakes, so trapped and taken,   121
For theirs, forgotten and forsaken,
    Watch, sleep not, gird thyself with prayer.
Nay, where the heart of wrath is broken,
Where long love ends as a thing spoken,
    How shall thy crying enter there?

Though the iron sides of the old world falter,   127
The likeness of them shall not alter
    For all the rumour of periods,
The stars and seasons that come after,
The tears of latter men, the laughter
    Of the old unalterable gods.

Far up above the years and nations,   133
The high gods, clothed and crowned with patience,
    Endure through days of deathlike date;
They bear the witness of things hidden;
Before their eyes all life stands chidden,
    As they before the eyes of Fate.

Not for their love shall Fate retire,   139
Nor they relent for our desire,
    Nor the graves open for their call.
The end is more than joy and anguish,
Than lives that laugh and lives that languish,
    The poppied sleep, the end of all.

Hermaphroditus

I

1   LIFT up thy lips, turn round, look back for love,
     Blind love that comes by night and casts out rest;
     Of all things tired thy lips look weariest,
Save the long smile that they are wearied of.
Ah sweet, albeit no love be sweet enough,
     Choose of two loves and cleave unto the best;
Two loves at either blossom of thy breast
8   Strive until one be under and one above.
Their breath is fire upon the amorous air,
     Fire in thine eyes and where thy lips suspire:
And whosoever hath seen thee, being so fair;
     Two things turn all his life and blood to fire;
A strong desire begot on great despair,
     A great despair cast out by strong desire.

II

15   Where between sleep and life some brief space is,
     With love like gold bound round about the head,
     Sex to sweet sex with lips and limbs is wed,
Turning the fruitful feud of hers and his
To the waste wedlock of a sterile kiss;

Hermaphroditus: the offspring of Aphrodite and of Hermes, ancient Greek god of fertility, whose cult-monument could be the phallus, and also of roads (hence messenger of the gods). In Asia Minor at Halikarnossos was a spring which had the peculiar power of enervating any man who bathed in it. The nymph of that spring, Salmacis, fell in love with Hermaphroditus, who rejected her. She implored the gods to unite her with him, and they did so. The two became one, half man, half woman. The famous statue in the Louvre, which inspired these sonnets, shows the god lying on one side and displaying both the breasts of a woman and the genitals of a man. Swinburne uses the figure as a symbol of bisexual love.

Yet from them something like as fire is shed
That shall not be assuaged till death be dead,
Though neither life nor sleep can find out this. 22
Love made himself of flesh that perisheth
A pleasure-house for all the loves his kin;
But on the one side sat a man like death,
And on the other a woman sat like sin.
So with veiled eyes and sobs between his breath
Love turned himself and would not enter in.

III

Love, is it love or sleep or shadow or light 29
That lies between thine eyelids and thine eyes?
Like a flower laid upon a flower it lies,
Or like the night's dew laid upon the night.
Love stands upon thy left hand and thy right,
Yet by no sunset and by no moonrise
Shall make thee man and ease a woman's sighs,
Or make thee woman for a man's delight. 36
To what strange end hath some strange god made fair
The double blossom of two fruitless flowers?
Hid love in all the folds of all thy hair,
Fed thee on summers, watered thee with showers,
Given all the gold that all the seasons wear
To thee that art a thing of barren hours?

IV

Yea, love, I see; it is not love but fear. 43
Nay, sweet, it is not fear but love, I know;
Or wherefore should thy body's blossom blow
So sweetly, or thine eyelids leave so clear
Thy gracious eyes that never made a tear—

23. *Love:* Here the son of Venus, Cupid, traditionally presented as a beautiful and winged young man.

Though for their love our tears like blood should flow,
Though love and life and death should come and go,
50   So dreadful, so desirable, so dear?
Yea, sweet, I know; I saw in what swift wise
    Beneath the woman's and the water's kiss
    Thy moist limbs melted into Salmacis,
And the large light turned tender in thine eyes,
And all thy boy's breath softened into sighs;
    But Love being blind, how should he know of this?

Au Musée du Louvre, Mars 1863.

57. "At the Museum of the Louvre, March, 1863."

Fragoletta

O LOVE! what shall be said of thee?
The son of grief begot by joy?
Being sightless, wilt thou see?
Being sexless, wilt thou be
Maiden or boy?   5

I dreamed of strange lips yesterday
And cheeks wherein the ambiguous blood
Was like a rose's—yea,
A rose's when it lay
Within the bud.   10

What fields have bred thee, or what groves
Concealed thee, O mysterious flower,
O double rose of Love's,
With leaves that lure the doves
From bud to bower?   15

I dare not kiss it, lest my lip
Press harder than an indrawn breath,
And all the sweet life slip
Forth, and the sweet leaves drip,
Bloodlike, in death.   20

O sole desire of my delight!
O sole delight of my desire!
Mine eyelids and eyesight

Fragoletta: Diminutive for the Italian *fragola*, "strawberry." The poem continues the bisexual theme of "Hermaphroditus," with a strong implication of male homosexuality.

1. *Love:* See note to "Hermaphroditus," line 23.

Feed on thee day and night
25   Like lips of fire.

Lean back thy throat of carven pearl,
Let thy mouth murmur like the dove's;
Say, Venus hath no girl,
No front of female curl,
30   Among her Loves.

Thy sweet low bosom, thy close hair,
Thy strait soft flanks and slenderer feet,
Thy virginal strange air,
Are these not over fair
35   For Love to greet?

How should he greet thee? what new name,
Fit to move all men's hearts, could move
Thee, deaf to love or shame,
Love's sister, by the same
40   Mother as Love?

Ah sweet, the maiden's mouth is cold,
Her breast-blossoms are simply red,
Her hair mere brown or gold,
Fold over simple fold
45   Binding her head.

Thy mouth is made of fire and wine,
Thy barren bosom takes my kiss
And turns my soul to thine
And turns thy lip to mine,
50   And mine it is.

Thou hast a serpent in thine hair,
In all the curls that close and cling;
And ah, thy breast-flower!

Ah love, thy mouth too fair
To kiss and sting!   55

Cleave to me, love me, kiss mine eyes,
Satiate thy lips with loving me;
Nay, for thou shalt not rise;
Lie still as Love that dies
For love of thee.   60

Mine arms are close about thine head,
My lips are fervent on thy face,
And where my kiss hath fed
Thy flower-like blood leaps red
To the kissed place.   65

O bitterness of things too sweet!
O broken singing of the dove!
Love's wings are over fleet,
And like the panther's feet
The feet of Love.   70

Rondel

1   THESE many years since we began to be,
What have the gods done with us? what with me,
What with my love? they have shown me fates and fears,
Harsh springs, and fountains bitterer than the sea,
Grief a fixed star, and joy a vane that veers,
    These many years.

7   With her, my love, with her have they done well?
But who shall answer for her? who shall tell
Sweet things or sad, such things as no man hears?
May no tears fall, if no tears ever fell,
From eyes more dear to me than starriest spheres
    These many years!

13   But if tears ever touched, for any grief,
Those eyelids folded like a white-rose leaf,
Deep double shells wherethrough the eye-flower peers,
Let them weep once more only, sweet and brief,
Brief tears and bright, for one who gave her tears
    These many years.

Rondel: Something which forms a circle; here the rhyme scheme, particularly the repetition in the last line of each stanza of the opening words of the first.

Satia te Sanguine

IF you loved me ever so little,   1
    I could bear the bonds that gall,
I could dream the bonds were brittle;
    You do not love me at all.

O beautiful lips, O bosom   5
    More white than the moon's and warm,
A sterile, a ruinous blossom
    Is blown your way in a storm.

As the lost white feverish limbs   9
    Of the Lesbian Sappho, adrift
In foam where the sea-weed swims,
    Swam loose for the streams to lift,

My heart swims blind in a sea   13
    That stuns me; swims to and fro,
And gathers to windward and lee
    Lamentation, and mourning, and woe.

A broken, an emptied boat,   17
    Sea saps it, winds blow apart,
Sick and adrift and afloat,
    The barren waif of a heart.

Where, when the gods would be cruel,   21
    Do they go for a torture? where
Plant thorns, set pain like a jewel?
    Ah, not in the flesh, not there!

Satia te Sanguine: "Thou art glutted with blood."

10. *Lesbian Sappho:* See notes to "Anactoria."

25   The racks of earth and the rods
          Are weak as foam on the sands;
      In the heart is the prey for gods,
          Who crucify hearts, not hands.

29   Mere pangs corrode and consume,
          Dead when life dies in the brain;
      In the infinite spirit is room
          For the pulse of an infinite pain.

33   I wish you were dead, my dear;
          I would give you, had I to give,
      Some death too bitter to fear;
          It is better to die than live.

37   I wish you were stricken of thunder
          And burnt with a bright flame through,
      Consumed and cloven in sunder,
          I dead at your feet like you.

41   If I could but know after all,
          I might cease to hunger and ache,
      Though your heart were ever so small,
          If it were not a stone or a snake.

45   You are crueller, you that we love,
          Than hatred, hunger, or death;
      You have eyes and breasts like a dove,
          And you kill men's hearts with a breath.

49   As plague in a poisonous city
          Insults and exults on her dead,
      So you, when pallid for pity
          Comes love, and fawns to be fed.

53   As a tame beast writhes and wheedles,
          He fawns to be fed with wiles;

You carve him a cross of needles,
    And whet them sharp as your smiles.

He is patient of thorn and whip,   57
    He is dumb under axe or dart;
You suck with a sleepy red lip
    The wet red wounds in his heart.

You thrill as his pulses dwindle,   61
    You brighten and warm as he bleeds,
With insatiable eyes that kindle
    And insatiable mouth that feeds.

Your hands nailed love to the tree,   65
    You stript him, scourged him with rods,
And drowned him deep in the sea
    That hides the dead and their gods.

And for all this, die will he not;   69
    There is no man sees him but I;
You came and went and forgot;
    I hope he will some day die.

A Litany

ἐν οὐρανῷ φαεννὰς
κρύψω παρ' ὑμὶν αὐγὰς,
μίας πρὸ νυκτὸς ἑπτὰ νύκτας ἕξετε, κ.τ.λ.

Anth. Sac.

FIRST ANTIPHONE

1 ALL the bright lights of heaven
   I will make dark over thee;
   One night shall be as seven
   That its skirts may cover thee;
   I will send on thy strong men a sword,
   On thy remnant a rod;
   Ye shall know that I am the Lord,
   Saith the Lord God.

SECOND ANTIPHONE

9 All the bright lights of heaven
   Thou hast made dark over us;

A Litany: Part of a liturgical service, the prescribed procedure for public worship in the Christian church, in which an utterance by the priest or clergyman is responded to by the members of the congregation speaking together. However, Swinburne's use of "antiphone" (the more common English term is "anthem") indicates two responsive choirs, usually one of men and one of boys, taking the place of priest and congregation. Compare "Anactoria," lines 147–180. In the English Book of Common Prayer, the priest begins the Litany and the congregation, whose words are in italics here, responds: "O God the Father, of heaven; have mercy upon us miserable sinners. *O God the Father, of heaven; have mercy upon us miserable sinners.* O God the Son, Redeemer of the world: have mercy upon us miserable sinners. *O God the Son, Redeemer of the world: have mercy upon us miserable sinners.*" And so on, through the Holy Ghost. After a short time the congregation does not repeat the priest's utterance exactly. Swinburne's poem is filled with Biblical phrases.

Epigraph: "In heaven I shall hide the shining lights, you shall have seven nights in place of one." The *Anthologia Sacra* is an invention of Swinburne's.

92

One night has been as seven
  That its skirt might cover us;
Thou hast sent on our strong men a sword,
  On our remnant a rod;
We know that thou art the Lord,
  O Lord our God.

THIRD ANTIPHONE

As the tresses and wings of the wind   17
  Are scattered and shaken,
I will scatter all them that have sinned,
  There shall none be taken;
As a sower that scattereth seed,
  So will I scatter them;
As one breaketh and shattereth a reed,
  I will break and shatter them.

FOURTH ANTIPHONE

As the wings and the locks of the wind   25
  Are scattered and shaken,
Thou hast scattered all them that have sinned,
  There was no man taken;
As a sower that scattereth seed,
  So hast thou scattered us;
As one breaketh and shattereth a reed,
  Thou hast broken and shattered us.

FIFTH ANTIPHONE

From all thy lovers that love thee   33
  I God will sunder thee;
I will make darkness above thee,
  And thick darkness under thee;
Before me goeth a light,
  Behind me a sword;
Shall a remnant find grace in my sight?
  I am the Lord.

SIXTH ANTIPHONE

41   From all our lovers that love us
                    Thou God didst sunder us;
                Thou madest darkness above us,
                    And thick darkness under us;
                Thou hast kindled thy wrath for a light,
                    And made ready thy sword;
                Let a remnant find grace in thy sight,
                    We beseech thee, O Lord.

SEVENTH ANTIPHONE

49   Wilt thou bring fine gold for a payment
                    For sins on this wise?
                For the glittering of raiment
                    And the shining of eyes,
                For the painting of faces
                    And the sundering of trust,
                For the sins of thine high places
                    And delight of thy lust?

57   For your high things ye shall have lowly,
                    Lamentation for song;
                For, behold, I God am holy,
                    I the Lord am strong;
                Ye shall seek me and shall not reach me
                    Till the wine-press be trod;
                In that hour ye shall turn and beseech me,
                    Saith the Lord God.

EIGHTH ANTIPHONE

65   Not with fine gold for a payment,
                    But with coin of sighs,
                But with rending of raiment
                    And with weeping of eyes,
                But with shame of stricken faces
                    And with strewing of dust,

For the sin of stately places
   And lordship of lust;

With voices of men made lowly,   73
   Made empty of song,
O Lord God most holy,
   O God most strong,
We reach out hands to reach thee
   Ere the wine-press be trod;
We beseech thee, O Lord, we beseech thee,
   O Lord our God.

NINTH ANTIPHONE

In that hour thou shalt say to the night,   81
   Come down and cover us;
To the cloud on thy left and thy right,
   Be thou spread over us;
A snare shall be as thy mother,
   And a curse thy bride;
Thou shalt put her away, and another
   Shall lie by thy side.

Thou shalt neither rise up by day   89
   Nor lie down by night;
Would God it were dark! thou shalt say;
   Would God it were light!
And the sight of thine eyes shall be made
   As the burning of fire;
And thy soul shall be sorely afraid
   For thy soul's desire.

Ye whom your lords loved well,   97
   Putting silver and gold on you,
The inevitable hell
   Shall surely take hold on you;
Your gold shall be for a token,

Your staff for a rod;
With the breaking of bands ye are broken,
Saith the Lord God.

TENTH ANTIPHONE

105   In our sorrow we said to the night,
            Fall down and cover us;
        To the darkness at left and at right,
            Be thou shed over us;
        We had breaking of spirit to mother
            And cursing to bride;
        And one was slain, and another
            Stood up at our side.

113   We could not arise by day,
            Nor lie down by night;
        Thy sword was sharp in our way,
            Thy word in our sight;
        The delight of our eyelids was made
            As the burning of fire;
        And our souls became sorely afraid
            For our soul's desire.

121   We whom the world loved well,
            Laying silver and gold on us,
        The kingdom of death and of hell
            Riseth up to take hold on us;
        Our gold is turned to a token,
            Our staff to a rod;
        Yet shalt thou bind them up that were broken,
            O Lord our God.

A Lamentation

I

WHO hath known the ways of time
  Or trodden behind his feet?
    There is no such man among men.
For chance overcomes him, or crime
  Changes; for all things sweet   5
    In time wax bitter again.
Who shall give sorrow enough,
  Or who the abundance of tears?
Mine eyes are heavy with love
  And a sword gone through mine ears,   10
    A sound like a sword and fire,
    For pity, for great desire;
Who shall ensure me thereof,
  Lest I die, being full of my fears?

Who hath known the ways and the wrath,   15
  The sleepless spirit, the root
    And blossom of evil will,
    The divine device of a god?
Who shall behold it or hath?
  The twice-tongued prophets are mute,   20
    The many speakers are still;
    No foot has travelled or trod,

A Lamentation: Like the preceding "Litany," "Lamentation" is a Christian term, with specific reference to the Biblical book The Lamentations of Jeremiah, portions of which are traditionally sung on Thursday, Friday, and Saturday of Holy Week, the week before Easter, in both the Roman and Anglican churches. The general character of these three poems and their classical references suggests that Swinburne first planned them for an uncompleted Greek play in the manner of *Atalanta in Calydon*, or possibly for that work itself.

No hand has meted, his path.
    Man's fate is a blood-red fruit,
25   And the mighty gods have their fill
        And relax not the rein, or the rod.

Ye were mighty in heart from of old,
    Ye slew with the spear, and are slain.
Keen after heat is the cold,
30   Sore after summer is rain,
And melteth man to the bone.
    As water he weareth away,
    As a flower, as an hour in a day,
Fallen from laughter to moan.
35 But my spirit is shaken with fear
    Lest an evil thing begin,
New-born, a spear for a spear,
    And one for another sin.
Or ever our tears began,
40   It was known from of old and said;
One law for a living man,
    And another law for the dead.
For these are fearful and sad,
    Vain, and things without breath;
45   While he lives let a man be glad,
    For none hath joy of his death.

II

Who hath known the pain, the old pain of earth,
    Or all the travail of the sea,
The many ways and waves, the birth
50 Fruitless, the labour nothing worth?
    Who hath known, who knoweth, O gods? not we.
There is none shall say he hath seen,
    There is none he hath known.
Though he saith, Lo, a lord have I been,
55   I have reaped and sown;

I have seen the desire of mine eyes,
   The beginning of love,
The season of kisses and sighs
   And the end thereof.
I have known the ways of the sea,   60
   All the perilous ways,
Strange winds have spoken with me,
   And the tongues of strange days.
I have hewn the pine for ships;
   Where steeds run arow,   65
I have seen from their bridled lips
   Foam blown as the snow.
With snapping of chariot-poles
   And with straining of oars
I have grazed in the race the goals,   70
   In the storm the shores;
As a greave is cleft with an arrow
   At the joint of the knee,
I have cleft through the sea-straits narrow
   To the heart of the sea.   75
When air was smitten in sunder
   I have watched on high
The ways of the stars and the thunder
   In the night of the sky;
Where the dark brings forth light as a flower,   80
   As from lips that dissever;
One abideth the space of an hour,
   One endureth for ever.
Lo, what hath he seen or known,
   Of the way and the wave   85
Unbeholden, unsailed on, unsown,
   From the breast to the grave?

Or ever the stars were made, or skies,
   Grief was born, and the kinless night,
      Mother of gods without form or name.   90
And light is born out of heaven and dies,

And one day knows not another's light,
But night is one, and her shape the same.

But dumb the goddesses underground
95   Wait, and we hear not on earth if their feet
Rise, and the night wax loud with their wings;
Dumb, without word or shadow of sound;
And sift in scales and winnow as wheat
Men's souls, and sorrow of manifold things.

III

100   Nor less of grief than ours
The gods wrought long ago
To bruise men one by one;
But with the incessant hours
Fresh grief and greener woe
105   Spring, as the sudden sun
Year after year makes flowers;
And these die down and grow,
And the next year lacks none.

As these men sleep, have slept
110   The old heroes in time fled,
No dream-divided sleep;
And holier eyes have wept
Than ours, when on her dead
Gods have seen Thetis weep,
115   With heavenly hair far-swept
Back, heavenly hands outspread
Round what she could not keep,

Could not one day withhold,
One night; and like as these
120   White ashes of no weight,

114. *Thetis:* A Nereid, or sea-nymph, the mother of Achilles, who had hoped
to see him immortal but saw him killed in the struggle at Troy. She took the
body and buried it.

      Held not his urn the cold
        Ashes of Heracles?
         For all things born one gate
    Opens, no gate of gold;
        Opens; and no man sees   125
         Beyond the gods and fate.

---

122. *Heracles:* Like Achilles a child of a mortal and an immortal, he was famed for his great strength and his labors. Poisoned by the blood of a centaur, he had himself placed on his funeral pyre while still living.

Anima Anceps

1

TILL death have broken
Sweet life's love-token,
Till all be spoken
    That shall be said,
What dost thou praying,
O soul, and playing
With song and saying,
    Things flown and fled?

9

For this we know not—
That fresh springs flow not
And fresh griefs grow not
    When men are dead;
When strange years cover
Lover and lover,
And joys are over
    And tears are shed.

17

If one day's sorrow
Mar the day's morrow—
If man's life borrow
    And man's death pay—
If souls once taken,
If lives once shaken,
Arise, awaken,
    By night, by day—

25

Why with strong crying
And years of sighing,
Living and dying,
    Fast ye and pray?
For all your weeping,

Anima Anceps: "Twofold soul."

Waking and sleeping,
Death come to reaping
And takes away.

Though time rend after   33
Roof-tree from rafter,
A little laughter
    Is much more worth
Than thus to measure
The hour, the treasure,
The pain, the pleasure,
    The death, the birth;
Grief, when days alter,   41
Like joy shall falter;
Song-book and psalter,
    Mourning and mirth.
Live like the swallow;
Seek not to follow
Where earth is hollow
    Under the earth.

In the Orchard

(PROVENÇAL BURDEN)

LEAVE go my hands, let me catch breath and see;
Let the dew-fall drench either side of me;
   Clear apple-leaves are soft upon that moon
Seen sidelong like a blossom in the tree;
5   Ah God, ah God, that day should be so soon.

The grass is thick and cool, it lets us lie.
Kissed upon either cheek and either eye,
   I turn to thee as some green afternoon
Turns toward sunset, and is loth to die;
10   Ah God, ah God, that day should be so soon.

Lie closer, lean your face upon my side,
Feel where the dew fell that has hardly dried,
   Hear how the blood beats that went nigh to swoon;
The pleasure lives there when the sense has died;
15   Ah God, ah God, that day should be so soon.

O my fair lord, I charge you leave me this:
Is it not sweeter than a foolish kiss?
   Nay take it then, my flower, my first in June,
My rose, so like a tender mouth it is:
20   Ah God, ah God, that day should be so soon.

Love, till dawn sunder night from day with fire,
Dividing my delight and my desire,

Provençal burden: Provence, in southern France, was the area in which the tradition of European lyric poetry was formed in the early Middle Ages. "Burden" comes from the French *bourdon,* the verse repeated at the end of each
stanza.

The crescent life and love the plenilune,
Love me though dusk begin and dark retire;
   Ah God, ah God, that day should be so soon.   25

Ah, my heart fails, my blood draws back; I know,
When life runs over, life is near to go;
   And with the slain of love love's ways are strewn,
And with their blood, if love will have it so;
   Ah God, ah God, that day should be so soon.   30

Ah, do thy will now; slay me if thou wilt;
There is no building now the walls are built,
   No quarrying now the corner-stone is hewn,
No drinking now the vine's whole blood is spilt;
   Ah God, ah God, that day should be so soon.   35

Nay, slay me now; nay, for I will be slain;
Pluck thy red pleasure from the teeth of pain,
   Break down thy vine ere yet grape-gatherers prune,
Slay me ere day can slay desire again;
   Ah God, ah God, that day should be so soon.   40

Yea, with thy sweet lips, with thy sweet sword; yea,
Take life and all, for I will die, I say;
   Love, I gave love, is life a better boon?
For sweet night's sake I will not live till day;
   Ah God, ah God, that day should be so soon.   45

Nay, I will sleep then only; nay, but go.
Ah sweet, too sweet to me, my sweet, I know
   Love, sleep, and death go to the sweet same tune;
Hold my hair fast, and kiss me through it so.
   Ah God, ah God, that day should be so soon.   50

A Match

1   IF love were what the rose is,
      And I were like the leaf,
Our lives would grow together
In sad or singing weather,
Blown fields or flowerful closes,
      Green pleasure or grey grief;
If love were what the rose is,
      And I were like the leaf.

9   If I were what the words are,
      And love were like the tune,
With double sound and single
Delight our lips would mingle,
With kisses glad as birds are
      That get sweet rain at noon;
If I were what the words are,
      And love were like the tune.

17   If you were life, my darling,
      And I your love were death,
We'd shine and snow together
Ere March made sweet the weather
With daffodil and starling
      And hours of fruitful breath;
If you were life, my darling,
      And I your love were death.

25   If you were thrall to sorrow,
      And I were page to joy,
We'd play for lives and seasons
With loving looks and treasons

106

And tears of night and morrow
   And laughs of maid and boy;
If you were thrall to sorrow,
   And I were page to joy.

If you were April's lady,   33
   And I were lord in May,
We'd throw with leaves for hours
And draw for days with flowers,
Till day like night were shady
   And night were bright like day;
If you were April's lady,
   And I were lord in May.

If you were queen of pleasure,   41
   And I were king of pain,
We'd hunt down love together,
Pluck out his flying-feather,
And teach his feet a measure,
   And find his mouth a rein;
If you were queen of pleasure,
   And I were king of pain.

35–36. *throw:* As in dice.   *draw:* As in a game of cards.
45. *measure:* A sequence of dance steps.

Faustine

Ave Faustina Imperatrix, morituri te salutant.

1   LEAN back, and get some minutes' peace;
        Let your head lean
    Back to the shoulder with its fleece
        Of locks, Faustine.

5   The shapely silver shoulder stoops,
        Weighed over clean
    With state of splendid hair that droops
        Each side, Faustine.

9   Let me go over your good gifts
        That crown you queen;
    A queen whose kingdom ebbs and shifts
        Each week, Faustine.

13   Bright heavy brows well gathered up:
        White gloss and sheen;
    Carved lips that make my lips a cup
        To drink, Faustine,

17   Wine and rank poison, milk and blood,
        Being mixed therein

Faustine: Faustina was the wife of the Roman emperor Marcus Aurelius (reigned A.D. 161–180), traditionally the morally most perfect of the emperors. Faustina, probably unjustly, was given by the historians the reputation of being among the most licentious of Roman empresses. Swinburne's poem is actually addressed, not to the empress, but to a woman who reminds the speaker of her.

Epigraph: "We who are about to die salute you," the traditional greeting of the gladiators to the emperor and empress.

Since first the devil threw dice with God
    For you, Faustine.

Your naked new-born soul, their stake,   21
    Stood blind between;
God said "let him that wins her take
    And keep Faustine."

But this time Satan throve, no doubt;   25
    Long since, I ween,
God's part in you was battered out;
    Long since, Faustine.

The die rang sideways as it fell,   29
    Rang cracked and thin,
Like a man's laughter heard in hell
    Far down, Faustine,

A shadow of laughter like a sigh,   33
    Dead sorrow's kin;
So rang, thrown down, the devil's die
    That won Faustine.

A suckling of his breed you were,   37
    One hard to wean;
But God, who lost you, left you fair,
    We see, Faustine.

You have the face that suits a woman   41
    For her soul's screen—
The sort of beauty that's called human
    In hell, Faustine.

You could do all things but be good   45
    Or chaste of mien;
And that you would not if you could,
    We know, Faustine.

49   Even he who cast seven devils out
              Of Magdalene
          Could hardly do as much, I doubt,
              For you, Faustine.

53   Did Satan make you to spite God?
              Or did God mean
          To scourge with scorpions for a rod
              Our sins, Faustine?

57   I know what queen at first you were,
              As though I had seen
          Red gold and black imperious hair
              Twice crown Faustine.

61   As if your fed sarcophagus
              Spared flesh and skin,
          You come back face to face with us,
              The same Faustine.

65   She loved the games men played with death,
              Where death must win;
          As though the slain man's blood and breath
              Revived Faustine.

69   Nets caught the pike, pikes tore the net;
              Lithe limbs and lean
          From drained-out pores dripped thick red sweat
              To soothe Faustine.

73   She drank the steaming drift and dust
              Blown off the scene;

49–50. *he:* Christ. *Magdalene:* See note to "Laus Veneris," line 283.

61. *sarcophagus:* Literally, body-eater.

65. *she:* The Empress Faustina. The following lines (through line 80) refer to the gladiatorial combats in the Circus, that is, the Colosseum. (The Circus Maximus was a different structure, used for horse racing.)

Blood could not ease the bitter lust
   That galled Faustine.

All round the foul fat furrows reeked, 77
   Where blood sank in;
The circus splashed and seethed and shrieked
   All round Faustine.

But these are gone now: years entomb 81
   The dust and din;
Yea, even the bath's fierce reek and fume
   That slew Faustine.

Was life worth living then? and now 85
   Is life worth sin?
Where are the imperial years? and how
   Are you Faustine?

Your soul forgot her joys, forgot 89
   Her times of teen;
Yea, this life likewise will you not
   Forget, Faustine?

For in the time we know not of 93
   Did fate begin
Weaving the web of days that wove
   Your doom, Faustine.

The threads were wet with wine, and all 97
   Were smooth to spin;
They wove you like a Bacchanal,
   The first Faustine.

And Bacchus cast your mates and you 101
   Wild grapes to glean;

99–101. *Bacchanal:* The wild celebrations of the rites of Bacchus, or Dionysus, the god of wine. In the ancient Greek celebration, the maddened women
tore apart a youth as sacrificial victim.

Your flower-like lips were dashed with dew
    From his, Faustine.

105   Your drenched loose hands were stretched to hold
    The vine's wet green,
Long ere they coined in Roman gold
    Your face, Faustine.

109   Then after change of soaring feather
    And winnowing fin,
You woke in weeks of feverish weather,
    A new Faustine.

113   A star upon your birthday burned,
    Whose fierce serene
Red pulseless planet never yearned
    In heaven, Faustine.

117   Stray breaths of Sapphic song that blew
    Through Mitylene
Shook the fierce quivering blood in you
    By night, Faustine.

121   The shameless nameless love that makes
    Hell's iron gin
Shut on you like a trap that breaks
    The soul, Faustine.

125   And when your veins were void and dead,
    What ghosts unclean
Swarmed round the straitened barren bed
    That hid Faustine?

129   What sterile growths of sexless root
    Or epicene?

117–118. *Sapphic:* See note to "Anactoria."
118. *Mitylene:* The birthplace of Sappho.
122. *gin:* Trap.

What flower of kisses without fruit
　　Of love, Faustine?

What adders came to shed their coats?　　133
　　What coiled obscene
Small serpents with soft stretching throats
　　Caressed Faustine?

But the time came of famished hours,　　137
　　Maimed loves and mean,
This ghastly thin-faced time of ours,
　　To spoil Faustine.

You seem a thing that hinges hold,　　141
　　A love-machine
With clockwork joints of supple gold—
　　No more, Faustine.

Not godless, for you serve one God,　　145
　　The Lampsacene,
Who metes the gardens with his rod;
　　Your lord, Faustine.

If one should love you with real love　　149
　　(Such things have been,
Things your fair face knows nothing of,
　　It seems, Faustine) ;

That clear hair heavily bound back,　　153
　　The lights wherein
Shift from dead blue to burnt-up black;
　　Your throat, Faustine,

Strong, heavy, throwing out the face　　157
　　And hard bright chin

146. *Lampsacene:* Lampsacus, on the Hellespont in Asia Minor, was famous as a cult center for Priapus, a fertility deity, traditionally pictured or
carved with an enormous erect phallus. He was the protector of gardens.

And shameful scornful lips that grace
Their shame, Faustine,

161   Curled lips, long since half kissed away,
Still sweet and keen;
You'd give him—poison shall we say?
Or what, Faustine?

A Cameo

THERE was a graven image of Desire
    Painted with red blood on a ground of gold
    Passing between the young men and the old,
And by him Pain, whose body shone like fire,
And Pleasure with gaunt hands that grasped their hire.   5
    Of his left wrist, with fingers clenched and cold,
    The insatiable Satiety kept hold,
Walking with feet unshod that pashed the mire.
The senses and the sorrows and the sins,
    And the strange loves that suck the breasts of Hate   10
Till lips and teeth bite in their sharp indenture,
Followed like beasts with flap of wings and fins.
    Death stood aloof behind a gaping grate,
Upon whose lock was written *Peradventure*.

A Cameo: An ornament carved from any stone or shell with two layers of differing colors. The figure is in one color against a background of the other.

  8. *pashed:* Struck violently.
 14. *Peradventure:* Perhaps, possibly.

Song Before Death

(FROM THE FRENCH)

1795

1   SWEET mother, in a minute's span
        Death parts thee and my love of thee;
Sweet love, that yet art living man,
        Come back, true love, to comfort me.
Back, ah, come back! ah wellaway!
But my love comes not any day.

7   As roses, when the warm West blows,
        Break to full flower and sweeten spring,
My soul would break to a glorious rose
        In such wise at his whispering.
In vain I listen; wellaway!
My love says nothing any day.

13   You that will weep for pity of love
        On the low place where I am lain,
I pray you, having wept enough,
        Tell him for whom I bore such pain
That he was yet, ah! wellaway!
My true love to my dying day.

The subtitle and epigraph suggest that the song is to be imagined as being sung just before the singer is guillotined in the French Revolution. The poem is a translation of a song in Part VIII of *Aline et Valcour* by the Marquis de Sade (1793).

Rococo

TAKE hands and part with laughter;　　　　1
　　Touch lips and part with tears;
Once more and no more after,
　　Whatever comes with years.
We twain shall not remeasure
　　The ways that left us twain;
Nor crush the lees of pleasure
　　From sanguine grapes of pain.

We twain once well in sunder,　　　　　　9
　　What will the mad gods do
For hate with me, I wonder,
　　Or what for love with you?
Forget them till November,
　　And dream there's April yet;
Forget that I remember,
　　And dream that I forget.

Time found our tired love sleeping,　　　17
　　And kissed away his breath;
But what should we do weeping,
　　Though light love sleep to death?
We have drained his lips at leisure,
　　Till there's not left to drain
A single sob of pleasure,
　　A single pulse of pain.

Dream that the lips once breathless　　　25

Rococo: The style of ornament, furniture, and painting, and by extension all
the arts, of the mid-eighteenth century; thus, by a further extension, a symbol
of the French culture of the time, a period of hedonism, particularly in erotic
matters.

Might quicken if they would;
Say that the soul is deathless;
  Dream that the gods are good;
Say March may wed September,
  And time divorce regret;
But not that you remember,
  And not that I forget.

33   We have heard from hidden places
  What love scarce lives and hears:
We have seen on fervent faces
  The pallor of strange tears:
We have trod the wine-vat's treasure,
  Whence, ripe to steam and stain,
Foams round the feet of pleasure
  The blood-red must of pain.

41   Remembrance may recover
  And time bring back to time
The name of your first lover,
  The ring of my first rhyme;
But rose-leaves of December
  The frosts of June shall fret,
The day that you remember,
  The day that I forget.

49   The snake that hides and hisses
  In heaven we twain have known;
The grief of cruel kisses,
  The joy whose mouth makes moan;
The pulse's pause and measure,
  Where in one furtive vein
Throbs through the heart of pleasure
  The purpler blood of pain.

57   We have done with tears and treasons
  And love for treason's sake;

Room for the swift new seasons,
    The years that burn and break,
Dismantle and dismember
    Men's days and dreams, Juliette;
For love may not remember,
    But time will not forget.

Life treads down love in flying,   65
    Time withers him at root;
Bring all dead things and dying,
    Reaped sheaf and ruined fruit,
Where, crushed by three days' pressure,
    Our three days' love lies slain;
And earlier leaf of pleasure,
    And latter flower of pain.

Breathe close upon the ashes,   73
    It may be flame will leap;
Unclose the soft close lashes,
    Lift up the lids, and weep.
Light love's extinguished ember,
    Let one tear leave it wet
For one that you remember
    And ten that you forget.

62. *Juliette:* The title of a novel by the Marquis de Sade, and the name of
its heroine who learns to enjoy every possible kind of sexual behavior, including the combination of sex and murder.

Stage Love

WHEN the game began between them for a jest,
He played king and she played queen to match the best;
Laughter soft as tears, and tears that turned to laughter,
These were things she sought for years and sorrowed after.

5   Pleasure with dry lips, and pain that walks by night;
All the sting and all the stain of long delight;
These were things she knew not of, that knew not of her,
When she played at half a love with half a lover.

Time was chorus, gave them cues to laugh or cry;
10   They would kill, befool, amuse him, let him die;
Set him webs to weave to-day and break to-morrow,
Till he died for good in play, and rose in sorrow.

What the years mean; how time dies and is not slain;
How love grows and laughs and cries and wanes again;
15   These were things she came to know, and take their measure,
When the play was played out so for one man's pleasure.

A Ballad of Burdens

THE burden of fair women. Vain delight,　　　　　1
　　And love self-slain in some sweet shameful way,
And sorrowful old age that comes by night
　　As a thief comes that has no heart by day,
　　And change that finds fair cheeks and leaves them grey,
And weariness that keeps awake for hire,
　　And grief that says what pleasure used to say;
This is the end of every man's desire.

The burden of bought kisses. This is sore,　　　　9
　　A burden without fruit in childbearing;
Between the nightfall and the dawn threescore,
　　Threescore between the dawn and evening.
　　The shuddering in thy lips, the shuddering
In thy sad eyelids tremulous like fire,
　　Makes love seem shameful and a wretched thing.
This is the end of every man's desire.

The burden of sweet speeches. Nay, kneel down,　　17
　　Cover thy head, and weep; for verily
These market-men that buy thy white and brown
　　In the last days shall take no thought for thee.
　　In the last days like earth thy face shall be,
Yea, like sea-marsh made thick with brine and mire,
　　Sad with sick leavings of the sterile sea.
This is the end of every man's desire.

A Ballad of Burdens: "Ballad" is used in the older French sense of *ballade,*
not a folk poem but an elaborate poem of high culture. Swinburne's model was
the ballades of François Villon (1431–?). For "Burden" see note to "In the
Orchard"; here Swinburne uses the word in that sense as well as the more
common one.

25   The burden of long living.   Thou shalt fear
           Waking, and sleeping mourn upon thy bed;
        And say at night "Would God the day were here,"
           And say at dawn "Would God the day were dead."
           With weary days thou shalt be clothed and fed,
        And wear remorse of heart for thine attire,
           Pain for thy girdle and sorrow upon thine head;
        This is the end of every man's desire.

33   The burden of bright colours.   Thou shalt see
           Gold tarnished, and the grey above the green;
        And as the thing thou seest thy face shall be,
           And no more as the thing beforetime seen.
           And thou shalt say of mercy "It hath been,"
        And living, watch the old lips and loves expire,
           And talking, tears shall take thy breath between;
        This is the end of every man's desire.

41   The burden of sad sayings.   In that day
           Thou shalt tell all thy days and hours, and tell
        Thy times and ways and words of love, and say
           How one was dear and one desirable,
           And sweet was life to hear and sweet to smell,
        But now with lights reverse the old hours retire
           And the last hour is shod with fire from hell;
        This is the end of every man's desire.

49   The burden of four seasons.   Rain in spring,
           White rain and wind among the tender trees;
        A summer of green sorrows gathering,
           Rank autumn in a mist of miseries,
           With sad face set towards the year, that sees
        The charred ash drop out of the dropping pyre,
           And winter wan with many maladies;
        This is the end of every man's desire.

The burden of dead faces.   Out of sight   57
   And out of love, beyond the reach of hands,
Changed in the changing of the dark and light,
   They walk and weep about the barren lands
   Where no seed is nor any garner stands,
Where in short breaths the doubtful days respire,
   And time's turned glass lets through the sighing sands;
This is the end of every man's desire.

The burden of much gladness.   Life and lust   65
   Forsake thee, and the face of thy delight;
And underfoot the heavy hour strews dust,
   And overhead strange weathers burn and bite;
   And where the red was, lo the bloodless white,
And where truth was, the likeness of a liar,
   And where day was, the likeness of the night;
This is the end of every man's desire.

L'ENVOY

Princes, and ye whom pleasure quickeneth,   73
   Heed well this rhyme before your pleasure tire;
For life is sweet, but after life is death.
   This is the end of every man's desire.

72–73. *L'envoy:* Swinburne uses the medieval spelling. The *envoy* was the
sending of a poem on its way.

Before the Mirror

(VERSES WRITTEN UNDER A PICTURE)

Inscribed to J. A. Whistler

I

1
    WHITE rose in red rose-garden
      Is not so white;
    Snowdrops that plead for pardon
      And pine for fright
    Because the hard East blows
    Over their maiden rows
      Grow not as this face grows from pale to bright.

8
    Behind the veil, forbidden,
      Shut up from sight,
    Love, is there sorrow hidden,
      Is there delight?
    Is joy thy dower or grief,
    White rose of weary leaf,
      Late rose whose life is brief, whose loves are light?

Dedication: Whistler (1834–1903), the American artist, lived from 1855 on in Europe, principally, after his Parisian studies, in London, where he was a member of artistic and literary circles and knew Swinburne. In 1863 his "The White Girl," having been refused by the Royal Academy, was exhibited in Paris in the first Salon des Refusés, where it created a considerable scandal. In 1864 he painted "The Little White Girl," which inspired Swinburne's poem. ("Little" refers to the size of the painting, smaller than "The White Girl.") It shows a girl dressed in white, holding a Japanese fan and leaning on a white mantelpiece, one arm extended along it. On the end of the mantelpiece is a Japanese vase, which she is pensively contemplating. She is in profile, but her reflection, in three-quarters view, exhibits an entirely different facial character, one of sadness, even of suffering.

Soft snows that hard winds harden 15
  Till each flake bite
Fill all the flowerless garden
  Whose flowers took flight
Long since when summer ceased,
And men rose up from feast,
  And warm west wind grew east, and warm day night.

II

"Come snow, come wind or thunder 22
  High up in air,
I watch my face, and wonder
  At my bright hair;
Nought else exalts or grieves
The rose at heart, that heaves
  With love of her own leaves and lips that pair.

"She knows not loves that kissed her 29
  She knows not where.
Art thou the ghost, my sister,
  White sister there,
Am I the ghost, who knows?
My hand, a fallen rose,
  Lies snow-white on white snows, and takes no care.

"I cannot see what pleasures 36
  Or what pains were;
What pale new loves and treasures
  New years will bear;
What beam will fall, what shower,
What grief or joy for dower;
  But one thing knows the flower; the flower is fair."

III

Glad, but not flushed with gladness, 43
  Since joys go by;

Sad, but not bent with sadness,
  Since sorrows die;
Deep in the gleaming glass
She sees all past things pass,
  And all sweet life that was lie down and lie.

50   There glowing ghosts of flowers
            Draw down, draw nigh;
          And wings of swift spent hours
            Take flight and fly;
          She sees by formless gleams,
          She hears across cold streams,
            Dead mouths of many dreams that sing and sigh.

57   Face fallen and white throat lifted,
            With sleepless eye
          She sees old loves that drifted,
            She knew not why,
          Old loves and faded fears
          Float down a stream that hears
            The flowing of all men's tears beneath the sky.

Erotion

SWEET for a little even to fear, and sweet,
O love, to lay down fear at love's fair feet;
Shall not some fiery memory of his breath
Lie sweet on lips that touch the lips of death?
Yet leave me not; yet, if thou wilt, be free;   5
Love me no more, but love my love of thee.
Love where thou wilt, and live thy life; and I,
One thing I can, and one love cannot—die.
Pass from me; yet thine arms, thine eyes, thine hair,
Feed my desire and deaden my despair.   10
Yet once more ere time change us, ere my cheek
Whiten, ere hope be dumb or sorrow speak,
Yet once more ere thou hate me, one full kiss;
Keep other hours for others, save me this.
Yea, and I will not (if it please thee) weep,   15
Lest thou be sad; I will but sigh, and sleep.
Sweet, does death hurt? thou canst not do me wrong:
I shall not lack thee, as I loved thee, long.

Erotion: Greek name, meaning "dedicated to Eros," or to Love; see also
"Anactoria," line 21. This poem was written to accompany a picture by Simeon
Solomon (1840–1905), an artist of considerable talent who led an exceedingly
bohemian and dissipated life and who shared with Swinburne an interest in
sexual aberrations. In 1871 Swinburne published an article about him, "Simeon
Solomon's Vision of Love"—never reprinted by Swinburne—in which he said
of the picture that the figure of the woman is "full of the soft fear and secret
certitude which I have tried elsewhere to render in the verses called Erotion
written as a comment on this picture, with design to express the subtle passionate sense of mortality in love itself which wells up from the 'middle spring
of pleasures' yet cannot quite kill the day's delight or eat away with the bitter
poison of doubt the burning faith and self-abandoned fondness of the hour;
since at least though the future be for others and the love now here turn elsewhere to seek pastures in fresh field from other flowers, the vows and kisses of
this his present lips are not theirs but hers, as the memory of his love and the
shadow of his youth shall be hers for ever."

Hast thou not given me above all that live
20   Joy, and a little sorrow shalt not give?
What even though fairer fingers of strange girls
Pass nestling through thy beautiful boy's curls
As mine did, or those curled lithe lips of thine
Meet theirs as these, all theirs come after mine;
25   And though I were not, though I be not, best,
I have loved and love thee more than all the rest.
O love, O lover, loose or hold me fast,
I had thee first, whoever have thee last;
Fairer or not, what need I know, what care?
30   To thy fair bud my blossom once seemed fair.
Why am I fair at all before thee, why
At all desired? seeing thou art fair, not I.
I shall be glad of thee, O fairest head,
Alive, alone, without thee, with thee, dead;
35   I shall remember while the light lives yet,
And in the night-time I shall not forget.
Though (as thou wilt) thou leave me ere life leave,
I will not, for thy love I will not, grieve;
Not as they use who love not more than I,
40   Who love not as I love thee though I die;
And though thy lips, once mine, be oftener prest
To many another brow and balmier breast,
And sweeter arms, or sweeter to thy mind,
Lull thee or lure, more fond thou wilt not find.

In Memory of Walter Savage Landor

BACK to the flower-town, side by side,   1
　　The bright months bring,
New-born, the bridegroom and the bride,
　　Freedom and spring.

The sweet land laughs from sea to sea,   5
　　Filled full of sun;
All things come back to her, being free;
　　All things but one.

In many a tender wheaten plot   9
　　Flowers that were dead
Live, and old suns revive; but not
　　That holier head.

By this white wandering waste of sea,   13
　　Far north, I hear
One face shall never turn to me
　　As once this year:

Shall never smile and turn and rest   17
　　On mine as there,
Nor one most sacred hand be prest
　　Upon my hair.

In Memory of Walter Savage Landor: Landor (1775–1864), poet and artist in
prose, was one of the passions of Swinburne from the time when at the age of
twelve he first read *Hellenics* (1847) and Landor's other poems, as well as his
Imaginary Conversations (1824 and after). Landor's love of liberty, republicanism, and general social intransigence, as well as his fine classicism and his exquisite sense of style in verse and prose, endeared him to Swinburne. They
finally met on March 29, 1864, in Florence. Swinburne received permission to
dedicate *Atalanta in Calydon* to him, but the old man was too weak and tired to
see him again. He died September 17, 1864.

　　1. *flower-town:* Florence, in Italian *Firenze*, city of flowers.

21   I came as one whose thoughts half linger,
               Half run before;
       The youngest to the oldest singer
               That England bore.

25   I found him whom I shall not find
               Till all grief end,
       In holiest age our mightiest mind,
               Father and friend.

29   But thou, if anything endure,
               If hope there be,
       O spirit that man's life left pure,
               Man's death set free,

33   Not with disdain of days that were
               Look earthward now;
       Let dreams revive the reverend hair,
               The imperial brow;

37   Come back in sleep, for in the life
               Where thou art not
       We find none like thee.   Time and strife
               And the world's lot

41   Move thee no more; but love at least
               And reverent heart
       May move thee, royal and released,
               Soul, as thou art.

45   And thou, his Florence, to thy trust
               Receive and keep,
       Keep safe his dedicated dust,
               His sacred sleep.

49   So shall thy lovers, come from far,
               Mix with thy name
       As morning-star with evening-star
               His faultless fame.

To Victor Hugo

In the fair days when God   1
  By man as godlike trod,
And each alike was Greek, alike was free,
  God's lightning spared, they said,
  Alone the happier head
Whose laurels screened it; fruitless grace for thee,
  To whom the high gods gave of right
Their thunders and their laurels and their light.

Sunbeams and bays before   9
  Our master's servants wore,
For these Apollo left in all men's lands;
  But far from these ere now
  And watched with jealous brow
Lay the blind lightnings shut between God's hands,
  And only loosed on slaves and kings
The terror of the tempest of their wings.

Born in those younger years   17
  That shone with storms of spears
And shook in the wind blown from a dead world's pyre,
  When by her back-blown hair
  Napoleon caught the fair

To Victor Hugo: Hugo (1802–1885), like Landor (see preceding poem), was one of Swinburne's heroes, for much the same reason. Poet and novelist, to Swinburne he was particularly admirable for his opposition to the Emperor Napoleon III of France, who, elected president of France, had in Hugo's and Swinburne's eyes tricked the French people into accepting him as Emperor, principally on the far from adequate grounds that he was the nephew of the great Napoleon. Hugo was driven into exile, and could not return to France until the downfall of Napoleon III in 1870.

17–24. *those younger years:* Hugo was born not long before Napoleon I became First Consul of the French Republic and virtual dictator.

And fierce Republic with her feet of fire,
        And stayed with iron words and hands
Her flight, and freedom in a thousand lands:

25   Thou sawest the tides of things
                Close over heads of kings,
        And thine hand felt the thunder, and to thee
                Laurels and lightnings were
                As sunbeams and soft air
        Mixed each in other, or as mist with sea
                Mixed, or as memory with desire,
        Or the lute's pulses with the louder lyre.

33   For thee man's spirit stood
                Disrobed of flesh and blood,
        And bare the heart of the most secret hours;
                And to thine hand more tame
                Than birds in winter came
        High hopes and unknown flying forms of powers,
                And from thy table fed, and sang
        Till with the tune men's ears took fire and rang.

41   Even all men's eyes and ears
                With fiery sound and tears
        Waxed hot, and cheeks caught flame and eyelid light,
                At those high songs of thine
                That stung the sense like wine,
        Or fell more soft than dew or snow by night,
                Or wailed as in some flooded cave
        Sobs the strong broken spirit of a wave.

49   But we, our master, we
                Whose hearts uplift to thee,
        Ache with the pulse of thy remembered song,

26. *heads of kings:* Napoleon defeated at one time or another most of the kings of Europe.

We ask not nor await
From the clenched hands of fate,
As thou, remission of the world's old wrong;
Respite we ask not, nor release;
Freedom a man may have, he shall not peace.

Though thy most fiery hope 57
Storm heaven, to set wide ope
The all-sought-for gate whence God or Chance debars
All feet of men, all eyes—
The old night resumes her skies,
Her hollow hiding-place of clouds and stars,
Where nought save these is sure in sight;
And, paven with death, our days are roofed with night.

One thing we can; to be 65
Awhile, as men may, free;
But not by hope or pleasure the most stern
Goddess, most awful-eyed,
Sits, but on either side
Sit sorrow and the wrath of hearts that burn,
Sad faith that cannot hope or fear,
And memory grey with many a flowerless year.

Not that in stranger's wise 73
I lift not loving eyes
To the fair foster-mother France, that gave
Beyond the pale fleet foam
Help to my sires and home,
Whose great sweet breast could shelter those and save
Whom from her nursing breasts and hands
Their land cast forth of old on gentler lands.

73–80. Swinburne liked to say (what may have been true) that his an-
cestors were followers of the Stuarts and went into exile into France during
the Commonwealth, which ended in 1660 when the Swinburnes were created
baronets, and again as the aftermath of the Pretender, Charles III or Bonnie
Prince Charlie.

81   Not without thoughts that ache
               For theirs and for thy sake,
          I, born of exiles, hail thy banished head;
               I whose young song took flight
               Toward the great heat and light
          On me a child from thy far splendour shed,
               From thine high place of soul and song,
          Which, fallen on eyes yet feeble, made them strong.

89   Ah, not with lessening love
               For memories born hereof,
          I look to that sweet mother-land, and see
               The old fields and fair full streams,
               And skies, but fled like dreams
          The feet of freedom and the thought of thee;
               And all between the skies and graves
          The mirth of mockers and the shame of slaves.

97   She, killed with noisome air,
               Even she! and still so fair,
          Who said "Let there be freedom," and there was
               Freedom; and as a lance
               The fiery eyes of France
          Touched the world's sleep and as a sleep made pass
               Forth of men's heavier ears and eyes
          Smitten with fire and thunder from new skies.

105   Are they men's friends indeed
               Who watch them weep and bleed?
          Because thou hast loved us, shall the gods love thee?
               Thou, first of men and friend,
               Seest thou, even thou, the end?

---

83. In 1851 Napoleon III seized power in a coup d'état, and Hugo fled into
exile, first to Belgium and then to the islands of Jersey and then Guernsey, English islands in the English Channel.
    99. *"Let there be freedom"*: The French Revolution, with its liberty, equal-
ity, and fraternity.

Thou knowest what hath been, knowest thou what shall be?
  Evils may pass and hopes endure;
But fate is dim, and all the gods obscure.

  O nursed in airs apart,   113
  O poet highest of heart,
Hast thou seen time, who hast seen so many things?
  Are not the years more wise,
  More sad than keenest eyes,
The years with soundless feet and sounding wings?
  Passing we hear them not, but past
The clamour of them thrills us, and their blast.

  Thou art chief of us, and lord;   121
  Thy song is as a sword
Keen-edged and scented in the blade from flowers;
  Thou art lord and king; but we
  Lift younger eyes, and see
Less of high hope, less light on wandering hours;
  Hours that have borne men down so long,
Seen the right fail, and watched uplift the wrong.

  But thine imperial soul,   129
  As years and ruins roll
To the same end, and all things and all dreams
  With the same wreck and roar
  Drift on the dim same shore,
Still in the bitter foam and brackish streams
  Tracks the fresh water-spring to be
And sudden sweeter fountains in the sea.

  As once the high God bound   137
  With many a rivet round
Man's saviour, and with iron nailed him through,
  At the wild end of things,

137–144. *Man's saviour:* Prometheus, who was chained to the Caucasus by
Zeus, in punishment for his aid to mankind.

Where even his own bird's wings
Flagged, whence the sea shone like a drop of dew,
From Caucasus beheld below
Past fathoms of unfathomable snow;

145   So the strong God, the chance
Central of circumstance,
Still shows him exile who will not be slave;
All thy great fame and thee
Girt by the dim strait sea
With multitudinous walls of wandering wave;
Shows us our greatest from his throne
Fate-stricken, and rejected of his own.

153   Yea, he is strong, thou say'st,
A mystery many-faced,
The wild beasts know him and the wild birds flee;
The blind night sees him, death
Shrinks beaten at his breath,
And his right hand is heavy on the sea:
We know he hath made us, and is king;
We know not if he care for anything.

161   Thus much, no more, we know;
He bade what is be so,
Bade light be and bade night be, one by one;
Bade hope and fear, bade ill
And good redeem and kill,
Till all men be aweary of the sun
And his world burn in its own flame
And bear no witness longer of his name.

169   Yet though all this be thus,
Be those men praised of us
Who have loved and wrought and sorrowed and not sinned
For fame or fear or gold,

151. *our greatest:* Hugo.

Nor waxed for winter cold,
Nor changed for changes of the worldly wind;
Praised above men of men be these,
Till this one world and work we know shall cease.

Yea, one thing more than this,   177
We know that one thing is,
The splendour of a spirit without blame,
That not the labouring years
Blind-born, nor any fears,
Nor men nor any gods can tire or tame;
But purer power with fiery breath
Fills, and exalts above the gulfs of death.

Praised above men be thou,   185
Whose laurel-laden brow,
Made for the morning, droops not in the night;
Praised and beloved, that none
Of all thy great things done
Flies higher than thy most equal spirit's flight;
Praised, that nor doubt nor hope could bend
Earth's loftiest head, found upright to the end.

Before Dawn

1   Sweet life, if life were stronger,
     Earth clear of years that wrong her,
     Then two things might live longer,
         Two sweeter things than they;
     Delight, the rootless flower,
     And love, the bloomless bower;
     Delight that lives an hour,
         And love that lives a day.

9   From evensong to daytime,
     When April melts in Maytime,
     Love lengthens out his playtime,
         Love lessens breath by breath,
     And kiss by kiss grows older
     On listless throat or shoulder
     Turned sideways now, turned colder
         Than life that dreams of death.

17   This one thing once worth giving
     Life gave, and seemed worth living;
     Sin sweet beyond forgiving
         And brief beyond regret:
     To laugh and love together
     And weave with foam and feather
     And wind and words the tether
         Our memories play with yet.

25   Ah, one thing worth beginning,
     One thread in life worth spinning,
     Ah sweet, one sin worth sinning
         With all the whole soul's will;

To lull you till one stilled you,
To kiss you till one killed you,
To feed you till one filled you,
   Sweet lips, if love could fill;

To hunt sweet Love and lose him 33
Between white arms and bosom,
Between the bud and blossom,
   Between your throat and chin;
To say of shame—what is it?
Of virtue—we can miss it,
Of sin—we can but kiss it,
   And it's no longer sin:

To feel the strong soul, stricken 41
Through fleshly pulses, quicken
Beneath swift sighs that thicken,
   Soft hands and lips that smite;
Lips that no love can tire,
With hands that sting like fire,
Weaving the web Desire
   To snare the bird Delight.

But love so lightly plighted, 49
Our love with torch unlighted,
Paused near us unaffrighted,
   Who found and left him free;
None, seeing us cloven in sunder,
Will weep or laugh or wonder;
Light love stands clear of thunder,
   And safe from winds at sea.

As, when late larks give warning 57
Of dying lights and dawning,
Night murmurs to the morning,
   "Lie still, O love, lie still;"
And half her dark limbs cover

The white limbs of her lover,
With amorous plumes that hover
And fervent lips that chill;

65   As scornful day represses
Night's void and vain caresses,
And from her cloudier tresses
    Unwinds the gold of his,
With limbs from limbs dividing
And breath by breath subsiding;
For love has no abiding,
    But dies before the kiss;

73   So hath it been, so be it;
For who shall live and flee it?
But look that no man see it
    Or hear it unaware;
Lest all who love and choose him
See Love, and so refuse him;
For all who find him lose him,
    But all have found him fair.

Dolores

COLD eyelids that hide like a jewel   1
    Hard eyes that grow soft for an hour;
The heavy white limbs, and the cruel
    Red mouth like a venomous flower;
When these are gone by with their glories,
    What shall rest of thee then, what remain,
O mystic and sombre Dolores,
    Our Lady of Pain?

Seven sorrows the priests give their Virgin;   9
    But thy sins, which are seventy times seven,
Seven ages would fail thee to purge in,
    And then they would haunt thee in heaven:
Fierce midnights and famishing morrows,
    And the loves that complete and control
All the joys of the flesh, all the sorrows
    That wear out the soul.

O garment not golden but gilded,   17
    O garden where all men may dwell,
O tower not of ivory, but builded
    By hands that reach heaven from hell;
O mystical rose of the mire,
    O house not of gold but of gain,
O house of unquenchable fire,
    Our Lady of Pain!

Dolores: From the Latin *dolor*, pain. The subtitle is a reference to the Seven
Sorrows of the Virgin Mary.

25   O lips full of lust and of laughter,
           Curled snakes that are fed from my breast,
        Bite hard, lest remembrance come after
           And press with new lips where you pressed.
        For my heart too springs up at the pressure,
           Mine eyelids too moisten and burn;
        Ah, feed me and fill me with pleasure,
           Ere pain come in turn.

33   In yesterday's reach and to-morrow's,
           Out of sight though they lie of to-day,
        There have been and there yet shall be sorrows
           That smite not and bite not in play.
        The life and the love thou despisest,
           These hurt us indeed, and in vain,
        O wise among women, and wisest,
           Our Lady of Pain.

41   Who gave thee thy wisdom? what stories
           That stung thee, what visions that smote?
        Wert thou pure and a maiden, Dolores,
           When desire took thee first by the throat?
        What bud was the shell of a blossom
           That all men may smell to and pluck?
        What milk fed thee first at what bosom?
           What sins gave thee suck?

49   We shift and bedeck and bedrape us,
           Thou art noble and nude and antique;
        Libitina thy mother, Priapus
           Thy father, a Tuscan and Greek.
        We play with light loves in the portal,
           And wince and relent and refrain;
         Loves die, and we know thee immortal,
           Our Lady of Pain.

     51. *Libitina:* Roman goddess of corpses. *Priapus:* See note to "Faustine,"
line 146.

Fruits fail and love dies and time ranges; 57
    Thou art fed with perpetual breath,
And alive after infinite changes,
    And fresh from the kisses of death;
Of languors rekindled and rallied,
    Of barren delights and unclean,
Things monstrous and fruitless, a pallid
    And poisonous queen.

Could you hurt me, sweet lips, though I hurt you? 65
    Men touch them, and change in a trice
The lilies and languors of virtue
    For the raptures and roses of vice;
Those lie where thy foot on the floor is,
    These crown and caress thee and chain,
O splendid and sterile Dolores,
    Our Lady of Pain.

There are sins it may be to discover, 73
    There are deeds it may be to delight.
What new work wilt thou find for thy lover,
    What new passions for daytime or night?
What spells that they know not a word of
    Whose lives are as leaves overblown?
What tortures undreamt of, unheard of,
    Unwritten, unknown?

Ah beautiful passionate body 81
    That never has ached with a heart!
On thy mouth though the kisses are bloody,
    Though they sting till it shudder and smart,
More kind than the love we adore is,
    They hurt not the heart or the brain,
O bitter and tender Dolores,
    Our Lady of Pain.

As our kisses relax and redouble, 89
    From the lips and the foam and the fangs

Shall no new sin be born for men's trouble,
  No dream of impossible pangs?
With the sweet of the sins of old ages
  Wilt thou satiate thy soul as of yore?
Too sweet is the rind, say the sages,
  Too bitter the core.

97   Hast thou told all thy secrets the last time,
  And bared all thy beauties to one?
Ah, where shall we go then for pastime,
  If the worst that can be has been done?
But sweet as the rind was the core is;
  We are fain of thee still, we are fain,
O sanguine and subtle Dolores,
  Our Lady of Pain.

105   By the hunger of change and emotion,
  By the thirst of unbearable things,
By despair, the twin-born of devotion,
  By the pleasure that winces and stings,
The delight that consumes the desire,
  The desire that outruns the delight,
By the cruelty deaf as a fire
  And blind as the night,

113   By the ravenous teeth that have smitten
  Through the kisses that blossom and bud,
By the lips intertwisted and bitten
  Till the foam has a savour of blood,
By the pulse as it rises and falters,
  By the hands as they slacken and strain,
I adjure thee, respond from thine altars,
  Our Lady of Pain.

121   Wilt thou smile as a woman disdaining
  The light fire in the veins of a boy?
But he comes to thee sad, without feigning,

Who has wearied of sorrow and joy;
Less careful of labour and glory
    Than the elders whose hair has uncurled;
And young, but with fancies as hoary
    And grey as the world.

I have passed from the outermost portal   129
    To the shrine where a sin is a prayer;
What care though the service be mortal?
    O our Lady of Torture, what care?
All thine the last wine that I pour is,
    The last in the chalice we drain,
O fierce and luxurious Dolores,
    Our Lady of Pain.

All thine the new wine of desire,   137
    The fruit of four lips as they clung
Till the hair and the eyelids took fire,
    The foam of a serpentine tongue,
The froth of the serpents of pleasure,
    More salt than the foam of the sea,
Now felt as a flame, now at leisure
    As wine shed for me.

Ah thy people, thy children, thy chosen,   145
    Marked cross from the womb and perverse!
They have found out the secret to cozen
    The gods that constrain us and curse;
They alone, they are wise, and none other;
    Give me place, even me, in their train,
O my sister, my spouse, and my mother,
    Our Lady of Pain.

For the crown of our life as it closes   153
    Is darkness, the fruit thereof dust;
No thorns go as deep as a rose's,
    And love is more cruel than lust.

Time turns the old days to derision,
　　Our loves into corpses or wives;
And marriage and death and division
　　Make barren our lives.

161 And pale from the past we draw nigh thee,
　　And satiate with comfortless hours;
And we know thee, how all men belie thee,
　　And we gather the fruit of thy flowers;
The passion that slays and recovers,
　　The pangs and the kisses that rain
On the lips and the limbs of thy lovers,
　　Our Lady of Pain.

169 The desire of thy furious embraces
　　Is more than the wisdom of years,
On the blossom though blood lie in traces,
　　Though the foliage be sodden with tears.
For the lords in whose keeping the door is
　　That opens on all who draw breath
Gave the cypress to love, my Dolores,
　　The myrtle to death.

177 And they laughed, changing hands in the measure,
　　And they mixed and made peace after strife;
Pain melted in tears, and was pleasure;
　　Death tingled with blood, and was life.
Like lovers they melted and tingled,
　　In the dusk of thine innermost fane;
In the darkness they murmured and mingled,
　　Our Lady of Pain.

185 In a twilight where virtues are vices,
　　In thy chapels, unknown of the sun,
To a tune that enthralls and entices,
　　They were wed, and the twain were as one.
For the tune from thine altar hath sounded

Since God bade the world's work begin,
And the fume of thine incense abounded,
   To sweeten the sin.

Love listens, and paler than ashes,   193
   Through his curls as the crown on them slips,
Lifts languid wet eyelids and lashes,
   And laughs with insatiable lips.
Thou shalt hush him with heavy caresses,
   With music that scares the profane;
Thou shalt darken his eyes with thy tresses,
   Our Lady of Pain.

Thou shalt blind his bright eyes though he wrestle,   201
   Thou shalt chain his light limbs though he strive;
In his lips all thy serpents shall nestle,
   In his hands all thy cruelties thrive.
In the daytime thy voice shall go through him,
   In his dreams he shall feel thee and ache;
Thou shalt kindle by night and subdue him
   Asleep and awake.

Thou shalt touch and make redder his roses   209
   With juice not of fruit nor of bud;
When the sense in the spirit reposes,
   Thou shalt quicken the soul through the blood.
Thine, thine the one grace we implore is,
   Who would live and not languish or feign,
O sleepless and deadly Dolores,
   Our Lady of Pain.

Dost thou dream, in a respite of slumber,   217
   In a lull of the fires of thy life,
Of the days without name, without number,
   When thy will stung the world into strife;
When, a goddess, the pulse of thy passion
   Smote kings as they revelled in Rome;

And they hailed thee re-risen, O Thalassian,
    Foam-white, from the foam?

225   When thy lips had such lovers to flatter;
    When the city lay red from thy rods,
And thine hands were as arrows to scatter
    The children of change and their gods;
When the blood of thy foemen made fervent
    A sand never moist from the main,
As one smote them, their lord and thy servant,
 ·   Our Lady of Pain.

233   On sands by the storm never shaken,
    Nor wet from the washing of tides;
Nor by foam of the waves overtaken,
    Nor winds that the thunder bestrides;
But red from the print of thy paces,
    Made smooth for the world and its lords,
Ringed round with a flame of fair faces,
    And splendid with swords.

241   There the gladiator, pale for thy pleasure,
    Drew bitter and perilous breath;
There torments laid hold on the treasure
    Of limbs too delicious for death;
When thy gardens were lit with live torches;
    When the world was a steed for thy rein;
When the nations lay prone in thy porches,
    Our Lady of Pain.

249   When, with flame all around him aspirant,
    Stood flushed, as a harp-player stands,
The implacable beautiful tyrant,
    Rose-crowned, having death in his hands;
And a sound as the sound of loud water
    Smote far through the flight of the fires,
And mixed with the lightning of slaughter
    A thunder of lyres.

Dost thou dream of what was and no more is, 257
    The old kingdoms of earth and the kings?
Dost thou hunger for these things, Dolores,
    For these, in a world of new things?
But thy bosom no fasts could emaciate,
    No hunger compel to complain
Those lips that no bloodshed could satiate,
    Our Lady of Pain.

As of old when the world's heart was lighter, 265
    Through thy garments the grace of thee glows,
The white wealth of thy body made whiter
    By the blushes of amorous blows,
And seamed with sharp lips and fierce fingers,
    And branded by kisses that bruise;
When all shall be gone that now lingers,
    Ah, what shall we lose?

Thou wert fair in the fearless old fashion, 273
    And thy limbs are as melodies yet,
And move to the music of passion
    With lithe and lascivious regret.
What ailed us, O gods, to desert you
    For creeds that refuse and restrain?
Come down and redeem us from virtue,
    Our Lady of Pain.

All shrines that were Vestal are flameless, 281
    But the flame has not fallen from this;
Though obscure be the god, and though nameless
    The eyes and the hair that we kiss;
Low fires that love sits by and forges
    Fresh heads for his arrows and thine;
Hair loosened and soiled in mid orgies
    With kisses and wine.

---

281. *Vestal:* The priestesses of Vesta, the Greek and Roman goddess of the
sacred hearth, symbol of the home and the tribe, were virgins.

289   Thy skin changes country and colour,
                   And shrivels or swells to a snake's.
             Let it brighten and bloat and grow duller,
                   We know it, the flames and the flakes,
             Red brands on it smitten and bitten,
                   Round skies where a star is a stain,
             And the leaves with thy litanies written,
                   Our Lady of Pain.

297   On thy bosom though many a kiss be,
                   There are none such as knew it of old.
             Was it Alciphron once or Arisbe,
                   Male ringlets or feminine gold,
             That thy lips met with under the statue,
                   Whence a look shot out sharp after thieves
             From the eyes of the garden-god at you
                   Across the fig-leaves?

305   Then still, through dry seasons and moister,
                   One god had a wreath to his shrine;
             Then love was the pearl of his oyster,*
                   And Venus rose red out of wine.
             We have all done amiss, choosing rather
                   Such loves as the wise gods disdain;
             Intercede for us thou with thy father,
                   Our Lady of Pain.

313   In spring he had crowns of his garden,
                   Red corn in the heat of the year,
             Then hoary green olives that harden
                   When the grape-blossom freezes with fear;

---

* Nam te præcipuè in suis urbibus colit ora
Hellespontia, cæteris osteosior oris.
CATULL. *Carm*. xviii.

299. *Alciphron:* Greek author of letters, but here, since Arisbe is an invention, merely a classical male name.
303. *garden-god:* Priapus.

And milk-budded myrtles with Venus
        And vine-leaves with Bacchus he trod;
And ye said, "We have seen, he hath seen us,
        A visible God."

What broke off the garlands that girt you?   321
        What sundered you spirit and clay?
Weak sins yet alive are as virtue
        To the strength of the sins of that day.
For dried is the blood of thy lover,
        Ipsithilla, contracted the vein;
Cry aloud, "Will he rise and recover,
        Our Lady of Pain?"

Cry aloud; for the old world is broken: 329
        Cry out; for the Phrygian is priest,
And rears not the bountiful token
        And spreads not the fatherly feast.
From the midmost of Ida, from shady
        Recesses that murmur at morn,
They have brought and baptized her, Our Lady,
        A goddess new-born.

And the chaplets of old are above us,   337
        And the oyster-bed teems out of reach;

317–318. *Venus . . . Bacchus:* Divinities of love and of wine.
329–362. *Cybele:* The Great Mother, the goddess of nature and as Rhea
mother of the gods—in short, the goddess of the inexhaustible productivity of
the natural world. Her center of worship was on Mount Dindymus on the Propontis. Her chariot was drawn by lions, symbols of the forces of nature which
bring man into existence and also destroy him. In 204 B.C. her sacred stone was
transported to Rome and the worship of Cybele was established there. Her
priests castrated themselves in memory of Attis, of whom an extraordinary story
is told. Cybele was born bisexual, but the gods reduced her to femininity by
cutting off her male genitals. From these sprang an almond tree from which a
nymph plucked a blossom, placed it in her bosom, and found herself pregnant.
Her child was Attis, whom Cybele loved frantically. When he attempted to
marry or to make love to a nymph, Cybele drove him mad, and he castrated
himself. The story is made use of in Catullus, *Carmen* 63, Roman poet of the
first century B.C., famous for his frank erotic love poetry.

Old poets outsing and outlove us,
 And Catullus makes mouths at our speech.
Who shall kiss, in thy father's own city,
 With such lips as he sang with, again?
Intercede for us all of thy pity,
 Our Lady of Pain.

345   Out of Dindymus heavily laden
     Her lions draw bound and unfed
    A mother, a mortal, a maiden,
      A queen over death and the dead.
    She is cold, and her habit is lowly,
      Her temple of branches and sods;
    Most fruitful and virginal, holy,
      A mother of gods.

353   She hath wasted with fire thine high places,
     She hath hidden and marred and made sad
    The fair limbs of the Loves, the fair faces
      Of gods that were goodly and glad.
    She slays, and her hands are not bloody;
      She moves as a moon in the wane,
    White-robed, and thy raiment is ruddy,
      Our Lady of Pain.

361   They shall pass and their places be taken,
     The gods and the priests that are pure.
    They shall pass, and shalt thou not be shaken?
      They shall perish, and shalt thou endure?
    Death laughs, breathing close and relentless
      In the nostrils and eyelids of lust,
    With a pinch in his fingers of scentless
      And delicate dust.

369   But the worm shall revive thee with kisses;
     Thou shalt change and transmute as a god,
    As the rod to a serpent that hisses,

As the serpent again to a rod.
Thy life shall not cease though thou doff it;
　Thou shalt live until evil be slain,
And good shall die first, said thy prophet,
　Our Lady of Pain.

Did he lie? did he laugh? does he know it,　377
　Now he lies out of reach, out of breath,
Thy prophet, thy preacher, thy poet,
　Sin's child by incestuous Death?
Did he find out in fire at his waking,
　Or discern as his eyelids lost light,
When the bands of the body were breaking
　And all came in sight?

Who has known all the evil before us,　385
　Or the tyrannous secrets of time?
Though we match not the dead men that bore us
　At a song, at a kiss, at a crime—
Though the heathen outface and outlive us,
　And our lives and our longings are twain—
Ah, forgive us our virtues, forgive us,
　Our Lady of Pain.

Who are we that embalm and embrace thee　393
　With spices and savours of song?
What is time, that his children should face thee?
　What am I, that my lips do thee wrong?
I could hurt thee—but pain would delight thee;
　Or caress thee—but love would repel;
And the lovers whose lips would excite thee
　Are serpents in hell.

Who now shall content thee as they did,　401
　Thy lovers, when temples were built

379. *Thy prophet, thy preacher, thy poet:* The Marquis de Sade.

And the hair of the sacrifice braided
And the blood of the sacrifice spilt,
In Lampsacus fervent with faces,
In Aphaca red from thy reign,
Who embraced thee with awful embraces,
Our Lady of Pain?

409   Where are they, Cotytto or Venus,
Astarte or Ashtaroth, where?
Do their hands as we touch come between us?
Is the breath of them hot in thy hair?
From their lips have thy lips taken fever,
With the blood of their bodies grown red?
Hast thou left upon earth a believer
If these men are dead?

417   They were purple of raiment and golden,
Filled full of thee, fiery with wine,
Thy lovers, in haunts unbeholden,
In marvellous chambers of thine.
They are fled, and their footprints escape us,
Who appraise thee, adore, and abstain,
O daughter of Death and Priapus,
Our Lady of Pain.

425   What ails us to fear overmeasure,
To praise thee with timorous breath,

---

405. *Lampsacus:* See "Faustine," line 146.

406. *Aphaca:* This may be a misprint for Aphaea, or Aphaia, also known as Britomartis and Diktynna, forms of Artemis. She was worshipped at Aigina and was probably there a fertility goddess. *Aphaca* means in Greek and Latin the wild dandelion, and Swinburne may have simply been inventing a name which, in context, would be sufficiently effective simply because absolutely unknown to most readers.

409. *Cotytto:* A Thracian goddess, associated with Cybele and worshipped with sexual orgies.

410. *Astarte . . . Ashtaroth:* Goddesses of love from the Near East, actually two forms of the same name.

O mistress and mother of pleasure,
  The one thing as certain as death?
We shall change as the things that we cherish,
  Shall fade as they faded before,
As foam upon water shall perish,
  As sand upon shore.

We shall know what the darkness discovers,
  If the grave-pit be shallow or deep;
And our fathers of old, and our lovers,
  We shall know if they sleep not or sleep.
We shall see whether hell be not heaven,
  Find out whether tares be not grain,
And the joys of thee seventy times seven,
  Our Lady of Pain.

433

The Garden of Proserpine

1   HERE, where the world is quiet;
           Here, where all trouble seems
        Dead winds' and spent waves' riot
           In doubtful dreams of dreams;
        I watch the green field growing
        For reaping folk and sowing,
        For harvest-time and mowing,
           A sleepy world of streams.

9   I am tired of tears and laughter,
           And men that laugh and weep;
        Of what may come hereafter
           For men that sow to reap:
        I am weary of days and hours,
        Blown buds of barren flowers,
        Desires and dreams and powers
           And everything but sleep.

17   Here life has death for neighbour,
           And far from eye or ear
        Wan waves and wet winds labour,
           Weak ships and spirits steer;
        They drive adrift, and whither
        They wot not who make thither;
        But no such winds blow hither,
           And no such things grow here.

25   No growth of moor or coppice,
           No heather-flower or vine,
         But bloomless buds of poppies,

The Garden of Proserpine: See "Hymn to Proserpine" above; the world of the happy dead.

Green grapes of Proserpine,
Pale beds of blowing rushes
Where no leaf blooms or blushes
Save this whereout she crushes
For dead men deadly wine.

Pale, without name or number,   33
In fruitless fields of corn,
They bow themselves and slumber
All night till light is born;
And like a soul belated,
In hell and heaven unmated,
By cloud and mist abated
Comes out of darkness morn.

Though one were strong as seven,   41
He too with death shall dwell,
Nor wake with wings in heaven,
Nor weep for pains in hell;
Though one were fair as roses,
His beauty clouds and closes;
And well though love reposes,
In the end it is not well.

Pale, beyond porch and portal,   49
Crowned with calm leaves, she stands
Who gathers all things mortal
With cold immortal hands;
Her languid lips are sweeter
Than love's who fears to greet her
To men that mix and meet her
From many times and lands.

She waits for each and other,   57
She waits for all men born;
Forgets the earth her mother,
The life of fruits and corn;
And spring and seed and swallow
Take wing for her and follow

Where summer song rings hollow
And flowers are put to scorn.

65   There go the loves that wither,
The old loves with wearier wings;
And all dead years draw thither,
And all disastrous things;
Dead dreams of days forsaken,
Blind buds that snows have shaken,
Wild leaves that winds have taken,
Red strays of ruined springs.

73   We are not sure of sorrow,
And joy was never sure;
To-day will die to-morrow;
Time stoops to no man's lure;
And love, grown faint and fretful,
With lips but half regretful
Sighs, and with eyes forgetful
Weeps that no loves endure.

81   From too much love of living,
From hope and fear set free,
We thank with brief thanksgiving
Whatever gods may be
That no life lives for ever;
That dead men rise up never;
That even the weariest river
Winds somewhere safe to sea.

89   Then star nor sun shall waken,
Nor any change of light:
Nor sound of waters shaken,
Nor any sound or sight:
Nor wintry leaves nor vernal,
Nor days nor things diurnal;
Only the sleep eternal
In an eternal night.

Hesperia

OUT of the golden remote wild west where the sea without shore is,
  Full of the sunset, and sad, if at all, with the fulness of joy,
As a wind sets in with the autumn that blows from the region of
    stories,
  Blows with a perfume of songs and of memories beloved from
    a boy,
Blows from the capes of the past oversea to the bays of the present,   5
  Filled as with shadow of sound with the pulse of invisible feet,
Far out to the shallows and straits of the future, by rough ways or
    pleasant,
  Is it thither the wind's wings beat? is it hither to me, O my sweet?
For thee, in the stream of the deep tide-wind blowing in with the
    water,
  Thee I behold as a bird borne in with the wind from the west,   10
Straight from the sunset, across white waves whence rose as a
    daughter
  Venus thy mother, in years when the world was a water at rest.
Out of the distance of dreams, as a dream that abides after slumber,
  Strayed from the fugitive flock of the night, when the moon over-
    head
Wanes in the wan waste heights of the heaven, and stars without   15
    number
  Die without sound, and are spent like lamps that are burnt by the
    dead,
Comes back to me, stays by me, lulls me with touch of forgotten
    caresses,
  One warm dream clad about with a fire as of life that endures;

Hesperia: The land of the West, that is, of the happy dead and of memories;
also, the goddess of that place, or Proserpine (see preceding poem).

12. *Venus thy mother:* See "Anactoria," line 57.

The delight of thy face, and the sound of thy feet, and the wind of
    thy tresses,
20   And all of a man that regrets, and all of a maid that allures.
But thy bosom is warm for my face and profound as a manifold
    flower,
    Thy silence as music, thy voice as an odour that fades in a flame;
Not a dream, not a dream is the kiss of thy mouth, and the bountiful
    hour
    That makes me forget what was sin, and would make me forget
    were it shame.
25 Thine eyes that are quiet, thine hands that are tender, thy lips that
    are loving,
    Comfort and cool me as dew in the dawn of a moon like a dream;
And my heart yearns baffled and blind, moved vainly toward thee,
    and moving
    As the refluent seaweed moves in the languid exuberant stream,
Fair as a rose is on earth, as a rose under water in prison,
30   That stretches and swings to the slow passionate pulse of the sea,
Closed up from the air and the sun, but alive, as a ghost rearisen,
    Pale as the love that revives as a ghost rearisen in me.
From the bountiful infinite west, from the happy memorial places
    Full of the stately repose and the lordly delight of the dead,
35 Where the fortunate islands are lit with the light of ineffable faces,
    And the sound of a sea without wind is about them, and sunset is
    red,
Come back to redeem and release me from love that recalls and
    represses,
    That cleaves to my flesh as a flame, till the serpent has eaten his
    fill;
From the bitter delights of the dark, and the feverish, the furtive
    caresses
40   That murder the youth in a man or ever his heart have its will.
Thy lips cannot laugh and thine eyes cannot weep; thou art pale as
    a rose is,
    Paler and sweeter than leaves that cover the blush of the bud;
And the heart of the flower is compassion, and pity the core it
    encloses,

Pity, not love, that is born of the breath and decays with the blood.
As the cross that a wild nun clasps till the edge of it bruises her   45
    bosom,
So love wounds as we grasp it, and blackens and burns as a flame;
I have loved overmuch in my life; when the live bud bursts with the
    blossom,
Bitter as ashes or tears is the fruit, and the wine thereof shame.
As a heart that its anguish divides is the green bud cloven asunder;
    As the blood of a man self-slain is the flush of the leaves that   50
    allure;
And the perfume as poison and wine to the brain, a delight and a
    wonder;
    And the thorns are too sharp for a boy, too slight for a man, to
    endure.
Too soon did I love it, and lost love's rose; and I cared not for
    glory's:
    Only the blossoms of sleep and of pleasure were mixed in my hair.
Was it myrtle or poppy thy garland was woven with, O my   55
    Dolores?
    Was it pallor of slumber, or blush as of blood, that I found in
    thee fair?
For desire is a respite from love, and the flesh not the heart is her
    fuel;
    She was sweet to me once, who am fled and escaped from the rage
    of her reign;
Who behold as of old time at hand as I turn, with her mouth growing
    cruel,
    And flushed as with wine with the blood of her lovers, Our Lady   60
    of Pain.
Low down where the thicket is thicker with thorns than with leaves
    in the summer,
    In the brake is a gleaming of eyes and a hissing of tongues that I
    knew;
And the lithe long throats of her snakes reach round her, their
    mouths overcome her,

55–60. *Dolores . . . Our Lady of Pain:* See "Dolores."

And her lips grow cool with their foam, made moist as a desert
    with dew.
65 With the thirst and the hunger of lust though her beautiful lips be
    so bitter,
    With the cold foul foam of the snakes they soften and redden and
    smile;
    And her fierce mouth sweetens, her eyes wax wide and her eyelashes
    glitter,
    And she laughs with a savour of blood in her face, and a savour
    of guile.
    She laughs, and her hands reach hither, her hair blows hither and
    hisses,
70 As a low-lit flame in a wind, back-blown till it shudder and leap;
    Let her lips not again lay hold on my soul, nor her poisonous kisses,
    To consume it alive and divide from thy bosom, Our Lady of
    Sleep.
    Ah daughter of sunset and slumber, if now it return into prison,
    Who shall redeem it anew? but we, if thou wilt, let us fly;
75 Let us take to us, now that the white skies thrill with a moon
    unarisen,
    Swift horses of fear or of love, take flight and depart and not die.
    They are swifter than dreams, they are stronger than death; there is
    none that hath ridden,
    None that shall ride in the dim strange ways of his life as we ride;
    By the meadows of memory, the highlands of hope, and the shore
    that is hidden,
80 Where life breaks loud and unseen, a sonorous invisible tide;
    By the sands where sorrow has trodden, the salt pools bitter and
    sterile,
    By the thundering reef and the low sea-wall and the channel of
    years,
    Our wild steeds press on the night, strain hard through pleasure
    and peril,
    Labour and listen and pant not or pause for the peril that nears;
85 And the sound of them trampling the way cleaves night as an arrow
    asunder,

    72. *Our Lady of Sleep:* Hesperia, or Proserpine.

And slow by the sand-hill and swift by the down with its glimpses
    of grass,
Sudden and steady the music, as eight hoofs trample and thunder,
    Rings in the ear of the low blind wind of the night as we pass;
Shrill shrieks in our faces the blind bland air that was mute as a
    maiden,
    Stung into storm by the speed of our passage, and deaf where   90
    we past;
And our spirits too burn as we bound, thine holy but mine heavy-
    laden,
    As we burn with the fire of our flight; ah love, shall we win at the
    last?

Love at Sea

1   WE are in love's land to-day;
       Where shall we go?
    Love, shall we start or stay,
       Or sail or row?
    There's many a wind and way,
    And never a May but May;
    We are in love's hand to-day;
       Where shall we go?

9   Our landwind is the breath
    Of sorrows kissed to death
       And joys that were;
       Our ballast is a rose;
    Our way lies where God knows
       And love knows where.
          We are in love's hand to-day—

16   Our seamen are fledged Loves,

A free imitation of "Barcarolle" by the French poet Théophile Gautier (1811–1872). The following verse translation was made by S. C. de Sumichrast (*The Complete Works of Théophile Gautier*, London, 1902, XII, 194).

Tell me, beautiful maiden,
  Whither wouldst thou away,
To what shore blossom-laden,
  Through the wind and the spray?
Oars of ivory are gleaming,
Silken banners are streaming,
  Golden-bright is the prow.
I've a page fair and minion,
For a sail a saint's pinion,
  And for ballast a bough.
Tell me, beautiful maiden, etc.
Tell me, what is thy pleasure,

A wide ocean to measure?
  A far island to claim?
Wreaths of snow-flowers to fashion,
Or to linger with passion
  Near the flower of the flame?
Tell me, beautiful maiden, etc.
"To the land ever vernal,
Where love liveth eternal,
  Ah, take me!" she sighs.
Sweet, this land of thy seeing
Hath no place and no being,
  Under any love skies!

Our masts are bills of doves,
Our decks fine gold;
Our ropes are dead maids' hair,
Our stores are love-shafts fair
And manifold.
We are in love's land to-day—

Where shall we land you, sweet?   23
On fields of strange men's feet,
Or fields near home?
Or where the fire-flowers blow,
Or where the flowers of snow
Or flowers of foam?
We are in love's hand to-day—

Land me, she says, where love   30
Shows but one shaft, one dove,
One heart, one hand.
—A shore like that, my dear,
Lies where no man will steer,
No maiden land.

Imitated from Théophile Gautier.

April

FROM THE FRENCH OF THE
VIDAME DE CHARTRES

12 — ?

WHEN the fields catch flower
   And the underwood is green,
And from bower unto bower
   The songs of the birds begin,
5   I sing with sighing between.
When I laugh and sing,
   I am heavy at heart for my sin;
I am sad in the spring
   For my love that I shall not win,
10   For a foolish thing.

This profit I have of my woe,
   That I know, as I sing,
I know he will needs have it so
   Who is master and king,
15   Who is lord of the spirit of spring.
I will serve her and will not spare
   Till her pity awake
Who is good, who is pure, who is fair,
   Even her for whose sake
20   Love hath ta'en me and slain unaware.

O my lord, O Love,
   I have laid my life at thy feet;

A translation of "Saluts d'Amour, VI" by the French poet of the thirteenth century, Guillaume de Ferrières, vidame (French feudal officer) of Chartres, whose works were edited and published in 1856.

Have thy will thereof,
   Do as it please thee with it,
   For what shall please thee is sweet. 25
I am come unto thee
   To do thee service, O Love;
Yet cannot I see
   Thou wilt take any pity thereof,
Any mercy on me. 30

But the grace I have long time sought
   Comes never in sight,
If in her it abideth not,
   Through thy mercy and might,
   Whose heart is the world's delight. 35
Thou hast sworn without fail I shall die,
   For my heart is set
On what hurts me, I wot not why,
   But cannot forget
What I love, what I sing for and sigh. 40

She is worthy of praise,
   For this grief of her giving is worth
All the joy of my days
   That lie between death's day and birth,
   All the lordship of things upon earth. 45
Nay, what have I said?
   I would not be glad if I could;
My dream and my dread
   Are of her, and for her sake I would
That my life were fled. 50

Lo, sweet, if I durst not pray to you,
   Then were I dead;
If I sang not a little to say to you,
   (Could it be said)
   O my love, how my heart would be fed; 55
Ah sweet who hast hold of my heart,
   For thy love's sake I live,

> Do but tell me, ere either depart,
>   What a lover may give
60   For a woman so fair as thou art.
>
> The lovers that disbelieve,
>   False rumours shall grieve
> And evil-speaking shall part.

Félise

Mais où sont les neiges d'antan?

WHAT shall be said between us here
 Among the downs, between the trees,
In fields that knew our feet last year,
 In sight of quiet sands and seas,
 This year, Félise?   5

Who knows what word were best to say?
 For last year's leaves lie dead and red
On this sweet day, in this green May,
 And barren corn makes bitter bread.
 What shall be said?   10

Epigraph: "Where are the snows of yesteryear?" from the "Ballade des dames
des temps jadis" or "Ballade of Dead Ladies" by the French poet François
Villon (1431– ?).
   From a letter to John Ruskin (?March 21, 1866), in Lang, *The Swinburne
Letters*, I, 160: "I recalcitrate vigorously against your opinion of 'Félise,' which
is rather a favourite child of mine. As to the subject, I thought it clear enough,
and likely to recall to most people a similar passage of experience. A young
fellow is left alone with a woman rather older, whom a year since he violently loved. Meantime he has been in town, she in the country; and in the
year's lapse they had time, he to become tired of her memory, she to fall in love
with his. Surely I have expressed this plainly and 'cynically' enough! Last year
I loved you, and you were puzzled, and didn't love me—quite. This year (I
perceive) you love me, and I feel puzzled, and don't love you—quite. 'Sech is
life,' as Mrs. Gamp says [in Dickens' *Martin Chuzzlewit*] ; *'Deus vult;* it can't
be helped.' As to the flowers and hours, they rhyme naturally, being the sweetest
and most transient things that exist—when they *are* sweet. And the poem, it
seems to me, is not long enough to explain what it has to say."
   From a letter to W. M. Rossetti, October 9, 1866, in Lang, I, 193. "As to
the antitheism of 'Félise' I know of course that *you* know that the verses represent a mood of mind and phase of thought not unfamiliar to me; but I must
nevertheless maintain that no reader (*as* a reader) has a right (whatever he
may conjecture) to assert that this is *my* faith. . . . Of course it is a more serious expression of feeling; and of course this is evident; but it is not less for-
mally dramatic than the others."

Here as last year the fields begin,
    A fire of flowers and glowing grass;
The old fields we laughed and lingered in,
    Seeing each our souls in last year's glass,
15   Félise, alas!

Shall we not laugh, shall we not weep,
    Not we, though this be as it is?
For love awake or love asleep
    Ends in a laugh, a dream, a kiss,
20   A song like this.

I that have slept awake, and you
    Sleep, who last year were well awake.
Though love do all that love can do,
    My heart will never ache or break
25   For your heart's sake.

The great sea, faultless as a flower,
    Throbs, trembling under beam and breeze,
And laughs with love of the amorous hour.
    I found you fairer once, Félise,
30   Than flowers or seas.

We played at bondsman and at queen;
    But as the days change men change too;
I find the grey sea's notes of green,
    The green sea's fervent flakes of blue,
35   More fair than you.

Your beauty is not over fair
    Now in mine eyes, who am grown up wise.
The smell of flowers in all your hair
    Allures not now; no sigh replies
40   If your heart sighs.

But you sigh seldom, you sleep sound,
    You find love's new name good enough.

Less sweet I find it than I found
    The sweetest name that ever love
    Grew weary of.   45

My snake with bright bland eyes, my snake
    Grown tame and glad to be caressed,
With lips athirst for mine to slake
    Their tender fever! who had guessed
    You loved me best?   50

I had died for this last year, to know
    You loved me.   Who shall turn on fate?
I care not if love come or go
    Now, though your love seek mine for mate.
    It is too late.   55

The dust of many strange desires
    Lies deep between us; in our eyes
Dead smoke of perishable fires
    Flickers, a fume in air and skies,
    A steam of sighs.   60

You loved me and you loved me not;
    A little, much, and overmuch.
Will you forget as I forgot?
    Let all dead things lie dead; none such
    Are soft to touch.   65

I love you and I do not love,
    Too much, a little, not at all;
Too much, and never yet enough.
    Birds quick to fledge and fly at call
    Are quick to fall.   70

And these love longer now than men,
    And larger loves than ours are these.
No diver brings up love again

Dropped once, my beautiful Félise,
75   In such cold seas.

Gone deeper than all plummets sound,
    Where in the dim green dayless day
The life of such dead things lies bound
    As the sea feeds on, wreck and stray
80   And castaway.

Can I forget? yea, that can I,
    And that can all men; so will you,
Alive, or later, when you die.
    Ah, but the love you plead was true?
85   Was mine not too?

I loved you for that name of yours
    Long ere we met, and long enough.
Now that one thing of all endures—
    The sweetest name that ever love
90   Waxed weary of.

Like colours in the sea, like flowers,
    Like a cat's splendid circled eyes
That wax and wane with love for hours,
    Green as green flame, blue-grey like skies,
95   And soft like sighs—

And all these only like your name,
    And your name full of all of these.
I say it, and it sounds the same—
    Save that I say it now at ease,
100   Your name, Félise.

I said "she must be swift and white,
    And subtly warm, and half perverse,
And sweet like sharp soft fruit to bite,

And like a snake's love lithe and fierce."
Men have guessed worse.   105

What was the song I made of you
    Here where the grass forgets our feet
As afternoon forgets the dew?
    Ah that such sweet things should be fleet,
    Such fleet things sweet!   110

As afternoon forgets the dew,
    As time in time forgets all men,
As our old place forgets us two,
    Who might have turned to one thing then,
    But not again.   115

        O lips that mine have grown into
            Like April's kissing May,
        O fervent eyelids letting through
        Those eyes the greenest of things blue,
            The bluest of things grey,   120

        If you were I and I were you,
            How could I love you, say?
        How could the roseleaf love the rue,
        The day love nightfall and her dew,
            Though night may love the day?   125

You loved it may be more than I;
    We know not; love is hard to seize,
And all things are not good to try;
    And lifelong loves the worst of these
    For us, Félise.   130

Ah, take the season and have done,
    Love well the hour and let it go:
Two souls may sleep and wake up one,
    Or dream they wake and find it so,
    And then—you know.   135

Kiss me once hard as though a flame
　　Lay on my lips and made them fire;
The same lips now, and not the same;
　　What breath shall fill and re-inspire
140　　　A dead desire?

The old song sounds hollower in mine ear
　　Than thin keen sounds of dead men's speech—
A noise one hears and would not hear;
　　Too strong to die, too weak to reach
145　　　From wave to beach.

We stand on either side the sea,
　　Stretch hands, blow kisses, laugh and lean
I toward you, you toward me;
　　But what hears either save the keen
150　　　Grey sea between?

A year divides us, love from love,
　　Though you love now, though I loved then.
The gulf is strait, but deep enough;
　　Who shall recross, who among men
155　　　Shall cross again?

Love was a jest last year, you said,
　　And what lives surely, surely dies.
Even so; but now that love is dead,
　　Shall love rekindle from wet eyes,
160　　　From subtle sighs?

For many loves are good to see;
　　Mutable loves, and loves perverse;
But there is nothing, nor shall be,
　　So sweet, so wicked, but my verse
165　　　Can dream of worse.

For we that sing and you that love
　　Know that which man may, only we.

The rest live under us; above,
   Live the great gods in heaven, and see
What things shall be. 170

So this thing is and must be so;
   For man dies, and love also dies.
Though yet love's ghost moves to and fro
   The sea-green mirrors of your eyes,
   And laughs, and lies. 175

Eyes coloured like a water-flower,
   And deeper than the green sea's glass;
Eyes that remember one sweet hour—
   In vain we swore it should not pass;
   In vain, alas! 180

Ah my Félise, if love or sin,
   If shame or fear could hold it fast,
Should we not hold it?   Love wears thin,
   And they laugh well who laugh the last.
   Is it not past? 185

The gods, the gods are stronger; time
   Falls down before them, all men's knees
Bow, all men's prayers and sorrows climb
   Like incense towards them; yea, for these
   Are gods, Félise. 190

Immortal are they, clothed with powers,
   Not to be comforted at all;
Lords over all the fruitless hours;
   Too great to appease, too high to appal,
   Too far to call. 195

For none shall move the most high gods,
   Who are most sad, being cruel; none
Shall break or take away the rods

Wherewith they scourge us, not as one
200   That smites a son.

By many a name of many a creed
    We have called upon them, since the sands
Fell through time's hour-glass first, a seed
    Of life; and out of many lands
205   Have we stretched hands.

When have they heard us? who hath known
    Their faces, climbed unto their feet,
Felt them and found them?   Laugh or groan,
    Doth heaven remurmur and repeat
210   Sad sounds or sweet?

Do the stars answer? in the night
    Have ye found comfort? or by day
Have ye seen gods?   What hope, what light,
    Falls from the farthest starriest way
215   On you that pray?

Are the skies wet because we weep,
    Or fair because of any mirth?
Cry out; they are gods; perchance they sleep;
    Cry; thou shalt know what prayers are worth,
220   Thou dust and earth.

O earth, thou art fair; O dust, thou art great;
    O laughing lips and lips that mourn,
Pray, till ye feel the exceeding weight
    Of God's intolerable scorn,
225   Not to be borne.

Behold, there is no grief like this;
    The barren blossom of thy prayer,
Thou shalt find out how sweet it is.
    O fools and blind, what seek ye there,
230   High up in the air?

Ye must have gods, the friends of men,
    Merciful gods, compassionate,
And these shall answer you again.
    Will ye beat always at the gate,
    Ye fools of fate?   235

Ye fools and blind; for this is sure,
    That all ye shall not live, but die.
Lo, what thing have ye found endure?
    Or what thing have ye found on high
    Past the blind sky?   240

The ghosts of words and dusty dreams,
    Old memories, faiths infirm and dead.
Ye fools; for which among you deems
    His prayer can alter green to red
    Or stones to bread?   245

Why should ye bear with hopes and fears
    Till all these things be drawn in one,
The sound of iron-footed years,
    And all the oppression that is done
    Under the sun?   250

Ye might end surely, surely pass
    Out of the multitude of things,
Under the dust, beneath the grass,
    Deep in dim death, where no thought stings,
    No record clings.   255

No memory more of love or hate,
    No trouble, nothing that aspires,
No sleepless labour thwarting fate,
    And thwarted; where no travail tires,
    Where no faith fires.   260

All passes, nought that has been is,
    Things good and evil have one end.

Can anything be otherwise
    Though all men swear all things would mend
265   With God to friend?

Can ye beat off one wave with prayer,
    Can ye move mountains? bid the flower
Take flight and turn to a bird in the air?
    Can ye hold fast for shine or shower
270   One wingless hour?

Ah sweet, and we too, can we bring
    One sigh back, bid one smile revive?
Can God restore one ruined thing,
    Or he who slays our souls alive
275   Make dead things thrive?

Two gifts perforce he has given us yet,
    Though sad things stay and glad things fly;
Two gifts he has given us, to forget
    All glad and sad things that go by,
280   And then to die.

We know not whether death be good,
    But life at least it will not be:
Men will stand saddening as we stood,
    Watch the same fields and skies as we
285   And the same sea.

Let this be said between us here,
    One love grows green when one turns grey;
This year knows nothing of last year;
    To-morrow has no more to say
290   To yesterday.

Live and let live, as I will do,
    Love and let love, and so will I.
But, sweet, for me no more with you:
    Not while I live, not though I die.
295   Goodnight, goodbye.

An Interlude

In the greenest growth of the Maytime,　　　　　　1
　　I rode where the woods were wet,
Between the dawn and the daytime;
　　The spring was glad that we met.

There was something the season wanted,　　　　　5
　　Though the ways and the woods smelt sweet;
The breath at your lips that panted,
　　The pulse of the grass at your feet.

You came, and the sun came after,　　　　　　　9
　　And the green grew golden above;
And the flag-flowers lightened with laughter,
　　And the meadow-sweet shook with love.

Your feet in the full-grown grasses　　　　　　13
　　Moved soft as a weak wind blows;
You passed me as April passes,
　　With face made out of a rose.

By the stream where the stems were slender,　　17
　　Your bright foot paused at the sedge;
It might be to watch the tender
　　Light leaves in the springtime hedge,

On boughs that the sweet month blanches　　　21
　　With flowery frost of May:
It might be a bird in the branches,
　　It might be a thorn in the way.

I waited to watch you linger　　　　　　　　25
　　With foot drawn back from the dew,

Till a sunbeam straight like a finger
    Struck sharp through the leaves at you.

29   And a bird overhead sang *Follow*,
    And a bird to the right sang *Here*;
And the arch of the leaves was hollow,
    And the meaning of May was clear.

33   I saw where the sun's hand pointed,
    I knew what the bird's note said;
By the dawn and the dewfall anointed,
    You were queen by the gold on your head.

37   As the glimpse of a burnt-out ember
    Recalls a regret of the sun,
I remember, forget, and remember
    What Love saw done and undone.

41   I remember the way we parted,
    The day and the way we met;
You hoped we were both broken-hearted,
    And knew we should both forget.

45   And May with her world in flower
    Seemed still to murmur and smile
As you murmured and smiled for an hour;
    I saw you turn at the stile.

49   A hand like a white wood-blossom
    You lifted, and waved, and passed,
With head hung down to the bosom,
    And pale, as it seemed, at last.

53   And the best and the worst of this is
    That neither is most to blame
If you've forgotten my kisses
    And I've forgotten your name.

Hendecasyllabics

In the month of the long decline of roses
I, beholding the summer dead before me,
Set my face to the sea and journeyed silent,
Gazing eagerly where above the sea-mark
Flame as fierce as the fervid eyes of lions   5
Half divided the eyelids of the sunset;
Till I heard as it were a noise of waters
Moving tremulous under feet of angels
Multitudinous, out of all the heavens;
Knew the fluttering wind, the fluttered foliage,   10
Shaken fitfully, full of sound and shadow;
And saw, trodden upon by noiseless angels,
Long mysterious reaches fed with moonlight,
Sweet sad straits in a soft subsiding channel,
Blown about by the lips of winds I knew not,   15
Winds not born in the north nor any quarter,
Winds not warm with the south nor any sunshine;
Heard between them a voice of exultation,
"Lo, the summer is dead, the sun is faded,
Even like as a leaf the year is withered,   20
All the fruits of the day from all her branches
Gathered, neither is any left to gather.
All the flowers are dead, the tender blossoms,
All are taken away; the season wasted,
Like an ember among the fallen ashes.   25
Now with light of the winter days, with moonlight,
Light of snow, and the bitter light of hoarfrost,
We bring flowers that fade not after autumn,
Pale white chaplets and crowns of latter seasons,

Hendecasyllabics: Latin verse of eleven syllables, found especially in Catullus
(see "Dolores," lines 329–362).

181

30   Fair false leaves (but the summer leaves were falser),
            Woven under the eyes of stars and planets
            When low light was upon the windy reaches
            Where the flower of foam was blown, a lily
            Dropt among the sonorous fruitless furrows
35   And green fields of the sea that make no pasture:
            Since the winter begins, the weeping winter,
            All whose flowers are tears, and round his temples
            Iron blossom of frost is bound for ever."

Sapphics

ALL the night sleep came not upon my eyelids,　　　　　1
Shed not dew, nor shook nor unclosed a feather,
Yet with lips shut close and with eyes of iron
　　Stood and beheld me.

Then to me so lying awake a vision　　　　　5
Came without sleep over the seas and touched me,
Softly touched mine eyelids and lips; and I too,
　　Full of the vision,

Saw the white implacable Aphrodite,　　　　　9
Saw the hair unbound and the feet unsandalled
Shine as fire of sunset on western waters;
　　Saw the reluctant

Feet, the straining plumes of the doves that drew her,　　　　　13
Looking always, looking with necks reverted,
Back to Lesbos, back to the hills whereunder
　　Shone Mitylene;

Heard the flying feet of the Loves behind her　　　　　17
Make a sudden thunder upon the waters,
As the thunder flung from the strong unclosing
　　Wings of a great wind.

So the goddess fled from her place, with awful　　　　　21
Sound of feet and thunder of wings around her;

Sapphics: As with the preceding poem, the prosodic form is imitated from
classical metrics, here the strophe, or stanza, invented by Sappho. See "Anactoria" for Sappho and the subject matter.

16. *Mitylene:* Birthplace of Sappho on Lesbos.

While behind a clamour of singing women
Severed the twilight.

25   Ah the singing, ah the delight, the passion!
All the Loves wept, listening; sick with anguish,
Stood the crowned nine Muses about Apollo;
    Fear was upon them,

29   While the tenth sang wonderful things they knew not.
Ah the tenth, the Lesbian! the nine were silent,
None endured the sound of her song for weeping;
    Laurel by laurel,

33   Faded all their crowns; but about her forehead,
Round her woven tresses and ashen temples
White as dead snow, paler than grass in summer,
    Ravaged with kisses,

37   Shone a light of fire as a crown for ever.
Yea, almost the implacable Aphrodite
Paused, and almost wept; such a song was that song.
    Yea, by her name too

41   Called her, saying, "Turn to me, O my Sappho;"
Yet she turned her face from the Loves, she saw not
Tears for laughter darken immortal eyelids,
    Heard not about her

45   Fearful fitful wings of the doves departing,
Saw not how the bosom of Aphrodite
Shook with weeping, saw not her shaken raiment,
    Saw not her hands wrung;

49   Saw the Lesbians kissing across their smitten
Lutes with lips more sweet than the sound of lute-strings,
Mouth to mouth and hand upon hand, her chosen,
    Fairer than all men;

Only saw the beautiful lips and fingers, 53
Full of songs and kisses and little whispers,
Full of music; only beheld among them
    Soar, as a bird soars

Newly fledged, her visible song, a marvel, 57
Made of perfect sound and exceeding passion,
Sweetly shapen, terrible, full of thunders,
    Clothed with the wind's wings.

Then rejoiced she, laughing with love, and scattered 61
Roses, awful roses of holy blossom;
Then the Loves thronged sadly with hidden faces
    Round Aphrodite,

Then the Muses, stricken at heart, were silent; 65
Yea, the gods waxed pale; such a song was that song.
All reluctant, all with a fresh repulsion,
    Fled from before her.

All withdrew long since, and the land was barren, 69
Full of fruitless women and music only.
Now perchance, when winds are assuaged at sunset,
    Lulled at the dewfall,

By the grey sea-side, unassuaged, unheard of, 73
Unbeloved, unseen in the ebb of twilight,
Ghosts of outcast women return lamenting,
    Purged not in Lethe,

Clothed about with flame and with tears, and singing 77
Songs that move the heart of the shaken heaven,
Songs that break the heart of the earth with pity,
    Hearing, to hear them.

76. *Lethe:* River of forgetfulness, crossed by the dead on the way to Hades.

Love and Sleep

LYING asleep between the strokes of night
 I saw my love lean over my sad bed,
 Pale as the duskiest lily's leaf or head,
Smooth-skinned and dark, with bare throat made to bite,
5 Too wan for blushing and too warm for white,
  But perfect-coloured without white or red.
 And her lips opened amorously, and said—
I wist not what, saving one word—Delight.
And all her face was honey to my mouth,
10 And all her body pasture to mine eyes;
   The long lithe arms and hotter hands than fire,
The quivering flanks, hair smelling of the south,
  The bright light feet, the splendid supple thighs
  And glittering eyelids of my soul's desire.

Madonna Mia

UNDER green apple-boughs
That never a storm will rouse,
My lady hath her house
　　Between two bowers;
In either of the twain
Red roses full of rain;
She hath for bondwomen
　　All kind of flowers.

She hath no handmaid fair
To draw her curled gold hair
Through rings of gold that bear
　　Her whole hair's weight;
She hath no maids to stand
Gold-clothed on either hand;
In all the great green land
　　None is so great.

She hath no more to wear
But one white hood of vair
Drawn over eyes and hair,
　　Wrought with strange gold,
Made for some great queen's head,
Some fair great queen since dead;
And one strait gown of red
　　Against the cold.

Beneath her eyelids deep
Love lying seems asleep,
Love, swift to wake, to weep,

Madonna Mia: "My lady."

To laugh, to gaze;
Her breasts are like white birds,
And all her gracious words
As water-grass to herds
     In the June-days.

33   To her all dews that fall
And rains are musical;
Her flowers are fed from all,
     Her joy from these;
In the deep-feathered firs
Their gift of joy is hers,
In the least breath that stirs
     Across the trees.

41   She grows with greenest leaves,
Ripens with reddest sheaves,
Forgets, remembers, grieves,
     And is not sad;
The quiet lands and skies
Leave light upon her eyes;
None knows her, weak or wise,
     Or tired or glad.

49   None knows, none understands,
What flowers are like her hands;
Though you should search all lands
     Wherein time grows,
What snows are like her feet,
Though his eyes burn with heat
Through gazing on my sweet,
     Yet no man knows.

57   Only this thing is said;
That white and gold and red,
God's three chief words, man's bread
     And oil and wine,

Were given her for dowers,
And kingdom of all hours,
And grace of goodly flowers
   And various vine.

This is my lady's praise: 65
God after many days
Wrought her in unknown ways,
   In sunset lands;
This was my lady's birth;
God gave her might and mirth
And laid his whole sweet earth
   Between her hands.

Under deep apple-boughs   73
My lady hath her house;
She wears upon her brows
   The flower thereof;
All saying but what God saith
To her is as vain breath;
She is more strong than death,
   Being strong as love.

The King's Daughter

1   WE were ten maidens in the green corn,
        Small red leaves in the mill-water:
      Fairer maidens never were born,
        Apples of gold for the king's daughter.

5   We were ten maidens by a well-head,
        Small white birds in the mill-water:
      Sweeter maidens never were wed,
        Rings of red for the king's daughter.

9   The first to spin, the second to sing,
        Seeds of wheat in the mill-water;
      The third may was a goodly thing,
        White bread and brown for the king's daughter.

13   The fourth to sew and the fifth to play,
        Fair green weed in the mill-water;
      The sixth may was a goodly may,
        White wine and red for the king's daughter.

17   The seventh to woo, the eighth to wed,
        Fair thin reeds in the mill-water;
      The ninth had gold work on her head,
        Honey in the comb for the king's daughter.

21   The ninth had gold work round her hair,
        Fallen flowers in the mill-water;
      The tenth may was goodly and fair,
        Golden gloves for the king's daughter.

25   We were ten maidens in a field green,
        Fallen fruit in the mill-water;

Written in the style of the *Border Ballads*.

Fairer maidens never have been,
    Golden sleeves for the king's daughter.

By there comes the king's young son,   29
    A little wind in the mill-water;
"Out of ten maidens ye'll grant me one,"
    A crown of red for the king's daughter.

"Out of ten mays ye'll give me the best,"   33
    A little rain in the mill-water;
A bed of yellow straw for all the rest,
    A bed of gold for the king's daughter.

He's ta'en out the goodliest,   37
    Rain that rains in the mill-water;
A comb of yellow shell for all the rest,
    A comb of gold for the king's daughter.

He's made her bed to the goodliest,   41
    Wind and hail in the mill-water;
A grass girdle for all the rest,
    A girdle of arms for the king's daughter.

He's set his heart to the goodliest,   45
    Snow that snows in the mill-water;
Nine little kisses for all the rest,
    An hundredfold for the king's daughter.

He's ta'en his leave at the goodliest,   49
    Broken boats in the mill-water;
Golden gifts for all the rest,
    Sorrow of heart for the king's daughter.

"Ye'll make a grave for my fair body,"   53
    Running rain in the mill-water;
"And ye'll streek my brother at the side of me,"
    The pains of hell for the king's daughter.

The Bloody Son

(FINNISH)

1   "O WHERE have ye been the morn sae late,
      My merry son, come tell me hither?
    O where have ye been the morn sae late?
      And I wot I hae not anither."
    "By the water-gate, by the water-gate,
      O dear mither."

7   "And whatten kin' o' wark had ye there to make,
      My merry son, come tell me hither?
    And whatten kin' o' wark had ye there to make?
      And I wot I hae not anither."
    "I watered my steeds with water frae the lake,
      O dear mither."

13   "Why is your coat sae fouled the day,
      My merry son, come tell me hither?
    Why is your coat sae fouled the day?
      And I wot I hae not anither."
    "The steeds were stamping sair by the weary banks of clay,
      O dear mither."

19   "And where gat ye thae sleeves of red,
      My merry son, come tell me hither?
    And where gat ye thae sleeves of red?
      And I wot I hae not anither."
    "I have slain my ae brither by the weary waterhead,
      O dear mither."

This is Swinburne's attempt to recreate a Swedish ballad mentioned in Bishop Percy's *Reliques of Ancient Poetry* (1765). The poem is inspired by the famous "Edward, Edward," a ballad published by Percy.

"And where will ye gang to mak your mend,   25
   My merry son, come tell me hither?
And where will ye gang to mak your mend?
   And I wot I hae not anither."
"The warldis way, to the warldis end,
   O dear mither."

"And what will ye leave your father dear,   31
   My merry son, come tell me hither?
And what will ye leave your father dear?
   And I wot I hae not anither."
"The wood to fell and the logs to bear,
For he'll never see my body mair,
   O dear mither."

"And what will ye leave your mither dear,   38
   My merry son, come tell me hither?
And what will ye leave your mither dear?
   And I wot I hae not anither."
"The wool to card and the wool to wear,
For ye'll never see my body mair,
   O dear mither."

"And what will ye leave for your wife to take,   45
   My merry son, come tell me hither?
And what will ye leave for your wife to take?
   And I wot I hae not anither."
"A goodly gown and a fair new make,
For she'll do nae mair for my body's sake,
   O dear mither."

"And what will ye leave your young son fair,   52
   My merry son, come tell me hither?
And what will ye leave your young son fair?
   And I wot ye hae not anither."
"A twiggen school-rod for his body to bear,
Though it garred him greet he'll get nae mair,
   O dear mither."

59   "And what will ye leave your little daughter sweet,
              My merry son, come tell me hither?
          And what will ye leave your little daughter sweet?
              And I wot ye hae not anither."
          "Wild mulberries for her mouth to eat,
          She'll get nae mair though it garred her greet,
              O dear mither."

66   "And when will ye come back frae roamin',
              My merry son, come tell me hither?
          And when will ye come back frae roamin'?
              And I wot I hae not anither."
          "When the sunrise out of the north is comen,
              O dear mither."

72   "When shall the sunrise on the north side be,
              My merry son, come tell me hither?
          When shall the sunrise on the north side be?
              And I wot I hae not anither."
          "When chuckie-stanes shall swim in the sea,
              O dear mither."

78   "When shall stanes in the sea swim,
              My merry son, come tell me hither?
          When shall stanes in the sea swim?
              And I wot I hae not anither."
          "When birdies' feathers are as lead therein,
              O dear mither."

84   "When shall feathers be as lead,
              My merry son, come tell me hither?
          When shall feathers be as lead?
              And I wot I hae not anither."
          "When God shall judge between the quick and dead,
              O dear mither."

Dedication

1865

THE sea gives her shells to the shingle,   1
    The earth gives her streams to the sea;
They are many, but my gift is single,
    My verses, the firstfruits of me.
Let the wind take the green and the grey leaf,
    Cast forth without fruit upon air;
Take rose-leaf and vine-leaf and bay-leaf
    Blown loose from the hair.

The night shakes them round me in legions,   9
    Dawn drives them before her like dreams;
Time sheds them like snows on strange regions,
    Swept shoreward on infinite streams;
Leaves pallid and sombre and ruddy,
    Dead fruits of the fugitive years;
Some stained as with wine and made bloody,
    And some as with tears.

Some scattered in seven years' traces,   17
    As they fell from the boy that was then;
Long left among idle green places,
    Or gathered but now among men;
On seas full of wonder and peril,
    Blown white round the capes of the north;
Or in islands where myrtles are sterile
    And loves bring not forth.

Dedication: See "In Memory of Walter Savage Landor."

25   O daughters of dreams and of stories
    That life is not wearied of yet,
   Faustine, Fragoletta, Dolores,
    Félise and Yolande and Juliette,
   Shall I find you not still, shall I miss you,
    When sleep, that is true or that seems,
   Comes back to me hopeless to kiss you,
    O daughters of dreams?

33   They are past as a slumber that passes,
    As the dew of a dawn of old time;
   More frail than the shadows on glasses,
    More fleet than a wave or a rhyme.
   As the waves after ebb drawing seaward,
    When their hollows are full of the night,
   So the birds that flew singing to me-ward
    Recede out of sight.

41   The songs of dead season, that wander
    On wings of articulate words;
   Lost leaves that the shore-wind may squander,
    Light flocks of untameable birds;
   Some sang to me dreaming in class-time
    And truant in hand as in tongue;
   For the youngest were born of boy's pastime,
    The eldest are young.

49   Is there shelter while life in them lingers,
    Is there hearing for songs that recede,
   Tunes touched from a harp with man's fingers
    Or blown with boy's mouth in a reed?
   Is there place in the land of your labour,
    Is there room in your world of delight,
   Where change has not sorrow for neighbor
    And day has not night?

57   In their wings though the sea-wind yet quivers,
    Will you spare not a space for them there

Made green with the running of rivers
    And gracious with temperate air;
In the fields and the turreted cities,
    That cover from sunshine and rain
Fair passions and bountiful pities
    And loves without stain?

In a land of clear colours and stories,   65
    In a region of shadowless hours,
Where earth has a garment of glories
    And a murmur of musical flowers;
In woods where the spring half uncovers
    The flush of her amorous face,
By the waters that listen for lovers,
    For these is there place?

For the song-birds of sorrow, that muffle   73
    Their music as clouds do their fire:
For the storm-birds of passion, that ruffle
    Wild wings in a wind of desire;
In the stream of the storm as it settles
    Blown seaward, borne far from the sun,
Shaken loose on the darkness like petals
    Dropt one after one?

Though the world of your hands be more gracious   81
    And lovelier in lordship of things
Clothed round by sweet art with the spacious
    Warm heaven of her imminent wings,
Let them enter, unfledged and nigh fainting,
    For the love of old loves and lost times;
And receive in your palace of painting
    This revel of rhymes.

Though the seasons of man full of losses   89
    Make empty the years full of youth,
If but one thing be constant in crosses,

Change lays not her hand upon truth;
Hopes die, and their tombs are for token
That the grief as the joy of them ends
Ere time that breaks all men has broken
The faith between friends.

97

Though the many lights dwindle to one light,
There is help if the heaven has one;
Though the skies be discrowned of the sunlight
And the earth dispossessed of the sun,
They have moonlight and sleep for repayment,
When, refreshed as a bride and set free,
With stars and sea-winds in her raiment,
Night sinks on the sea.

Atalanta

in

Calydon

A Tragedy

Τοὺς ζῶντας εὖ δρᾶν · κατθανὼν δὲ πᾶς ἀνὴρ
Γῆ καὶ σκιά · τὸ μηδὲν εἰς οὐδὲν ῥέπει

EUR. *Fr. Mel.* 20 (537)

Epigraph: ". . . to do good to the living; each man, dying, is earth and shadow; the nothing sinks into nothingness." A fragment (now numbered fragment 532) from the lost *Meleager* by Euripides. Translated by W. R. Rutland.

TO THE MEMORY
OF
WALTER SAVAGE LANDOR

I NOW DEDICATE, WITH EQUAL AFFECTION, REVERENCE, AND REGRET,
A POEM INSCRIBED TO HIM WHILE YET ALIVE IN WORDS WHICH ARE
NOW RETAINED BECAUSE THEY WERE LAID BEFORE HIM; AND TO
WHICH, RATHER THAN CANCEL THEM, I HAVE ADDED SUCH OTHERS
AS WERE EVOKED BY THE NEWS OF HIS DEATH: THAT THOUGH LOS-
ING THE PLEASURE I MAY NOT LOSE THE HONOUR OF INSCRIBING IN
FRONT OF MY WORK THE HIGHEST OF CONTEMPORARY NAMES.

[I]

ὤχεο δὴ Βορέηθεν ἀπότροπος· ἀλλά σε Νύμφαι
ἤγαγον ἀσπασίαν ἡδύπνοοι καθ' ἅλα,
πληροῦσαι μέλιτος θεόθεν στόμα, μή τι Ποσειδῶν
βλάψῃ, ἐν ὠσὶν ἔχων σὴν μελίγηρυν ὄπα.
τοῖος ἀοιδὸς ἔφυς· ἡμεῖς δ' ἔτι κλαίομεν, οἳ σου
δευόμεθ' οἰχομένου, καί σε ποθοῦμεν ἀεί.
εἶπε δὲ Πιερίδων τις ἀναστρεφθεῖσα πρὸς ἄλλην·
ἦλθεν, ἰδού, πάντων φίλτατος ἦλθε βροτῶν,
στέμματα δρεψάμενος νεοθηλέα χερσὶ γεραιαῖς,
καὶ πολιὸν δάφναις ἀμφεκάλυψε κάρα,   10
ἡδύ τι Σικελικαῖς ἐπὶ πηκτίσιν, ἡδύ τι χόρδαις,
ἁσόμενος· πολλὴν γὰρ μετέβαλλε λύραν,
πολλάκι δ' ἐν βήσσαισι καθήμενον εὗρεν Ἀπόλλων,
ἄνθεσι δ' ἔστεψεν, τερπνὰ δ' ἔδωκε λέγειν,
Πᾶνα τ' ἀείμνηστόν τε Πίτυν Κόρυθόν τε δύσεδρον,
ἥν τ' ἐφίλησε θεὰν θνητὸς Ἀμαδρύαδα·
πόντου δ' ἐν μεγάροισιν ἐκοίμισε Κυμοδάμειαν,
τήν τ' Ἀγαμεμνονίαν παῖδ' ἀπέδωκε πατρί,
πρὸς δ' ἱεροὺς Δελφοὺς θεόπληκτον ἔτεμψεν Ὀρέστην,
τειρόμενον στυγεραῖς ἔνθα καὶ ἔνθα θεαῖς.   20

Dedicatory Poem I: "Thou didst depart, exiled from the north; but thee the
sweetly breathing nymphs led over the pleasant sea, filling thy mouth with
honey from the gods, that Poseidon might harm thee not when he heard thine
honey-sweet voice. Such a singer wast thou. We yet sorrow who are bereft of
thee now thou art departed, ever we yearn for thee. And a Muse cried, turning
to her sister, 'He that hath gone, lo, the dearest of all mortals hath gone, having
plucked fresh budding garlands with his old hands and covered his hoary head
with laurels, to sing some sweet song upon Sicilian harps, upon Sicilian strings:
for he was wont often to change his lyre, and often Apollo found him seated
in the glades, and crowned him with flowers, and give him delightsome things
to sing—Pan ever memorable, and Pitys and ill-starred Corythos, and the
Hamadryad whom, though a Goddess, a mortal loved: and he lulled Cymodameia to sleep in the caverns of the sea, and restored the child of Agamemnon
to her father, and sent Orestes smitten-of-god to holy Delphi, goaded hither and

201

[II]

ᾤχεο δὴ καὶ ἄνευθε φίλων καὶ ἄνευθεν ἀοιδῆς,
  δρεψόμενος μαλακῆς ἄνθεα Περσεφόνης.
ᾤχεο· κοὐκ ἔτ' ἔσει, κοὐκ αὖ ποτέ σοι παρεδοῦμαι
  ἀζόμενος, χειρῶν χερσὶ θιγὼν ὁσίαις·
νῦν δ' αὖ μνησάμενον γλυκύπικρος ὑπήλυθεν αἰδώς,
  οἷα τυχὼν οἵου πρὸς σέθεν οἷος ἔχω·
οὔποτε σοῖς, γέρον, ὄμμα φίλοις φίλον ὄμμασι τέρψω,
  σῆς, γέρον, ἀψάμενος, φίλτατε, δεξιτερᾶς.
ἢ ψαφαρὰ κόνις, ἢ ψαφαρὸς βίος ἐστι· τί τούτων
10   μεῖον ἐφημερίων; οὐ κόνις ἀλλὰ βίος.
ἀλλά μοι ἡδύτερός γε πέλεις πολὺ τῶν ἔτ' ἐόντων,
  ἔπλεο γάρ· σοὶ μὴν ταῦτα θανόντι φέρω,
παῦρα μὲν, ἀλλ' ἀπὸ κῆρος ἐτήτυμα· μηδ' ἀποτρεφθῇς,
  πρὸς δὲ βαλὼν ἔτι νῦν ἥσυχον ὄμμα δέχου.

---

thither by loathsome Furies.' " Translated by W. R. Rutland (see Bibliography).

fresh budding garlands: Landor published *Heroic Idylls* in 1863 at the age of 88.

Sicilian: Landor composed both English and Latin verse in the style of the Greek pastoral poets Theocritus, Moschus, and Bion, of whom the first two were born in Sicily. He wrote an "Ode to Sicily" published in *Italics* (1848) and *Last Fruit off an Old Tree* (1853), and "A Friend to Theocritos in Egypt," *Heroic Idylls.*

change his lyre: Landor wrote in a great variety of verse forms and genres.

Pan, Pitys, Corythos, the Hamadryad, Cymodameia: Subjects of poems in *Heroic Idylls.*

the child of Agamemnon (Iphigenia), *Orestes:* Subjects of early poems by Landor, reprinted in *Heroic Idylls.*

Dedicatory Poem II: "Thou didst depart, friendless and unsung, to gather blossoms of gentle Persephone. Thou didst depart; never again wilt thou have being; never again at any time shall I sit beside thee in awe, touching thy hands with reverent hands. And now bitter-sweet shame has stolen into my heart when I remember what I received at thy hands, and what manner of man thou wast, and what I am. Never more, old man, shall I delight my eyes, so dear to thee, with sight of eyes so dear to me, holding thy hand the while, old man most well beloved. Ah, fugitive is dust, fugitive is life. Which of these transient things is the lesser? Not dust but life. Nevertheless thou art far dearer to me than those yet living, for thou wast wont to be. To thee, dead, I bring these gifts, which, though few, are true and from the heart. Turn not away, but re-

οὐ γὰρ ἔχω, μέγα δή τι θέλων, σέθεν ἄξια δοῦναι,
θαπτομένου περ ἀπών· οὐ γὰρ ἔνεστιν ἔμοι·
οὐδὲ μελικρήτου παρέχειν γάνος · εἰ γὰρ ἐνείη
καί σε χεροῖν ψαῦσαι καί σέ ποτ᾿ αὖθις ἰδεῖν,
δάκρυσί τε σπονδαῖς τε κάρα φίλον ἀμφιπολεύειν
ὀφθαλμούς θ᾿ ἱερούς σοὺς ἱερόν τε δέμας.   20
εἴθ᾿ ὄφελον· μάλα γὰρ τάδ᾿ ἂν ἀμπαύσειε μερίμνης·
νῦν δὲ πρόσωθεν ἄνευ σήματος οἶκτον ἄγω·
οὐδ᾿ ἐπιτυμβίδιον θρηνῶ μέλος, ἀλλ᾿ ἀπαμυνθεὶς,
ἀλλ᾿ ἀπάνευθεν ἔχων ἀμφιδακρυτὰ πάθη.
ἀλλὰ σὺ χαῖρε θανὼν, καὶ ἔχων γέρας ἴσθι πρὸς ἀνδρῶν
πρός τε θεῶν, ἐνέροις εἴ τις ἔπεοτι θεός.
χαῖρε γέρον, φίλε χαῖρε πατὲρ, πολὺ φέρτατ᾿ ἀοιδῶν
ὧν ἴδομεν, πολὺ δὴ φέρτατ᾿ ἀεισομένων·
χαῖρε, καὶ ὄλβον ἔχοις, οἷόν γε θανόντες ἔχουσιν,
ἡσυχίαν ἔχθρας καὶ φιλότητος ἄτερ·   30
σήματος οἰχομένου σοι μνήματ᾿ ἐς ὕστερον ἔσται,
σοί τε φιλὴ μνήμη μνήματος οἰχομένου·
ὃν Χάριτες κλαίουσι θεαὶ, κλαίει δ᾿ Ἀφροδίτη
καλλιχόροις Μουσῶν τερψαμένη στεφάνοις.
οὐ γὰρ ἅπαξ ἱερούς ποτε γῆρας ἔτριψεν ἀοιδούς·
τήνδε τὸ σόν φαίνει μνῆμα τόδ᾿ ἀγλαΐαν.

---

ceive them, bending on me even now thy tranquil gaze. For, greatly though I desire it, nothing can I give thee worthy of thee, absent though I was when thou wast buried, for it is not in my power. Nor can I even bring thee the lovely libation of milk and honey. Would that I could touch thee with mine hands, see thee yet again, tend with tears and libations thy dear head, thine hallowed eyes, thine hallowed body! Ah, would that I might! For these things truly would me surcease from sorrow. Now from afar off without any sign I make lamentation. Not even over thy tomb sing I my lament, but kept apart, sorrowing from far away in tears. But thou, rejoice in death. Keep thine honour at the hands of men and gods, if there be any god among shadows. Farewell, old man, farewell, father beloved, by far the greatest of poets we have seen, yea, by far the greatest of poets yet to be. Farewell; and mayest thou have such happiness as the dead have—rest without hatred and without love. When thy tomb hath vanished there will still be memorials of thee, and when every memorial is gone, the beloved memory of thee will remain; thee whom the divine Graces mourn, and Aphrodite, who delighted in the Muses' garlands for fair choruses. Never once yet hath old age worn away inspired poets. This splendour this memorial of thine maketh manifest. Truly thou wast a mortal dear to the

ἢ φίλος ἧς μακάρεσσι βροτός, σοὶ δ' εἴ τινι Νύμφαι
δῶρα ποθεινὰ νέμειν, ὕστατα δῶρ', ἔδοσαν.
τὰς νῦν χάλκεος ὕπνος ἔβη καὶ ἀνήνεμος αἰών,
40   καὶ συνθαπτομέναι μοῖραν ἔχουσι μίαν.
εὕδεις καὶ σὺ, καλὸν καὶ ἀγάκλυτον ἐν χθονὶ κοίλῃ
ὕπνον ἐφικόμενος, σῆς ἀπόνοσφι πάτρας,
τῆλε παρὰ ξανθοῦ Τυρσηνικὸν οἶδμα καθεύδεις
νάματος, ἡ δ' ἔτι σὴ μαῖά σε γαῖα ποθεῖ,
ἀλλ' ἀπέχεις, καὶ πρόσθε φιλόπτολις ὧν περ ἀπεῖπας·
εὖδε· μάκαρ δ' ἡμῖν οὐδ' ἀμέγαρτος ἔσει.
βαιὸς ἐπιχθονίων γε χρόνος καὶ μοῖρα κρατήσει,
τοὺς δέ ποτ' εὐφροσύνη τοὺς δέ τοτ' ἄλγος ἔχει·
πολλάκι δ' ἢ βλάπτει φάος ἢ οκότος ἀμφικαλύπτει
50   μυρομένους, δάκνει δ' ὕπνος ἐγρηγορότας·
οὐδ' ἔθ' ὅτ' ἐν τύμβοισι κατέδραθεν ὄμμα θανόντων
ἢ σκότος ἤ τι φάος δήξεται ἠελίου·
οὐδ' ὄναρ ἐννύχιον καὶ ἐνύπνιον οὐδ' ὕπαρ ἔσται
ἤ ποτε τερπομένοις ἤ ποτ' ὀδυρομένοις·
ἀλλ' ἕνα πάντες ἀεὶ θᾶκον συνέχουσι καὶ ἕδραν
ἀντὶ βροτῆς ἄβροτον, κάλλιμον ἀντὶ κακῆς.

---

blessed ones; and to thee, if to any man, the Nymphs granted the possession
of longed-for gifts, their last gifts. To them now has come the iron sleep of
death, and windless eternity, and buried together they share a common lot.
Thou too sleepest, having attained slumber lovely and renowned in the hollow
earth far from thy country. In a far land thou sleepest, by the surge of the yellow Tyrrhenian wave, but the earth that nursed thee still longs for thee. Yet
thou art far away, and long ago, albeit a lover of thy country, thou didst re-
nounce her. Sleep on. In our eyes thou wilt be blessed not wretched. Brief time
and fate will conquer mortals. Now they have pleasure and now pain; and ever
the light harmeth them, or the darkness covereth them, weeping. And the sleep
of death snatcheth them away waking. But for these of the dead that have closed
in the grave, neither darkness nor light of the sun shall wound them again. Nor
ever unto those who rejoice, nor ever unto those who mourn shall come a vision
of dreams in sleep, or a reality waking. But they all for ever have one abiding
place, immortal in place of mortality and beautiful in place of evil." Translated
by W. R. Rutland (see Bibliography).

The Argument

ALTHÆA, daughter of Thestius and Eurythemis, queen of Calydon, being with child of Meleager her first-born son, dreamed that she brought forth a brand burning; and upon his birth came the three Fates and prophesied of him three things, namely these; that he should have great strength of his hands, and good fortune in this life, and that he should live no longer when the brand then in the fire were consumed: wherefore his mother plucked it forth and kept it by her. And the child being a man grown sailed with Jason after the fleece of gold, and won himself great praise of all men living; and when the tribes of the north and west made war upon Ætolia, he fought against their army and scattered it. But Artemis, having at the first stirred up these tribes to war against Œneus king of Calydon, because he had offered sacrifice to all the gods saving her alone, but her he had forgotten to honour, was yet more wroth because of the destruction of this army, and sent upon the land of Calydon a wild boar which slew many and wasted all their increase, but him could none slay, and many went against him and perished. Then were all the chief men of Greece gathered together, and among them Atalanta daughter of Iasius the Arcadian, a virgin; for whose sake Artemis let slay the boar, seeing she favoured the maiden greatly; and Meleager having despatched it gave the spoil thereof to Atalanta, as one beyond measure enamoured of her; but the brethren of Althæa his mother, Toxeus and Plexippus, with such others as misliked that she only should bear off the praise whereas many had borne the labour, laid wait for her to take away her spoil; but Meleager fought against them and slew them: whom when Althæa their sister beheld and knew to be slain of her son, she waxed for wrath and sorrow like as one

Argument: See Appendix for translations of Swinburne's sources, and Appendix 10 for locations of places mentioned.

mad, and taking the brand whereby the measure of her son's life was meted to him, she cast it upon a fire; and with the wasting thereof his life likewise wasted away, that being brought back to his father's house he died in a brief space; and his mother also endured not long after for very sorrow; and this was his end, and the end of that hunting.

The Persons

CHIEF HUNTSMAN
CHORUS
ALTHÆA
MELEAGER
ŒNEUS
ATALANTA
TOXEUS
PLEXIPPUS
HERALD
MESSENGER
SECOND MESSENGER

Althæa: Queen of Calydon and mother of Meleager; daughter of Thestios king of Pleuron, and sister of Leda.

Meleager: Son of the king of Calydon.

Œneus: King of Calydon and father of Meleager.

Atalanta: Maiden of Arcadia, a huntress, dedicated to virginity and to Artemis; daughter of Iasios, son of Lykurgos king of Tegea, a city in Arcadia.

Toxeus, Plexippus: Brothers of Althæa.

ἴοτω δ' ὅστις οὐχ ὑπόπτερος
φροντίσιν δαεὶς,
τὰν ἁ παιδολύμας τάλαινα Θεστιὰς μήσατο
πυρδαῆ τινα πρόνοιαν,
καταίθουσα παιδὸς δαφοινὸν
δαλὸν ἥλικ', ἐπεὶ μολὼν
ματρόθεν κελάδησε;
σύμμετρόν τε διαὶ βίου
μοιρόκραντον ἐς ἁμαρ.

ÆSCH. *Cho.* 602–612.

From Æschylus, *Chœphorœ* (*The Libation Bearers*), the second part of the trilogy on Orestes, of which the other two parts are *Agamemnon* and *Eumenides*. "Let him, who goes not on flimsy wings of thought, learn from her, Althæa, Thestius' daughter: who maimed her child, and hard of heart, in deliberate guile set fire to the bloody torch, her own son's agemate, that from the day he emerged from the mother's womb crying shared the measure of all his life down to the marked death day." Translated by Richmond Lattimore (Chicago, 1959.) Reprinted by permission of University of Chicago Press.

208

Atalanta in Calydon

[Before the columned porch of the palace in Calydon.
Enter Chief Huntsman.]

CHIEF HUNTSMAN

MAIDEN, and mistress of the months and stars
Now folded in the flowerless fields of heaven,
Goddess whom all gods love with threefold heart,
Being treble in thy divided deity,
A light for dead men and dark hours, a foot   5
Swift on the hills as morning, and a hand
To all things fierce and fleet that roar and range
Mortal, with gentler shafts than snow or sleep;
Hear now and help and lift no violent hand,
But favourable and fair as thine eye's beam   10
Hidden and shown in heaven; for I all night
Amid the king's hounds and the hunting men
Have wrought and worshipped toward thee; nor shall man
See goodlier hounds or deadlier edge of spears;
But for the end, that lies unreached at yet   15
Between the hands and on the knees of gods.
O fair-faced sun, killing the stars and dews
And dreams and desolation of the night!
Rise up, shine, stretch thine hand out, with thy bow
Touch the most dimmest height of trembling heaven,   20
And burn and break the dark about thy ways,
Shot through and through with arrows; let thine hair

Swinburne published the play without stage-directions, as Greek plays are
ordinarily published. The present editor has added the stage-directions.
    1. *Maiden:* Eos, or Aurora, goddess of the sunrise.
    4–8. Swinburne means that as goddess of morning, accompanied by the
Hours when she sets forth, Aurora is also goddess of time and hence of death.
    17. The huntsman now addresses Apollo, god of the sun.

Lighten as flame above that flameless shell
Which was the moon, and thine eyes fill the world
25   And thy lips kindle with swift beams; let earth
Laugh, and the long sea fiery from thy feet
Through all the roar and ripple of streaming springs
And foam in reddening flakes and flying flowers
Shaken from hands and blown from lips of nymphs
30   Whose hair or breast divides the wandering wave
With salt close tresses cleaving lock to lock,
All gold, or shuddering and unfurrowed snow;
And all the winds about thee with their wings,
And fountain-heads of all the watered world;
35   Each horn of Acheloüs, and the green
Euenus, wedded with the straitening sea.
For in fair time thou comest; come also thou,
Twin-born with him, and virgin, Artemis,
And give our spears their spoil, the wild boar's hide,
40   Sent in thine anger against us for sin done
And bloodless altars without wine or fire.
Him now consume thou; for thy sacrifice
With sanguine-shining steam divides the dawn,
And one, the maiden rose of all thy maids,
45   Arcadian Atalanta, snowy-souled,
Fair as the snow and footed as the wind,
From Ladon and well-wooded Mænalus
Over the firm hills and the fleeting sea
Hast thou drawn hither, and many an armèd king,
50   Heroes, the crown of men, like gods in fight.
Moreover out of all the Ætolian land,

35–36. *Acheloüs . . . Euenus:* Acheloüs is the largest river of Greece. After the events of the play Heracles fought the god the river in the form of a bull and broke off one of his horns. The contest was over Deianeira, daughter of Oeneus. The Euenus flowed through Aetolia and past Calydon. When Heracles came to this river, it was flooded, and the centaur Nessus offered to carry Deianeira across on his back. When he tried to assault her, Heracles shot him.
38. *Artemis:* Goddess of the moon, of virginity, and of the hunt.
47. *Ladon . . . Mænalus:* A river and a mountain in Arcadia.
51. *Ætolian land:* Calydon was a city in Aetolia.

From the full-flowered Lelantian pasturage
To what of fruitful field the son of Zeus
Won from the roaring river and labouring sea
When the wild god shrank in his horn and fled   55
And foamed and lessened through his wrathful fords
Leaving clear lands that steamed with sudden sun,
These virgins with the lightening of the day
Bring thee fresh wreaths and their own sweeter hair,
Luxurious locks and flower-like mixed with flowers,   60
Clean offering, and chaste hymns; but me the time
Divides from these things; whom do thou not less
Help and give honour, and to mine hounds good speed,
And edge to spears, and luck to each man's hand.

                                                  [Exit.]

        [Enter chorus of Calydonian maidens.]

CHORUS

When the hounds of spring are on winter's traces,   65
    The mother of months in meadow or plain
Fills the shadows and windy places
    With lisp of leaves and ripple of rain;
And the brown bright nightingale amorous
Is half assuaged for Itylus,   70
For the Thracian ships and the foreign faces,
    The tongueless vigil, and all the pain.

Come with bows bent and with emptying of quivers,
    Maiden most perfect, lady of light,

---

52. *Lelantian pasturage:* The Lelantian fields, a plain where the Lelantus River of the island Euboea flows into the Eurenus, the strait between Euboea and Bœotia.

52–55. The Legend of Alkmeon tells of new lands formed at the mouth of the Acheloüs; the river had two mouths or horns, and one of these was shut off. Swinburne, apparently, invents the detail of Heracles' winning the lands in his fight with the river (see note to line 35).

66. *Mother of months:* The moon, that is, Artemis. The chorus invokes her because she has sent the Calydonian boar.

70–73. See notes to "Itylus" in *Poems and Ballads*.

75   With a noise of winds and many rivers,
           With a clamour of waters, and with might;
       Bind on thy sandals, O thou most fleet,
       Over the splendour and speed of thy feet;
       For the faint east quickens, the wan west shivers,
80   Round the feet of the day and the feet of the night.

       Where shall we find her, how shall we sing to her,
           Fold our hands round her knees, and cling?
       O that man's heart were as fire and could spring to her,
           Fire, or the strength of the streams that spring!
85   For the stars and the winds are unto her
       As raiment, as songs of the harp-player;
       For the risen stars and the fallen cling to her,
           And the southwest-wind and the west-wind sing.

       For winter's rains and ruins are over,
90   And all the season of snows and sins;
       The days dividing lover and lover,
           The light that loses, the night that wins;
       And time remembered is grief forgotten,
       And frosts are slain and flowers begotten,
95   And in green underwood and cover
           Blossom by blossom the spring begins.

       The full streams feed on flower of rushes,
           Ripe grasses trammel a travelling foot,
       The faint fresh flame of the young year flushes
100   From leaf to flower and flower to fruit;
       And fruit and leaf are as gold and fire,
       And the oat is heard above the lyre,
       And the hoofèd heel of a satyr crushes
           The chestnut-husk at the chestnut-root.

---

   102. *oat . . . lyre:* The countryman's music, made on pipes made of oat
stalks, is louder than the sophisticated music of the townsman, performed on
the lyre; or the music of Pan is louder than that of Apollo.
   103–108. *Satyr:* Satyrs were minor divinities with goats' horns and horses'
tails.

And Pan by noon and Bacchus by night, 105
    Fleeter of foot than the fleet-foot kid,
Follows with dancing and fills with delight
    The Mænad and the Bassarid;
And soft as lips that laugh and hide
The laughing leaves of the trees divide, 110
And screen from seeing and leave in sight
    The god pursuing, the maiden hid.

The ivy falls with the Bacchanal's hair
    Over her eyebrows hiding her eyes;
The wild vine slipping down leaves bare 115
    Her bright breast shortening into sighs;
The wild vine slips with the weight of its leaves,
But the berried ivy catches and cleaves
To the limbs that glitter, the feet that scare
    The wolf that follows, the fawn that flies. 120

[*Enter Althaea.*]

ALTHÆA

What do ye singing? what is this ye sing?

CHORUS

Flowers bring we, and pure lips that please the gods,
And raiment meet for service: lest the day
Turn sharp with all its honey in our lips.

ALTHÆA

Night, a black hound, follows the white fawn day, 125
Swifter than dreams the white flown feet of sleep;

108. *Mænad and the Bassarid:* Human women who were servitors and followers of Dionyos or Bacchus, god of wine, revelry, and licentiousness. In their
celebrations, accompanied by the satyrs, the Mænads tore apart both men and
animals; they were also protectors of animals.

Will ye pray back the night with any prayers?
And though the spring put back a little while
Winter, and snows that plague all men for sin,
130   And the iron time of cursing, yet I know
Spring shall be ruined with the rain, and storm
Eat up like fire the ashen autumn days.
I marvel what men do with prayers awake
Who dream and die with dreaming; any god,
135   Yea the least god of all things called divine,
Is more than sleep and waking; yet we say,
Perchance by praying a man shall match his god.
For if sleep have no mercy, and man's dreams
Bite to the blood and burn into the bone,
140   What shall this man do waking?   By the gods,
He shall not pray to dream sweet things to-night,
Having dreamt once more bitter things than death.

CHORUS

Queen, but what is it that hath burnt thine heart?
For thy speech flickers like a blown-out flame.

ALTHÆA

145   Look, ye say well, and know not what ye say;
For all my sleep is turned into a fire,
And all my dreams to stuff that kindles it.

CHORUS

Yet one doth well being patient of the gods.

ALTHÆA

Yea, lest they smite us with some four-foot plague.

CHORUS

150   But when time spreads find out some herb for it.

ALTHÆA

And with their healing herbs infect our blood.

CHORUS

What ails thee to be jealous of their ways?

ALTHÆA

What if they give us poisonous drinks for wine?

CHORUS

They have their will; much talking mends it not.

ALTHÆA

And gall for milk, and cursing for a prayer?   155

CHORUS

Have they not given life, and the end of life?

ALTHÆA

Lo, where they heal, they help not; thus they do,
They mock us with a little piteousness,
And we say prayers, and weep; but at the last,
Sparing awhile, they smite and spare no whit.   160

CHORUS

Small praise man gets dispraising the high gods:
What have they done that thou dishonourest them?

ALTHÆA

First Artemis for all this harried land
I praise not, and for wasting of the boar
That mars with tooth and tusk and fiery feet   165

Green pasturage and the grace of standing corn
And meadow and marsh with springs and unblown leaves,
Flocks and swift herds and all that bite sweet grass,
I praise her not; what things are these to praise?

CHORUS

170 But when the king did sacrifice, and gave
Each god fair dues of wheat and blood and wine,
Her not with bloodshed nor burnt-offering
Revered he, nor with salt or cloven cake;
Wherefore being wroth she plagued the land; but now
175 Takes off from us fate and her heavy things.
Which deed of these twain were not good to praise?
For a just deed looks always either way
With blameless eyes, and mercy is no fault.

ALTHÆA

Yea, but a curse she hath sent above all these
180 To hurt us where she healed us; and hath lit
Fire where the old fire went out, and where the wind
Slackened, hath blown on us with deadlier air.

CHORUS

What storm is this that tightens all our sail?

ALTHÆA

Love, a thwart sea-wind full of rain and foam.

CHORUS

185 Whence blown, and born under what stormier star?

ALTHÆA

Southward across Euenus from the sea.

186. *Euenus:* See line 35.

CHORUS

Thy speech turns toward Arcadia like blown wind.

ALTHÆA

Sharp as the north sets when the snows are out.

CHORUS

Nay, for this maiden hath no touch of love.

ALTHÆA

I would she had sought in some cold gulf of sea   190
Love, or in dens where strange beasts lurk, or fire,
Or snows on the extreme hills, or iron land
Where no spring is; I would she had sought therein
And found, or ever love had found her here.

CHORUS

She is holier than all holy days or things,   195
The sprinkled water or fume of perfect fire;
Chaste, dedicated to pure prayers, and filled
With higher thoughts than heaven; a maiden clean,
Pure iron, fashioned for a sword; and man
She loves not; what should one such do with love?   200

ALTHÆA

Look you, I speak not as one light of wit,
But as a queen speaks, being heart-vexed; for oft
I hear my brothers wrangling in mid hall,
And am not moved; and my son chiding them,
And these things nowise move me, but I know   205
Foolish and wise men must be to the end,
And feed myself with patience; but this most,
This moves me, that for wise men as for fools
Love is one thing, an evil thing, and turns

210   Choice words and wisdom into fire and air.
           And in the end shall no joy come, but grief,
           Sharp words and soul's division and fresh tears
           Flower-wise upon the old root of tears brought forth,
           Fruit-wise upon the old flower of tears sprung up,
215   Pitiful sighs, and much regrafted pain.
           These things are in my presage, and myself
           Am part of them and know not; but in dreams
           The gods are heavy on me, and all the fates
           Shed fire across my eyelids mixed with night,
220   And burn me blind, and disilluminate
           My sense of seeing, and my perspicuous soul
           Darken with vision; seeing I see not, hear
           And hearing am not holpen, but mine eyes
           Stain many tender broideries in the bed
225   Drawn up about my face that I may weep
           And the king wake not; and my brows and lips
           Tremble and sob in sleeping, like swift flames
           That tremble, or water when it sobs with heat
           Kindled from under; and my tears fill my breast
230   And speck the fair dyed pillows round the king
           With barren showers and salter than the sea,
           Such dreams divide me dreaming; for long since
           I dreamed that out of this my womb had sprung
           Fire and a firebrand; this was ere my son,
235   Meleager, a goodly flower in fields of fight,
           Felt the light touch him coming forth, and wailed
           Childlike; but yet he was not; and in time
           I bare him, and my heart was great; for yet
           So royally was never strong man born,
240   Nor queen so nobly bore as noble a thing
           As this my son was: such a birth God sent
           And such a grace to bear it.   Then came in
           Three weaving women, and span each a thread,
           Saying This for strength and That for luck, and one

---

243. *Three weaving women:* The three Fates, Clotho, Lachesis, and Atropos.
Strictly, they were spinners, spinning off the thread of each man's life from
the distaff, the staff on which was twirled the raw wool.

Saying Till the brand upon the hearth burn down,   245
So long shall this man see good days and live.
And I with gathered raiment from the bed
Sprang, and drew forth the brand, and cast on it
Water, and trod the flame bare-foot, and crushed
With naked hand spark beaten out of spark   250
And blew against and quenched it; for I said,
These are the most high Fates that dwell with us,
And we find favour a little in their sight,
A little, and more we miss of, and much time
Foils us; howbeit they have pitied me, O son,   255
And thee most piteous, thee a tenderer thing
Than any flower of fleshly seed alive.
Wherefore I kissed and hid him with my hands,
And covered under arms and hair, and wept,
And feared to touch him with my tears, and laughed;   260
So light a thing was this man, grown so great
Men cast their heads back, seeing against the sun
Blaze the armed man carven on his shield, and hear
The laughter of little bells along the brace
Ring, as birds singing or flutes blown, and watch,   265
High up, the cloven shadow of either plume
Divide the bright light of the brass, and make
His helmet as a windy and wintering moon
Seen through blown cloud and plume-like drift, when ships
Drive, and men strive with all the sea, and oars   270
Break, and the beaks dip under, drinking death;
Yet was he then but a span long, and moaned
With inarticulate mouth inseparate words,
And with blind lips and fingers wrung my breast
Hard, and thrust out with foolish hands and feet,   275
Murmuring; but those grey women with bound hair
Who fright the gods frighted not him; he laughed
Seeing them, and pushed out hands to feel and haul
Distaff and thread, intangible; but they
Passed, and I hid the brand, and in my heart   280
Laughed likewise, having all my will of heaven.
But now I know not if to left or right

The gods have drawn us hither; for again
I dreamt, and saw the black brand burst on fire
285   As a branch bursts in flower, and saw the flame
Fade flower-wise, and Death came and with dry lips
Blew the charred ash into my breast; and Love
Trampled the ember and crushed it with swift feet.
This I have also at heart; that not for me,
290   Not for me only or son of mine, O girls,
The gods have wrought life, and desire of life,
Heart's love and heart's division; but for all
There shines one sun and one wind blows till night.
And when night comes the wind sinks and the sun,
295   And there is no light after, and no storm,
But sleep and much forgetfulness of things.
In such wise I gat knowledge of the gods
Years hence, and heard high sayings of one most wise,
Eurythemis my mother, who beheld
300   With eyes alive and spake with lips of these
As one on earth disfleshed and disallied
From breath or blood corruptible; such gifts
Time gave her, and an equal soul to these
And equal face to all things; thus she said.
305   But whatsoever intolerable or glad
The swift hours weave and unweave, I go hence
Full of mine own soul, perfect of myself,
Toward mine and me sufficient; and what chance
The gods cast lots for and shake out on us,
310   That shall we take, and that much bear withal.
And now, before these gather to the hunt,
I will go arm my son and bring him forth,
Lest love or some man's anger work him harm.

[Exit.]

---

299. *Eurythemis:* Wife of Thestios, king of Aetolia. Her sister was Leda, mother of Kastor and Pollux (or Polydeukes), of Helen of Troy, and of Clytemnestra. Clytemnestra married and eventually murdered Agamemnon, king of Mycenae. His brother Menelaus, king of Sparta, married Helen.

CHORUS

Before the beginning of years
  There came to the making of man   315
Time, with a gift of tears;
  Grief, with a glass that ran;
Pleasure, with pain for leaven;
  Summer, with flowers that fell;
Remembrance fallen from heaven,   320
  And madness risen from hell;
Strength without hands to smite;
  Love that endures for a breath:
Night, the shadow of light,
  And life, the shadow of death.   325

And the high gods took in hand
  Fire, and the falling of tears,
And a measure of sliding sand
  From under the feet of the years;
And froth and drift of the sea;   330
  And dust of the labouring earth;
And bodies of things to be
  In the houses of death and of birth;
And wrought with weeping and laughter,
  And fashioned with loathing and love.   335
With life before and after
  And death beneath and above,
For a day and a night and a morrow,
  That his strength might endure for a span
With travail and heavy sorrow,   340
  The holy spirit of man.

From the winds of the north and the south
  They gathered as unto strife;
They breathed upon his mouth,
  They filled his body with life;   345
Eyesight and speech they wrought

For the veils of the soul therein,
A time for labour and thought,
A time to serve and to sin;
350   They gave him light in his ways,
    And love, and a space for delight,
  And beauty and length of days,
    And night, and sleep in the night.
His speech is a burning fire;
355   With his lips he travaileth;
In his heart is a blind desire,
  In his eyes foreknowledge of death;
He weaves, and is clothed with derision;
  Sows, and he shall not reap;
360 His life is a watch or a vision
  Between a sleep and a sleep.

[*Enter Althaea and Meleager.*]

MELEAGER

O sweet new heaven and air without a star,
Fair day, be fair and welcome, as to men
With deeds to do and praise to pluck from thee.
365 Come forth a child, born with clear sound and light,
With laughter and swift limbs and prosperous looks;
That this great hunt with heroes for the hounds
May leave thee memorable and us well sped.

ALTHÆA

Son, first I praise thy prayer, then bid thee speed;
370 But the gods hear men's hands before their lips,
And heed beyond all crying and sacrifice
Light of things done and noise of labouring men.
But thou, being armed and perfect for the deed,
Abide; for like rain-flakes in a wind they grow,
375 The men thy fellows, and the choice of the world,

Bound to root out the tuskèd plague, and leave
Thanks and safe days and peace in Calydon.

MELEAGER

For the whole city and all the low-lying land
Flames, and the soft air sounds with them that come;
The gods give all these fruit of all their works.   380

ALTHÆA

Set thine eye thither and fix thy spirit and say
Whom there thou knowest; for sharp mixed shadow and
          wind
Blown up between the morning and the mist,
With steam of steeds and flash of bridle or wheel,
And fire, and parcels of the broken dawn,   385
And dust divided by hard light, and spears
That shine and shift as the edge of wild beasts' eyes,
Smite upon mine; so fiery their blind edge
Burns, and bright points break up and baffle day.

MELEAGER

The first, for many I know not, being far off,   390
Peleus the Larissæan, couched with whom
Sleeps the white sea-bred wife and silver-shod,
Fair as fled foam, a goddess; and their son
Most swift and splendid of men's children born,
Most like a god, full of the future fame.   395

ALTHÆA

Who are these shining like one sundered star?

391. *Peleus:* Father of Achilles by Thetis, the sea-nymph. He is called
Larissaean after Larissa in Thessaly, part of which, Phthia, he ruled.

MELEAGER

Thy sister's sons, a double flower of men.

ALTHÆA

O sweetest kin to me in all the world,
O twin-born blood of Leda, gracious heads

400 Like kindled lights in untempestuous heaven,
Fair flower-like stars on the iron foam of fight,
With what glad heart and kindliness of soul,
Even to the staining of both eyes with tears
And kindling of warm eyelids with desire,

405 A great way off I greet you, and rejoice
Seeing you so fair, and moulded like as gods.
Far off ye come, and least in years of these,
But lordliest, but worth love to look upon.

MELEAGER

Even such (for sailing hither I saw far hence,

410 And where Eurotas hollows his moist rock
Nigh Sparta with a strenuous-hearted stream)
Even such I saw their sisters; one swan-white,
The little Helen, and less fair than she
Fair Clytæmnestra, grave as pasturing fawns

415 Who feed and fear some arrow; but at whiles,
As one smitten with love or wrung with joy,
She laughs and lightens with her eyes, and then
Weeps; whereat Helen, having laughed, weeps too,
And the other chides her, and she being chid speaks nought,

420 But cheeks and lips and eyelids kisses her,
Laughing; so fare they, as in their bloomless bud
And full of unblown life, the blood of gods.

397. *Thy sister's sons:* Castor and Pollux (see note to line 299).
399. *Leda:* See note to line 299.
410. *Eurotas:* The river that flows past Sparta.
413–414. *Helen . . . Clytæmnestra:* See note to line 299.

ALTHÆA

Sweet days befall them and good loves and lords,
And tender and temperate honours of the hearth,
Peace, and a perfect life and blameless bed.   425
But who shows next an eagle wrought in gold,
That flames and beats broad wings against the sun
And with void mouth gapes after emptier prey?

MELEAGER

Know by that sign the reign of Telamon
Between the fierce mouths of the encountering brine   430
On the strait reefs of twice-washed Salamis.

ALTHÆA

For like one great of hand he bears himself,
Vine-chapleted, with savours of the sea,
Glittering as wine and moving as a wave.
But who girt round there roughly follows him?   435

MELEAGER

Ancæus, great of hand, an iron bulk,
Two-edged for fight as the axe against his arm,
Who drives against the surge of stormy spears
Full-sailed; him Cepheus follows, his twin-born,
Chief name next his of all Arcadian men.   440

ALTHÆA

Praise be with men abroad; chaste lives with us,
Home-keeping days and household reverences.

429. *Telamon:* King of Salamis and brother of Peleus (see note to line 391).
436–439. *Ancæus . . . Cepheus:* Arcadian heroes, sons of Lycurgus, king of
Tegea, and uncles of Atalanta.

MELEAGER

Next by the left unsandalled foot know thou
The sail and oar of this Ætolian land,
445   Thy brethren, Toxeus and the violent-souled
Plexippus, over-swift with hand and tongue;
For hands are fruitful, but the ignorant mouth
Blows and corrupts their work with barren breath.

ALTHÆA

Speech too bears fruit, being worthy; and air blows down
450   Things poisonous, and high-seated violences,
And with charmed words and songs have men put out
Wild evil, and the fire of tyrannies.

MELEAGER

Yea, all things have they, save the gods and love.

ALTHÆA

Love thou the law and cleave to things ordained.

MELEAGER

455   Law lives upon their lips whom these applaud.

ALTHÆA

How sayest thou these? what god applauds new things?

MELEAGER

Zeus, who hath fear and custom under foot.

443. *unsandalled foot:* It was the custom among the Aetolians to leave the
left foot unbooted but sandaled, to be freer in action. Swinburne is here inac-
curate. (See Appendix, Euripides, *Meleager* Fragment 530.)

ALTHÆA

But loves not laws thrown down and lives awry.

MELEAGER

Yet is not less himself than his own law.

ALTHÆA

Nor shifts and shuffles old things up and down.   460

MELEAGER

But what he will remoulds and discreates.

ALTHÆA

Much, but not this, that each thing live its life.

MELEAGER

Nor only live, but lighten and lift up higher.

ALTHÆA

Pride breaks itself, and too much gained is gone.

MELEAGER

Things gained are gone, but great things done endure.   465

ALTHÆA

Child, if a man serve law through all his life
And with his whole heart worship, him all gods
Praise; but who loves it only with his lips,
And not in heart and deed desiring it
Hides a perverse will with obsequious words,   470
Him heaven infatuates and his twin-born fate
Tracks, and gains on him, scenting sins far off,
And the swift hounds of violent death devour.
Be man at one with equal-minded gods,

475   So shall he prosper; not through laws torn up,
      Violated rule and a new face of things.
      A woman armed makes war upon herself,
      Unwomanlike, and treads down use and wont
      And the sweet common honour that she hath,
480   Love, and the cry of children, and the hand
      Trothplight and mutual mouth of marriages.
      This doth she, being unloved; whom if one love,
      Not fire nor iron and the wide-mouthed wars
      Are deadlier than her lips or braided hair.
485   For of the one comes poison, and a curse
      Falls from the other and burns the lives of men.
      But thou, son, be not filled with evil dreams,
      Nor with desire of these things; for with time
      Blind love burns out; but if one feed it full
490   Till some discolouring stain dyes all his life,
      He shall keep nothing praiseworthy, nor die
      The sweet wise death of old men honourable,
      Who have lived out all the length of all their years
      Blameless, and seen well-pleased the face of gods,
495   And without shame and without fear have wrought
      Things memorable, and while their days held out
      In sight of all men and the sun's great light
      Have gat them glory and given of their own praise
      To the earth that bare them and the day that bred,
500   Home friends and far-off hospitalities,
      And filled with gracious and memorial fame
      Lands loved of summer or washed by violent seas,
      Towns populous and many unfooted ways,
      And alien lips and native with their own.
505   But when white age and venerable death
      Mow down the strength and life within their limbs,
      Drain out the blood and darken their clear eyes,
      Immortal honour is on them, having past
      Through splendid life and death desirable

505–525. An allusion to Landor (see "In Memory of Walter Savage Landor"
in *Poems and Ballads*, the Dedication to *Atalanta*, and the dedicatory poems
in Greek).

To the clear seat and remote throne of souls, 510
Lands indiscoverable in the unheard-of west,
Round which the strong stream of a sacred sea
Rolls without wind for ever, and the snow
There shows not her white wings and windy feet,
Nor thunder nor swift rain saith anything, 515
Nor the sun burns, but all things rest and thrive;
And these, filled full of days, divine and dead,
Sages and singers fiery from the god,
And, best beloved of best men, liberty, 520
Free lives and lips, free hands of men free-born,
And whatsoever on earth was honourable
And such as loved their land and all things good
And whosoever of all the ephemeral seed,
Live there a life no liker to the gods
But nearer than their life of terrene days. 525
Love thou such life and look for such a death.
But from the light and fiery dreams of love
Spring heavy sorrows and a sleepless life,
Visions not dreams, whose lids no charm shall close
Nor song assuage them waking; and swift death 530
Crushes with sterile feet the unripening ear,
Treads out the timeless vintage; whom do thou
Eschewing embrace the luck of this thy life,
Not without honour; and it shall bear to thee
Such fruit as men reap from spent hours and wear, 535
Few men, but happy; of whom be thou, O son,
Happiest, if thou submit thy soul to fate,
And set thine eyes and heart on hopes high-born
And divine deeds and abstinence divine.
So shalt thou be toward all men all thy days 540
As light and might communicable, and burn
From heaven among the stars above the hours,
And break not as a man breaks nor burn down:
For to whom other of all heroic names
Have the gods given his life in hand as thine? 545

511. *Lands . . . in the . . . west:* See Appendix 9.

And gloriously hast thou lived, and made thy life
To me that bare thee and to all men born
Thankworthy, a praise for ever; and hast won fame
When wild wars broke all round thy father's house,
550   And the mad people of windy mountain ways
Laid spears against us like a sea, and all
Ætolia thundered with Thessalian hoofs;
Yet these, as wind baffles the foam, and beats
Straight back the relaxed ripple, didst thou break
555   And loosen all their lances, till undone
And man from man they fell; for ye twain stood
God against god, Ares and Artemis,
And thou the mightier; wherefore she unleashed
A sharp-toothed curse thou too shalt overcome;
560   For in the greener blossom of thy life
Ere the full blade caught flower, and when time gave
Respite, thou didst not slacken soul nor sleep,
But with great hand and heart seek praise of men
Out of sharp straits and many a grievous thing,
565   Seeing the strange foam of undivided seas
On channels never sailed in, and by shores
Where the old winds cease not blowing, and all the night
Thunders, and day is no delight to men.

CHORUS

Meleager, a noble wisdom and fair words
570   The gods have given this woman; hear thou these.

MELEAGER

O mother, I am not fain to strive in speech
Nor set my mouth against thee, who art wise

---

552. The raid of the Thessalians, the horse-breeders, on Aetolia is apparently invented by Swinburne.

557. *Ares:* Some authorities say that Meleager was in fact the son of Ares, the god of war. Swinburne suggests that Artemis' first anger against the Calydonians was this opposition by Meleager.

565ff. This is a reference to the sailing of the Argonauts after the Golden Fleece, in which Meleager took part.

Even as they say and full of sacred words.
But one thing I know surely, and cleave to this;
That though I be not subtle of wit as thou   575
Nor womanlike to weave sweet words, and melt
Mutable minds of wise men as with fire,
I too, doing justly and reverencing the gods,
Shall not want wit to see what things be right.
For whom they love and whom reject, being gods,   580
There is no man but seeth, and in good time
Submits himself, refraining all his heart.
And I too as thou sayest have seen great things;
Seen otherwhere, but chiefly when the sail
First caught between stretched ropes the roaring west,   585
And all our oars smote eastward, and the wind
First flung round faces of seafaring men
White splendid snow-flakes of the sundering foam,
And the first furrow in virginal green sea
Followed the plunging ploughshare of hewn pine,   590
And closed, as when deep sleep subdues man's breath
Lips close and heart subsides; and closing, shone
Sunlike with many a Nereid's hair, and moved
Round many a trembling mouth of doubtful gods,
Risen out of sunless and sonorous gulfs   595
Through waning water and into shallow light,
That watched us; and when flying the dove was snared
As with men's hands, but we shot after and sped
Clear through the irremeable Symplegades;
And chiefliest when hoar beach and herbless cliff   600
Stood out ahead from Colchis, and we heard
Clefts hoarse with wind, and saw through narrowing reefs
The lightning of the intolerable wave

585–615. This is Meleager's description of the expedition of the Argonauts.
593. *Nereid:* Sea-nymph.
597–599. *Irremeable:* That which cannot be rowed through.   *Symplegades:*
Two clashing rocks at the mouth of the Euxine or Black Sea. The Argonauts
got through by following a dove. See Appendix 9.
   601. *Colchis:* The Golden Fleece was in Colchis, the land of King Aetes, at
the eastern end of the Euxine. His daughter was Medea, who fell in love with
Jason and helped him to gain the Fleece in return for marrying her.

Flash, and the white wet flame of breakers burn
605 Far under a kindling south-wind, as a lamp
Burns and bends all its blowing flame one way;
Wild heights untravelled of the wind, and vales
Cloven seaward by their violent streams, and white
With bitter flowers and bright salt scurf of brine;
610 Heard sweep their sharp swift gales, and blowing birdwise
Shriek with birds' voices, and with furious feet
Tread loose the long skirts of a storm; and saw
The whole white Euxine clash together and fall
Full-mouthed, and thunderous from a thousand throats;
615 Yet we drew thither and won the fleece and won
Medea, deadlier than the sea; but there
Seeing many a wonder and fearful things to men
I saw not one thing like this one seen here,
Most fair and fearful, feminine, a god,
620 Faultless; whom I that love not, being unlike,
Fear, and give honour, and choose from all the gods.

[*Enter Oeneus.*]

ŒNEUS

Lady, the daughter of Thestius, and thou, son,
Not ignorant of your strife nor light of wit,
Scared with vain dreams and fluttering like spent fire,
625 I come to judge between you, but a king
Full of past days and wise from years endured.
Nor thee I praise, who art fain to undo things done:
Nor thee, who art swift to esteem them overmuch.
For what the hours have given is given, and this
630 Changeless; howbeit these change, and in good time
Devise new things and good, not one thing still.
Us have they sent now at our need for help
Among men armed a woman, foreign born,
Virgin, not like the natural flower of things
635 That grows and bears and brings forth fruit and dies;

616. *Medea:* See note to line 601.

Unlovable, no light for a husband's house,
Espoused; a glory among unwedded girls,
And chosen of gods who reverence maidenhood.
These too we honour in honouring her; but thou,
Abstain thy feet from following, and thine eyes   640
From amorous touch; nor set toward hers thine heart,
Son, lest hate bear no deadlier fruit than love.

ALTHÆA

O king, thou art wise, but wisdom halts; and just,
But the gods love not justice more than fate,
And smite the righteous and the violent mouth,   645
And mix with insolent blood the reverent man's,
And bruise the holier as the lying lips.
Enough; for wise words fail me, and my heart
Takes fire and trembles flamewise, O my son,
O child, for thine head's sake; mine eyes wax thick,   650
Turning toward thee, so goodly a weaponed man,
So glorious; and for love of thine own eyes
They are darkened, and tears burn them, fierce as fire,
And my lips pause and my soul sinks with love.
But by thine hand, by thy sweet life and eyes,   655
By thy great heart and these clasped knees, O son,
I pray thee that thou slay me not with thee.
For there was never a mother woman-born
Loved her sons better; and never a queen of men
More perfect in her heart toward whom she loved.   660
For what lies light on many and they forget,
Small things and transitory as a wind o' the sea,
I forget never; I have seen thee all thine years
A man in arms, strong and a joy to men
Seeing thine head glitter and thine hand burn its way   665
Through a heavy and iron furrow of sundering spears;
But always also a flower of three suns old,
The small one thing that lying drew down my life
To lie with thee and feed thee; a child and weak,
Mine, a delight to no man, sweet to me.   670

Who then sought to thee? who gat help? who knew
If thou wert goodly? nay, no man at all.
Or what sea saw thee, or sounded with thine oar,
Child? or what strange land shone with war through thee?
675   But fair for me thou wert, O little life,
Fruitless, the fruit of mine own flesh, and blind,
More than much gold, ungrown, a foolish flower.
For silver nor bright snow nor feather of foam
Was whiter, and no gold yellower than thine hair,
680   O child, my child; and now thou art lordlier grown,
Not lovelier, nor a new thing in mine eyes,
I charge thee by thy soul and this my breast,
Fear thou the gods and me and thine own heart,
Lest all these turn against thee; for who knows
685   What wind upon what wave of altering time
Shall speak a storm and blow calamity?
And there is nothing stabile in the world
But the gods break it; yet not less, fair son,
If but one thing be stronger, if one endure,
690   Surely the bitter and the rooted love
That burns between us, going from me to thee,
Shall more endure than all things.   What dost thou,
Following strange loves? why wilt thou kill mine heart?
Lo, I talk wild and windy words, and fall
695   From my clear wits, and seem of mine own self
Dethroned, dispraised, disseated; and my mind,
That was my crown, breaks, and mine heart is gone,
And I am naked of my soul, and stand
Ashamed, as a mean woman; take thou thought:
700   Live if thou wilt, and if thou wilt not, look,
The gods have given thee life to lose or keep,
Thou shalt not die as men die, but thine end
Fallen upon thee shall break me unaware.

MELEAGER

Queen, my whole heart is molten with thy tears,
705   And my limbs yearn with pity of thee, and love

Compels with grief mine eyes and labouring breath;
For what thou art I know thee, and this thy breast
And thy fair eyes I worship, and am bound
Toward thee in spirit and love thee in all my soul.
For there is nothing terribler to men   710
Than the sweet face of mothers, and the might.
But what shall be let be! for us the day
Once only lives a little, and is not found.
Time and the fruitful hour are more than we,
And these lay hold upon us; but thou, God,   715
Zeus, the sole steersman of the helm of things,
Father, be swift to see us, and as thou wilt
Help: or if adverse, as thou wilt, refrain.

CHORUS

We have seen thee, O Love, thou art fair; thou art goodly, O
    Love;
Thy wings make light in the air as the wings of a dove.   720
Thy feet are as winds that divide the stream of the sea;
Earth is thy covering to hide thee, the garment of thee.
Thou art swift and subtle and blind as a flame of fire;
Before thee the laughter, behind thee the tears of desire;
And twain go forth beside thee, a man with a maid;   725
Her eyes are the eyes of a bride whom delight makes afraid;
As the breath in the buds that stir is her bridal breath:
But Fate is the name of her; and his name is Death.

For an evil blossom was born
    Of sea-foam and the frothing of blood,   730
       Blood-red and bitter of fruit,
          And the seed of it laughter and tears,
    And the leaves of it madness and scorn;
      A bitter flower from the bud,
        Sprung of the sea without root,   735
          Sprung without graft from the years.

729. For the birth of Venus see notes to lines 48–49 of "Anactoria," in
Poems and Ballads.

The weft of the world was untorn
  That is woven of the day on the night,
  The hair of the hours was not white
740 Nor the raiment of time overworn,
    When a wonder, a world's delight,
  A perilous goddess was born;
    And the waves of the sea as she came
Clove, and the foam at her feet,
745   Fawning, rejoiced to bring forth
    A fleshly blossom, a flame
Filling the heavens with heat
    To the cold white ends of the north.

And in air the clamorous birds,
750   And men upon earth that hear
Sweet articulate words
    Sweetly divided apart,
    And in shallow and channel and mere
The rapid and footless herds,
755   Rejoiced, being foolish of heart.

For all they said upon earth,
  She is fair, she is white like a dove,
    And the life of the world in her breath
Breathes, and is born at her birth;
760   For they knew thee for mother of love,
    And knew thee not mother of death.

What hadst thou to do being born,
  Mother, when winds were at ease,
As a flower of the springtime of corn,
765   A flower of the foam of the seas?
For bitter thou wast from thy birth,
    Aphrodite, a mother of strife;
For before thee some rest was on earth,
    A little respite from tears,
770   A little pleasure of life;

For life was not then as thou art,
    But as one that waxeth in years
    Sweet-spoken, a fruitful wife;
      Earth had no thorn, and desire
No sting, neither death any dart;   775
    What hadst thou to do amongst these,
      Thou, clothed with a burning fire,
Thou, girt with sorrow of heart,
    Thou, sprung of the seed of the seas
As an ear from a seed of corn,   780
      As a brand plucked forth of a pyre,
As a ray shed forth of the morn,
    For division of soul and disease,
For a dart and a sting and a thorn?
What ailed thee then to be born?   785

Was there not evil enough,
    Mother, and anguish on earth
      Born with a man at his birth,
Wastes underfoot, and above
    Storm out of heaven, and dearth   790
Shaken down from the shining thereof,
      Wrecks from afar overseas
    And peril of shallow and firth,
      And tears that spring and increase
In the barren places of mirth,   795
That thou, having wings as a dove,
    Being girt with desire for a girth,
      That thou must come after these,
That thou must lay on him love?

Thou shouldst not so have been born: 800
    But death should have risen with thee,
      Mother, and visible fear,
        Grief, and the wringing of hands,
And noise of many that mourn;

805   The smitten bosom, the knee
          Bowed, and in each man's ear
           A cry as of perishing lands,
     A moan as of people in prison,
        A tumult of infinite griefs;
810   And thunder of storm on the sands,
          And wailing of wives on the shore;
    And under thee newly arisen
        Loud shoals and shipwrecking reefs,
         Fierce air and violent light;
815   Sail rent and sundering oar,
         Darkness, and noises of night;
   Clashing of streams in the sea,
     Wave against wave as a sword,
       Clamour of currents, and foam;
820   Rains making ruin on earth,
       Winds that wax ravenous and roam
   As wolves in a wolfish horde;
 Fruits growing faint in the tree,
     And blind things dead in their birth;
825   Famine, and blighting of corn,
      When thy time was come to be born.

  All these we know of; but thee
   Who shall discern or declare?
 In the uttermost ends of the sea
830   The light of thine eyelids and hair,
     The light of thy bosom as fire
      Between the wheel of the sun
   And the flying flames of the air?
      Wilt thou turn thee not yet nor have pity,
835 But abide with despair and desire
    And the crying of armies undone,
      Lamentation of one with another
    And breaking of city by city;
  The dividing of friend against friend,
840   The severing of brother and brother;

Wilt thou utterly bring to an end?
Have mercy, mother!

For against all men from of old
Thou hast set thine hand as a curse,
And cast out gods from their places.   845
These things are spoken of thee.
Strong kings and goodly with gold
Thou hast found out arrows to pierce,
And made their kingdoms and races
As dust and surf of the sea.   850
All these, overburdened with woes
And with length of their days waxen weak,
Thou slewest; and sentest moreover
Upon Tyro an evil thing,
Rent hair and a fetter and blows   855
Making bloody the flower of the cheek,
Though she lay by a god as a lover,
Though fair, and the seed of a king.
For of old, being full of thy fire,
She endured not longer to wear   860
On her bosom a saffron vest,
On her shoulder an ashwood quiver;
Being mixed and made one through desire
With Enipeus, and all her hair
Made moist with his mouth, and her breast   865
Filled full of the foam of the river.

[Enter Atalanta.]

---

854. *Tyro:* Daughter of Salmoneus, whose second wife abused her. She loved
to wander by the banks of the river Enipeus in Thessaly and fell in love with
the river god. Poseidon, god of the sea, fell in love with her and, disguising
himself as Enipeus, overcame her in a great wave. Their children were Aeson
and Pelias. The former was the father of Jason, the leader of the Argonauts
(see line 565 etc.).

860–862. That is, she disdained to continue to be a virgin and worshipper
of Artemis.

ATALANTA

Sun, and clear light among green hills, and day
Late risen and long sought after, and you just gods
Whose hands divide anguish and recompense,
870   But first the sun's white sister, a maid in heaven,
On earth of all maids worshipped—hail, and hear,
And witness with me if not without sign sent,
Not without rule and reverence, I a maid
Hallowed, and huntress holy as whom I serve,
875   Here in your sight and eyeshot of these men
Stand, girt as they toward hunting, and my shafts
Drawn; wherefore all ye stand up on my side,
If I be pure and all ye righteous gods,
Lest one revile me, a woman, yet no wife,
880   That bear a spear for spindle, and this bow strung
For a web woven; and with pure lips salute
Heaven, and the face of all the gods, and dawn
Filling with maiden flames and maiden flowers
The starless fold o' the stars, and making sweet
885   The warm wan heights of the air, moon-trodden ways
And breathless gates and extreme hills of heaven.
Whom, having offered water and bloodless gifts,
Flowers, and a golden circlet of pure hair,
Next Artemis I bid be favourable
890   And make this day all golden, hers and ours,
Gracious and good and white to the unblamed end.
But thou, O well-beloved, of all my days
Bid it be fruitful, and a crown for all,
To bring forth leaves and bind round all my hair
895   With perfect chaplets woven for thine of thee.
For not without the word of thy chaste mouth,
For not without law given and clean command,
Across the white straits of the running sea
From Elis even to the Acheloïan horn.

---

899. *Elis:* Division of Greece northwest of Arcadia. Swinburne has Atalanta
sail from Elis to the horn or point of land formed by the river Acheloüs (see
note to line 35).

I with clear winds came hither and gentle gods, 900
Far off my father's house, and left uncheered
Iasius, and uncheered the Arcadian hills
And all their green-haired waters, and all woods
Disconsolate, to hear no horn of mine
Blown, and behold no flash of swift white feet. 905

MELEAGER

For thy name's sake and awe toward thy chaste head,
O holiest Atalanta, no man dares
Praise thee, though fairer than whom all men praise,
And godlike for thy grace of hallowed hair
And holy habit of thine eyes, and feet 910
That make the blown foam neither swift nor white
Though the wind winnow and whirl it; yet we praise
Gods, found because of thee adorable
And for thy sake praiseworthiest from all men:
Thee therefore we praise also, thee as these, 915
Pure, and a light lit at the hand of gods.

[*Enter Toxeus and Plexippus.*]

TOXEUS

How long will ye whet spears with eloquence,
Fight, and kill beasts dry-handed with sweet words?
Cease, or talk still and slay thy boars at home.

PLEXIPPUS

Why, if she ride among us for a man, 920
Sit thou for her and spin; a man grown girl
Is worth a woman weaponed; sit thou here.

MELEAGER

Peace, and be wise; no gods love idle speech.

902. *Iasius:* Father of Atalanta.

PLEXIPPUS

Nor any man a man's mouth woman-tongued.

MELEAGER

925   For my lips bite not sharper than mine hands.

PLEXIPPUS

Nay, both bite soft, but no whit softly mine.

MELEAGER

Keep thine hands clean; they have time enough to stain.

PLEXIPPUS

For thine shall rest and wax not red to-day.

MELEAGER

Have all thy will of words; talk out thine heart.

ALTHÆA

930   Refrain your lips, O brethren, and my son,
        Lest words turn snakes and bite you uttering them.

TOXEUS

Except she give her blood before the gods,
What profit shall a maid be among men?

PLEXIPPUS

Let her come crowned and stretch her throat for a knife,
935   Bleat out her spirit and die, and so shall men
        Through her too prosper and through prosperous gods,
        But nowise through her living; shall she live
        A flower-bud of the flower-bed, or sweet fruit
        For kisses and the honey-making mouth,

And play the shield for strong men and the spear? 940
Then shall the heifer and her mate lock horns,
And the bride overbear the groom, and men
Gods; for no less division sunders these;
Since all things made are seasonable in time,
But if one alter unseasonable are all. 945
But thou, O Zeus, hear me that I may slay
This beast before thee and no man halve with me
Nor woman, lest these mock thee, though a god,
Who hast made men strong, and thou being wise be held
Foolish; for wise is that thing which endures. 950

ATALANTA

Men, and the chosen of all this people, and thou,
King, I beseech you a little bear with me.
For if my life be shameful that I live,
Let the gods witness and their wrath; but these
Cast no such word against me.   Thou, O mine, 955
O holy, O happy goddess, if I sin
Changing the words of women and the works
For spears and strange men's faces, hast not thou
One shaft of all thy sudden seven that pierced
Seven through the bosom or shining throat or side, 960
All couched about one mother's loosening knees,
All holy born, engraffed of Tantalus?
But if toward any of you I am overbold
That take thus much upon me, let him think
How I, for all my forest holiness, 965
Fame, and this armed and iron maidenhood,
Pay thus much also; I shall have no man's love
For ever, and no face of children born
Or feeding lips upon me or fastening eyes
For ever, nor being dead shall kings my sons 970

959. *One shaft of all thy sudden seven:* Niobe, daughter of Tantalus, boasted
that with seven sons and seven daughters she was more worthy than Leto, the
mother of Apollo and Artemis. In revenge Apollo slew the sons and Artemis
the daughters.

Mourn me and bury, and tears on daughters' cheeks
Burn; but a cold and sacred life, but strange,
But far from dances and the back-blowing torch,
Far off from flowers or any bed of man,
975   Shall my life be for ever: me the snows
That face the first o' the morning, and cold hills
Full of the land-wind and sea-travelling storms
And many a wandering wing of noisy nights
That know the thunder and hear the thickening wolves—
980   Me the utmost pine and footless frost of woods
That talk with many winds and gods, the hours
Re-risen, and white divisions of the dawn,
Springs thousand-tongued with the intermitting reed
And streams that murmur of the mother snow—
985   Me these allure, and know me; but no man
Knows, and my goddess only.   Lo now, see
If one of all you these things vex at all.
Would God that any of you had all the praise
And I no manner of memory when I die,
990   So might I show before her perfect eyes
Pure, whom I follow, a maiden to my death.
But for the rest let all have all they will;
For is it a grief to you that I have part,
Being woman merely, in your male might and deeds
995   Done by main strength? yet in my body is throned
As great a heart, and in my spirit, O men,
I have not less of godlike.   Evil it were
That one a coward should mix with you, one hand
Fearful, one eye abase itself; and these
1000   Well might ye hate and well revile, not me.
For not the difference of the several flesh
Being vile or noble or beautiful or base
Makes praiseworthy, but purer spirit and heart
Higher than these meaner mouths and limbs, that feed,
1005   Rise, rest, and are and are not; and for me,
What should I say? but by the gods of the world
And this my maiden body, by all oaths

That bind the tongue of men and the evil will,
I am not mighty-minded, nor desire
Crowns, nor the spoil of slain things nor the fame;   1010
Feed ye on these, eat and wax fat; cry out,
Laugh, having eaten, and leap without a lyre,
Sing, mix the wind with clamour, smite and shake
Sonorous timbrels and tumultuous hair,
And fill the dance up with tempestuous feet,   1015
For I will none; but having prayed my prayers
And made thank-offering for prosperities,
I shall go hence and no man see me more.
What thing is this for you to shout me down,
What, for a man to grudge me this my life   1020
As it were envious of all yours, and I
A thief of reputations? nay, for now,
If there be any highest in heaven, a god
Above all thrones and thunders of the gods
Throned, and the wheel of the world roll under him,   1025
Judge he between me and all of you, and see
If I transgress at all: but ye, refrain
Transgressing hands and reinless mouths, and keep
Silence, lest by much foam of violent words
And proper poison of your lips ye die.   1030

ŒNEUS

O flower of Tegea, maiden, fleetest foot
And holiest head of women, have good cheer
Of thy good words: but ye, depart with her
In peace and reverence, each with blameless eye
Following his fate; exalt your hands and hearts,   1035
Strike, cease not, arrow on arrow and wound on wound,
And go with gods and with the gods return.

[*Exit Althaea to the palace; the rest to the hunt.*]

1031. *Tegea:* City in southeast Arcadia.

CHORUS

Who hath given man speech? or who hath set therein
A thorn for peril and a snare for sin?
1040 For in the word his life is and his breath,
      And in the word his death,
That madness and the infatuate heart may breed
      From the word's womb the deed
And life bring one thing forth ere all pass by,
1045 Even one thing which is ours yet cannot die—
Death.   Hast thou seen him ever anywhere,
Time's twin-born brother, imperishable as he
Is perishable and plaintive, clothed with care
      And mutable as sand,
1050 But death is strong and full of blood and fair
And perdurable and like a lord of land?
Nay, time thou seest not, death thou wilt not see
Till life's right hand be loosened from thine hand
      And thy life-days from thee.
1055 For the gods very subtly fashion
      Madness with sadness upon earth:
Not knowing in any wise compassion,
      Nor holding pity of any worth;
And many things they have given and taken,
1060   And wrought and ruined many things;
The firm land have they loosed and shaken,
      And sealed the sea with all her springs;
They have wearied time with heavy burdens
      And vexed the lips of life with breath:
1065 Set men to labour and given them guerdons,
      Death, and great darkness after death:
Put moans into the bridal measure
      And on the bridal wools a stain;
And circled pain about with pleasure,
1070   And girdled pleasure about with pain;
And strewed one marriage-bed with tears and fire
For extreme loathing and supreme desire.

What shall be done with all these tears of ours?
   Shall they make watersprings in the fair heaven
To bathe the brows of morning? or like flowers   1075
Be shed and shine before the starriest hours,
   Or made the raiment of the weeping Seven?
Or rather, O our masters, shall they be
Food for the famine of the grievous sea,
   A great well-head of lamentation   1080
Satiating the sad gods? or fall and flow
Among the years and seasons to and fro,
   And wash their feet with tribulation
And fill them full with grieving ere they go?
   Alas, our lords, and yet alas again,   1085
Seeing all your iron heaven is gilt as gold
   But all we smite thereat in vain;
Smite the gates barred with groanings manifold,
   But all the floors are paven with our pain.
Yea, and with weariness of lips and eyes,   1090
With breaking of the bosom, and with sighs,
   We labour, and are clad and fed with grief
And filled with days we would not fain behold
And nights we would not hear of; we wax old,
   All we wax old and wither like a leaf.   1095
We are outcast, strayed between bright sun and moon;
   Our light and darkness are as leaves of flowers,
Black flowers and white, that perish; and the noon
   As midnight, and the night as daylight hours.
   A little fruit a little while is ours,   1100
     And the worm finds it soon.

But up in heaven the high gods one by one
   Lay hands upon the draught that quickeneth,
Fulfilled with all tears shed and all things done,

1077. *The weeping seven:* The Pleiades, seven sisters pursued by the giant
hunter Orion. They were turned by the gods into doves and placed among the
stars. The constellation Orion is near that of the Pleiades.

1105   And stir with soft imperishable breath
     The bubbling bitterness of life and death,
    And hold it to our lips and laugh; but they
    Preserve their lips from tasting night or day,
     Lest they too change and sleep, the fates that spun,
1110   The lips that made us and the hands that slay;
     Lest all these change, and heaven bow down to none,
    Change and be subject to the secular sway
    And terrene revolution of the sun.
    Therefore they thrust it from them, putting time away.

1115   I would the wine of time, made sharp and sweet
     With multitudinous days and nights and tears
     And many mixing savours of strange years,
    Were no more trodden of them under feet,
     Cast out and spilt about their holy places:
1120   That life were given them as a fruit to eat
    And death to drink as water; that the light
    Might ebb, drawn backward from their eyes, and night
     Hide for one hour the imperishable faces.
    That they might rise up sad in heaven, and know
1125   Sorrow and sleep, one paler than young snow,
     One cold as blight of dew and ruinous rain;
    Rise up and rest and suffer a little, and be
    Awhile as all things born with us and we,
     And grieve as men, and like slain men be slain.

1130   For now we know not of them; but one saith
     The gods are gracious, praising God; and one,
    When hast thou seen? or hast thou felt his breath
     Touch, nor consume thine eyelids as the sun,
    Nor fill thee to the lips with fiery death?
1135   None hath beheld him, none
    Seen above other gods and shapes of things,
    Swift without feet and flying without wings,
    Intolerable, not clad with death or life,
     Insatiable, not known of night or day,

The lord of love and loathing and of strife 1140
   Who gives a star and takes a sun away;
Who shapes the soul, and makes her a barren wife
   To the earthly body and grievous growth of clay;
Who turns the large limbs to a little flame
   And binds the great sea with a little sand; 1145
Who makes desire, and slays desire with shame;
   Who shakes the heaven as ashes in his hand;
Who, seeing the light and shadow for the same,
   Bids day waste night as fire devours a brand,
Smites without sword, and scourges without rod; 1150
   The supreme evil, God.

Yea, with thine hate, O God, thou hast covered us,
   One saith, and hidden our eyes away from sight,
And made us transitory and hazardous,
   Light things and slight; 1155
Yet have men praised thee, saying, He hath made man thus,
   And he doeth right.
Thou hast kissed us, and hast smitten; thou hast laid
Upon us with thy left hand life, and said,
Live: and again thou hast said, Yield up your breath, 1160
And with thy right hand laid upon us death.
Thou hast sent us sleep, and stricken sleep with dreams,
   Saying, Joy is not, but love of joy shall be;
Thou hast made sweet springs for all the pleasant streams,
   In the end thou hast made them bitter with the sea. 1165
Thou hast fed one rose with dust of many men;
   Thou hast marred one face with fire of many tears;
Thou hast taken love, and give us sorrow again;
   With pain thou hast filled us full to the eyes and ears.
Therefore because thou art strong, our father, and we 1170
   Feeble; and thou art against us, and thine hand
Constrains us in the shallows of the sea
   And breaks us at the limits of the land;
Because thou hast bent thy lightnings as a bow,
   And loosed the hours like arrows; and let fall 1175

Sins and wild words and many a wingèd woe
   And wars among us, and one end of all;
Because thou hast made the thunder, and thy feet
   Are as a rushing water when the skies
1180   Break, but thy face as an exceeding heat
   And flames of fire the eyelids of thine eyes;
Because thou art over all who are over us;
   Because thy name is life and our name death;
Because thou art cruel and men are piteous,
1185   And our hands labour and thine hand scattereth;
Lo, with hearts rent and knees made tremulous,
   Lo, with ephemeral lips and casual breath,
     At least we witness of thee ere we die
That these things are not otherwise, but thus;
1190   That each man in his heart sigheth, and saith,
     That all men even as I,
All we are against thee, against thee, O God most high.

   But ye, keep ye on earth
   Your lips from over-speech,
1195   Loud words and longing are so little worth;
   And the end is hard to reach.
For silence after grievous things is good,
   And reverence, and the fear that makes men whole,
And shame, and righteous governance of blood,
1200   And lordship of the soul.
But from sharp words and wits men pluck no fruit,
And gathering thorns they shake the tree at root;
   For words divide and rend;
But silence is most noble till the end.

[Enter Althaea.]

ALTHÆA

1205   I heard within the house a cry of news
   And came forth eastward hither, where the dawn

Cheers first these warder gods that face the sun
And next our eyes unrisen; for unaware
Came clashes of swift hoofs and trampling feet
And through the windy pillared corridor   1210
Light sharper than the frequent flames of day
That daily fill it from the fiery dawn;
Gleams, and a thunder of people that cried out,
And dust and hurrying horsemen; lo their chief,
That rode with Œneus rein by rein, returned.   1215
What cheer, O herald of my lord the king?

[*Enter Herald.*]

HERALD

Lady, good cheer and great; the boar is slain.

CHORUS

Praised be all gods that look toward Calydon.

ALTHÆA

Good news and brief; but by whose happier hand?

HERALD

A maiden's and a prophet's and thy son's.   1220

ALTHÆA

Well fare the spear that severed him and life.

HERALD

Thine own, and not an alien, hast thou blest.

ALTHÆA

Twice be thou too for my sake blest and his.

HERALD

As the king's word I rode afoam for thine.

ALTHÆA

1225   Thou sayest he tarrieth till they bring the spoil?

HERALD

Hard by the quarry, where they breathe, O queen.

ALTHÆA

Speak thou their chance; but some bring flowers and crown
These gods and all the lintel, and shed wine,
Fetch sacrifice and slay; for heaven is good.

HERALD

1230   Some furlongs northward where the brakes begin
West of that narrowing range of warrior hills
Whose brooks have bled with battle when thy son
Smote Acarnania, there all they made halt,
And with keen eye took note of spear and hound,
1235   Royally ranked; Lærtes island-born,
The young Gerenian Nestor, Panopeus,
And Cepheus and Ancæus, mightiest thewed,
Arcadians; next, and evil-eyed of these,
Arcadian Atalanta, with twain hounds
1240   Lengthening the leash, and under nose and brow
Glittering with lipless tooth and fire-swift eye;
But from her white braced shoulder the plumed shafts

1233. *Acarnania:* The west coast of Aetolia; haunt of pirates.
1235. *Lærtes:* King of Ithaca, an island off the coast of Acarnania (see line 1233), and father of Odysseus.
1236. *Nestor:* King of Pylos or Gerenia in Messenia. Later he was the wise old advisor of the Greeks at Troy. *Panopeus:* One of the heroes of the hunt named by Ovid.
1237. *Cepheus and Ancæus:* See note to lines 436–439.

Rang, and the bow shone from her side; next her
Meleager, like a sun in spring that strikes
Branch into leaf and bloom into the world,   1245
A glory among men meaner; Iphicles,
And following him that slew the biform bull
Pirithous, and divine Eurytion,
And, bride-bound to the gods, Æacides.
Then Telamon his brother, and Argive-born   1250
The seer and sayer of visions and of truth,
Amphiaraus; and a four-fold strength,
Thine, even thy mother's and thy sister's sons.
And recent from the roar of foreign foam
Jason, and Dryas twin-begot with war,   1255
A blossom of bright battle, sword and man
Shining; and Idas, and the keenest eye
Of Lynceus, and Admetus twice-espoused,
And Hippasus and Hyleus, great in heart.
These having halted bade blow horns, and rode   1260
Through woods and waste lands cleft by stormy streams,
Past yew-trees and the heavy hair of pines,

1246. *Iphicles:* Althaea's brother.
1247. *him that slew the biform bull:* Theseus, slayer of the Minotaur (see
note to "Phædra," in *Poems and Ballads*).
1248. *Pirithous:* King of the Lapithæ of Thessaly, who defeated the cen-
taurs and drove them from their district about Mount Helicon. *Eurytion:*
Properly Eurytus, king of Oechalia, city in east Aetolia. Eurytus, grandson of
Mars, taught Heracles the use of the bow.
1249. *Æacides:* Peleus, husband of the sea-nymph Thetis and father of
Achilles.
1250. *Telamon:* See note to line 429.
1252. *Amphiaraus:* Invited to take part of the expedition of the Seven
against Thebes, Amphiaraus at first refused, since he foresaw the failure of
the expedition and his own death.
1255. *Jason:* Recently returned from the expedition of the Argonauts (see
line 565). *Dryas:* a hero of Thrace and son of Ares, or Mars.
1257. *Idas:* Father of Kleopatra, Meleager's wife according to one version of
the legend.
1258. *Admetus:* Husband of Alcestis, who died, having sacrificed herself
that he might live, but was restored to life when Heracles defeated Thanatos,
the messenger of death.
1259. *Hippasus . . . Hyleus:* Heroes mentioned by Ovid.

And where the dew is thickest under oaks,
This way and that; but questing up and down
1265   They saw no trail nor scented; and one said,
Plexippus, Help, or help not, Artemis,
And we will flay thy boarskin with male hands;
But saying, he ceased and said not that he would,
Seeing where the green ooze of a sun-struck marsh
1270   Shook with a thousand reeds untunable,
And in their moist and multitudinous flower
Slept no soft sleep, with violent visions fed,
The blind bulk of the immeasurable beast.
And seeing, he shuddered with sharp lust of praise
1275   Through all his limbs, and launched a double dart.
And missed; for much desire divided him,
Too hot of spirit and feebler than his will,
That his hand failed, though fervent; and the shaft,
Sundering the rushes, in a tamarisk stem
1280   Shook, and stuck fast; then all abode save one,
The Arcadian Atalanta; from her side
Sprang her hounds, labouring at the leash, and slipped,
And plashed ear-deep with plunging feet; but she
Saying, Speed it as I send it for thy sake,
1285   Goddess, drew bow and loosed; the sudden string
Rang, and sprang inward, and the waterish air
Hissed, and the moist plumes of the songless reeds
Moved as a wave which the wind moves no more.
But the boar heaved half out of ooze and slime
1290   His tense flank trembling round the barbèd wound,
Hateful; and fiery with invasive eyes
And bristling with intolerable hair
Plunged, and the hounds clung, and green flowers and white
Reddened and broke all round them where they came.
1295   And charging with sheer tusk he drove, and smote
Hyleus; and sharp death caught his sudden soul,
And violent sleep shed night upon his eyes.
Then Peleus, with strong strain of hand and heart,
Shot; but the sidelong arrow slid, and slew

His comrade born and loving countryman, 1300
Under the left arm smitten, as he no less
Poised a like arrow; and bright blood brake afoam,
And falling, and weighed back by clamorous arms,
Sharp rang the dead limbs of Eurytion.
Then one shot happier, the Cadmean seer, 1305
Amphiaraus; for his sacred shaft
Pierced the red circlet of one ravening eye
Beneath the brute brows of the sanguine boar,
Now bloodier from one slain; but he so galled
Sprang straight, and rearing cried no lesser cry 1310
Than thunder and the roar of wintering streams
That mix their own foam with the yellower sea;
And as a tower that falls by fire in fight
With ruin of walls and all its archery,
And breaks the iron flower of war beneath, 1315
Crushing charred limbs and molten arms of men;
So through crushed branches and the reddening brake
Clamoured and crashed the fervour of his feet,
And trampled, springing sideways from the tusk,
Too tardy a moving mould of heavy strength, 1320
Ancæus; and as flakes of weak-winged snow
Break, all the hard thews of his heaving limbs
Broke, and rent flesh fell every way, and blood
Flew, and fierce fragments of no more a man.
Then all the heroes drew sharp breath, and gazed, 1325
And smote not; but Meleager, but thy son,
Right in the wild way of the coming curse
Rock-footed, fair with fierce and fastened lips,
Clear eyes, and springing muscle and shortening limb—
With chin aslant indrawn to a tightening throat, 1330
Grave, and with gathered sinews, like a god,—
Aimed on the left side his well-handled spear
Grasped where the ash was knottiest hewn, and smote,
And with no missile wound, the monstrous boar
Right in the hairiest hollow of his hide 1335
Under the last rib, sheer through bulk and bone,

Deep in; and deeply smitten, and to death,
The heavy horror with his hanging shafts
Leapt, and fell furiously, and from raging lips
1340   Foamed out the latest wrath of all his life.
And all they praised the gods with mightier heart,
Zeus and all gods, but chiefliest Artemis,
Seeing; but Meleager bade whet knives and flay,
Strip and stretch out the splendour of the spoil;
1345   And hot and horrid from the work all these
Sat, and drew breath and drank and made great cheer
And washed the hard sweat off their calmer brows.
For much sweet grass grew higher than grew the reed,
And good for slumber, and every holier herb,
1350   Narcissus, and the low-lying melilote,
And all of goodliest blade and bloom that springs
Were, hid by heavier hyacinth, violet buds
Blossom and burn; and fire of yellower flowers
And light of crescent lilies, and such leaves
1355   As fear the Faun's and know the Dryad's foot;
Olive and ivy and poplar dedicate,
And many a well-spring overwatched of these,
There now they rest; but me the king bade bear
Good tidings to rejoice this town and thee.
1360   Wherefore be glad, and all ye give much thanks,
For fallen is all the trouble of Calydon.

ALTHÆA

Laud ye the gods; for this they have given is good,
And what shall be they hide until their time.
Much good and somewhat grievous hast thou said,
1365   And either well; but let all sad things be,
Till all have made before the prosperous gods
Burnt-offering, and poured out the floral wine.

1350. *melilote:* Sweet clover.
1355. *Faun:* Latin equivalent of the Greek satyr (see, for example, line
104). *Dryads:* Tree-nymphs.

Look fair, O gods, and favourable; for we
Praise you with no false heart or flattering mouth,
Being merciful, but with pure souls and prayer.   1370

HERALD

Thou hast prayed well; for whoso fears not these,
But once being prosperous waxes huge of heart,
Him shall some new thing unaware destroy.

[*Exit Herald. Exit Althaea to the palace.*]

CHORUS

O that I now, I too were
By deep wells and water-floods,   1375
Streams of ancient hills, and where
All the wan green places bear
Blossoms cleaving to the sod,
Fruitless fruit, and grasses fair,
Or such darkest ivy-buds   1380
As divide thy yellow hair,
Bacchus, and their leaves that nod
Round thy fawnskin brush the bare
Snow-soft shoulders of a god;
There the year is sweet, and there   1385
Earth is full of secret springs,
And the fervent rose-cheeked hours,
Those that marry dawn and noon,
There are sunless, there look pale
In dim leaves and hidden air,   1390
Pale as grass or latter flowers
Or the wild vine's wan wet rings
Full of dew beneath the moon,
And all day the nightingale
Sleeps, and all night sings;   1395

1382. *Bacchus:* Dionysus, god of wine.

There in cold remote recesses
That nor alien eyes assail,
Feet, nor imminence of wings,
Nor a wind nor any tune,
1400   Thou, O queen and holiest,
Flower the whitest of all things,
With reluctant lengthening tresses
And with sudden splendid breast
Save of maidens unbeholden,
1405   There art wont to enter, there
Thy divine swift limbs and golden
Maiden growth of unbound hair,
Bathed in waters white,
Shine, and many a maid's by thee
1410   In moist woodland or the hilly
Flowerless brakes where wells abound
Out of all men's sight;
Or in lower pools that see
All their marges clothed all round
1415   With the innumerable lily,
Whence the golden-girdled bee
Flits through flowering rush to fret
White or duskier violet,
Fair as those that in far years
1420   With their buds left luminous
And their little leaves made wet,
From the warmer dew of tears,
Mother's tears in extreme need,
Hid the limbs of Iamus,
1425   Of thy brother's seed;
For his heart was piteous

1400. *Thou, O queen:* Artemis.
1424. *Iamus:* Son of Apollo by Evadne, who was forced to abandon her infant. He was tended by serpents until he was found by his grandfather. According to Pindar (*Olympian Ode* II, 55–56) he was sheltered by pansies or,
as here, the wild iris.
1425. *brother's seed:* Apollo's child.

Toward him, even as thine heart now
Pitiful toward us;
Thine, O goddess, turning hither
A benignant blameless brow;   1430
Seeing enough of evil done
And lives withered as leaves wither
In the blasting of the sun;
Seeing enough of hunters dead,
Ruin enough of all our year,   1435
Herds and harvests slain and shed,
Herdsmen stricken many an one,
Fruits and flocks consumed together,
And great length of deadly days.
Yet with reverent lips and fear   1440
Turn we toward thee, turn and praise
For this lightening of clear weather,
And prosperities begun.
For not seldom, when all air
As bright water without breath   1445
Shines, and when men fear not, fate
Without thunder unaware
Breaks, and brings down death.
Joy with grief ye great gods give,
Good with bad, and overbear   1450
All the pride of us that live,
All the high estate,
As ye long since overbore,
As in old time long before,
Many a strong man and a great,   1455
All that were.
But do thou, sweet, otherwise,
Having heed of all our prayer,
Taking note of all our sighs;
We beseech thee by thy light,   1460
By thy bow, and thy sweet eyes,
And the kingdom of the night,
Be thou favourable and fair;

By thine arrows and thy might
1465   And Orion overthrown;
By the maiden thy delight,
By the indissoluble zone
And the sacred hair.

*[Enter Messenger followed by huntsmen bearing the
bodies of Toxeus and Plexippus.]*

MESSENGER

Maidens, if ye will sing now, shift your song,
1470   Bow down, cry, wail for pity; is this a time
For singing? nay, for strewing of dust and ash,
Rent raiment, and for bruising of the breast.

CHORUS

What new thing wolf-like lurks behind thy words?
What snake's tongue in thy lips? what fire in the eyes?

MESSENGER

1475   Bring me before the queen and I will speak.

CHORUS

Lo, she comes forth as from thank-offering made.

MESSENGER

A barren offering for a bitter gift.

[Enter Althaea.]

1465. *Orion:* The giant son of earth, killed by Artemis, whom he challenged
to throw the discus against him, or because he attempted to violate one of her
maidens.
1467. *indissoluble zone:* Girdle not to be untied, or inviolable virginity.

ALTHÆA

What are these borne on branches, and the face
Covered? no mean men living, but now slain
Such honour have they, if any dwell with death.   1480

MESSENGER

Queen, thy twain brethren and thy mother's sons.

ALTHÆA

Lay down your dead till I behold their blood
If it be mine indeed, and I will weep.

MESSENGER

Weep if thou wilt, for these men shall no more.

ALTHÆA

O brethren, O my father's sons, of me   1485
Well loved and well reputed, I should weep
Tears dearer than the dear blood drawn from you
But that I know you not uncomforted,
Sleeping no shameful sleep, however slain,
For my son surely hath avenged you dead.   1490

MESSENGER

Nay, should thine own seed slay himself, O queen?

ALTHÆA

Thy double word brings forth a double death.

MESSENGER

Know this then singly, by one hand they fell.

ALTHÆA

What mutterest thou with thine ambiguous mouth?

MESSENGER

1495   Slain by thy son's hand; is that saying so hard?

ALTHÆA

Our time is come upon us: it is here.

CHORUS

O miserable, and spoiled at thine own hand.

ALTHÆA

Wert thou not called Meleager from this womb?

CHORUS

A grievous huntsman hath it bred to thee.

ALTHÆA

1500   Wert thou born fire, and shalt thou not devour?

CHORUS

The fire thou madest, will it consume even thee?

ALTHÆA

My dreams are fallen upon me; burn thou too.

CHORUS

Not without God are visions born and die.

ALTHÆA

The gods are many about me; I am one.

CHORUS

She groans as men wrestling with heavier gods.   1505

ALTHÆA

They rend me, they divide me, they destroy.

CHORUS

Or one labouring in travail of strange births.

ALTHÆA

They are strong, they are strong; I am broken, and these
    prevail.

CHORUS

The god is great against her; she will die.

ALTHÆA

Yea, but not now; for my heart too is great.   1510
I would I were not here in sight of the sun.
But thou, speak all thou sawest, and I will die.

MESSENGER

O queen, for queenlike hast thou borne thyself,
A little word may hold so great mischance.
For in division of the sanguine spoil   1515
These men thy brethren wrangling bade yield up
The boar's head and the horror of the hide
That this might stand a wonder in Calydon,
Hallowed; and some drew toward them; but thy son
With great hands grasping all that weight of hair   1520
Cast down the dead heap clanging and collapsed
At female feet, saying This thy spoil not mine,
Maiden, thine own hand for thyself hath reaped;

And all this praise God gives thee: she thereat
1525   Laughed, as when dawn touches the sacred night
The sky sees laugh and redden and divide
Dim lips and eyelids virgin of the sun,
Hers, and the warm slow breasts of morning heave,
Fruitful, and flushed with flame from lamp-lit hours,
1530   And maiden undulation of clear hair
Colour the clouds; so laughed she from pure heart,
Lit with a low blush to the braided hair,
And rose-coloured and cold like very dawn,
Golden and godlike, chastely with chaste lips,
1535   A faint grave laugh; and all they held their peace,
And she passed by them.   Then one cried Lo now,
Shall not the Arcadian shoot out lips at us,
Saying all we were despoiled by this one girl?
And all they rode against her violently
1540   And cast the fresh crown from her hair, and now
They had rent her spoil away, dishonouring her,
Save that Meleager, as a tame lion chafed,
Bore on them, broke them, and as fire cleaves wood
So clove and drove them, smitten in twain; but she
1545   Smote not nor heaved up hand; and this man first,
Plexippus, crying out This for love's sake, sweet,
Drove at Meleager, who with spear straightening
Pierced his cheek through; then Toxeus made for him,
Dumb, but his spear spake; vain and violent words,
1550   Fruitless; for him too stricken through both sides
The earth felt falling, and his horse's foam
Blanched thy son's face, his slayer; and these being slain,
None moved nor spake; but Œneus bade bear hence
These made of heaven infatuate in their deaths,
1555   Foolish; for these would baffle fate, and fell.
And they passed on, and all men honoured her,
Being honourable, as one revered of heaven.

[Exit Messenger.]

ALTHÆA

What say you, women? is all this not well done?

CHORUS

No man doth well but God hath part in him.

ALTHÆA

But no part here; for these my brethren born   1560
Ye have no part in, these ye know not of
As I that was their sister, a sacrifice
Slain in their slaying.   I would I had died for these;
For this man dead walked with me, child by child,
And made a weak staff for my feebler feet   1565
With his own tender wrist and hand, and held
And led me softly and shewed me gold and steel
And shining shapes of mirror and bright crown
And all things fair; and threw light spears, and brought
Young hounds to huddle at my feet and thrust   1570
Tame heads against my little maiden breasts
And please me with great eyes; and those days went
And these are bitter and I a barren queen
And sister miserable, a grievous thing
And mother of many curses; and she too,   1575
My sister Leda, sitting overseas
With fair fruits round her, and her faultless lord,
Shall curse me, saying A sorrow and not a son,
Sister, thou barest, even a burning fire,
A brand consuming thine own soul and me.   1580
But ye now, sons of Thestius, make good cheer,
For ye shall have such wood to funeral fire
As no king hath; and flame that once burnt down
Oil shall not quicken or breath relume or wine
Refresh again; much costlier than fine gold,   1585
And more than many lives of wandering men.

CHORUS

O queen, thou hast yet with thee love-worthy things,
Thine husband, and the great strength of thy son.

ALTHÆA

Who shall get brothers for me while I live?
1590   Who bear them? who bring forth in lieu of these?
Are not our fathers and our brethren one,
And no man like them? are not mine here slain?
Have we not hung together, he and I,
Flowerwise feeding as the feeding bees,
1595   With mother-milk for honey? and this man too,
Dead, with my son's spear thrust between his sides,
Hath he not seen us, later born than he,
Laugh with lips filled, and laughed again for love?
There were no sons then in the world, nor spears,
1600   Nor deadly births of women; but the gods
Allowed us, and our days were clear of these.
I would I had died unwedded, and brought forth
No swords to vex the world; for these that spake
Sweet words long since and loved me will not speak
1605   Nor love nor look upon me; and all my life
I shall not hear nor see them living men.
But I too living, how shall I now live?
What life shall this be with my son, to know
What hath been and desire what will not be,
1610   Look for dead eyes and listen for dead lips,
And kill mine own heart with remembering them,
And with those eyes that see their slayer alive
Weep, and wring hands that clasp him by the hand?
How shall I bear my dreams of them, to hear
1615   False voices, feel the kisses of false mouths
And footless sound of perished feet, and then
Wake and hear only it may be their own hounds
Whine masterless in miserable sleep,
And see their boar-spears and their beds and seats

And all the gear and housings of their lives 1620
And not the men? shall hounds and horses mourn,
Pine with strange eyes, and prick up hungry ears,
Famish and fail at heart for their dear lords,
And I not heed at all? and those blind things
Fall off from life for love's sake, and I live? 1625
Surely some death is better than some life,
Better one death for him and these and me
For if the gods had slain them it may be
I had endured it; if they had fallen by war
Or by the nets and knives of privy death 1630
And by hired hands while sleeping, this thing too
I had set my soul to suffer; or this hunt,
Had this despatched them under tusk or tooth
Torn, sanguine, trodden, broken; for all deaths
Or honourable or with facile feet avenged 1635
And hands of swift gods following, all save this,
Are bearable; but not for their sweet land
Fighting, but not a sacrifice, lo these
Dead; for I had not then shed all mine heart
Out at mine eyes; then either with good speed, 1640
Being just, I had slain their slayer atoningly,
Or strewn with flowers their fire and on their tombs
Hung crowns, and over them a song, and seen
Their praise outflame their ashes: for all men,
All maidens, had come thither, and from pure lips 1645
Shed songs upon them, from heroic eyes
Tears; and their death had been a deathless life;
But now, by no man hired nor alien sword,
By their own kindred are they fallen, in peace,
After much peril, friendless among friends, 1650
By hateful hands they loved; and how shall mine
Touch these returning red and not from war,
These fatal from the vintage of men's veins,
Dead men my brethren? how shall these wash off
No festal stains of undelightful wine, 1655
How mix the blood, my blood on them, with me,

Holding mine hand? or how shall I say, son,
That am no sister? but by night and day
Shall we not sit and hate each other, and think
1660   Things hate-worthy? not live with shamefast eyes,
Brow-beaten, treading soft with fearful feet,
Each unupbraided, each without rebuke
Convicted, and without a word reviled
Each of another? and I shall let thee live
1665   And see thee strong and hear men for thy sake
Praise me, but these thou wouldest not let live
No man shall praise for ever? these shall lie
Dead, unbeloved, unholpen, all through thee?
Sweet were they toward me living, and mine heart
1670   Desired them, but was then well satisfied,
That now is as men hungered; and these dead
I shall want always to the day I die.
For all things else and all men may renew;
Yea, son for son the gods may give and take,
1675   But never a brother or sister any more.

CHORUS

Nay, for the son lies close about thine heart,
Full of thy milk, warm from thy womb, and drains
Life and the blood of life and all thy fruit,
Eats thee and drinks thee as who breaks bread and eats,
1680   Treads wine and drinks, thyself, a sect of thee;
And if he feed not, shall not thy flesh faint?
Or drink not, are not thy lips dead for thirst?
This thing moves more than all things, even thy son,
That thou cleave to him; and he shall honour thee,
1685   Thy womb that bare him and the breasts he knew,
Reverencing most for thy sake all his gods.

ALTHÆA

But these the gods too gave me, and these my son,
Not reverencing his gods nor mine own heart

Nor the old sweet years nor all venerable things,
But cruel, and in his ravin like a beast, 1690
Hath taken away to slay them: yea, and she
She the strange woman, she the flower, the sword,
Red from spilt blood, a mortal flower to men,
Adorable, detestable—even she
Saw with strange eyes and with strange lips rejoiced, 1695
Seeing these mine own slain of mine own, and me
Made miserable above all miseries made,
A grief among all women in the world,
A name to be washed out with all men's tears.

CHORUS

Strengthen thy spirit; is this not also a god, 1700
Chance, and the wheel of all necessities?
Hard things have fallen upon us from harsh gods,
Whom lest worse hap rebuke we not for these.

ALTHÆA

My spirit is strong against itself, and I
For these things' sake cry out on mine own soul 1705
That it endures outrage, and dolorous days,
And life, and this inexpiable impotence.
Weak am I, weak and shameful; my breath drawn
Shames me, and monstrous things and violent gods.
What shall atone? what heal me? what bring back 1710
Strength to the foot, light to the face? what herb
Assuage me? what restore me? what release?
What strange thing eaten or drunken, O great gods,
Make me as you or as the beasts that feed,
Slay and divide and cherish their own hearts? 1715
For these ye show us; and we less than these
Have not wherewith to live as all these things
Which all their lives fare after their own kind
As who doth well rejoicing; but we ill,
Weeping or laughing, we whom eyesight fails, 1720

Knowledge and light of face and perfect heart,
And hands we lack, and wit; and all our days
Sin, and have hunger, and die infatuated.
For madness have ye given us and not health,
1725   And sins whereof we know not; and for these
Death, and sudden destruction unaware.
What shall we say now? what thing comes of us?

CHORUS

Alas, for all this all men undergo.

ALTHÆA

Wherefore I will not that these twain, O gods,
1730   Die as a dog dies, eaten of creeping things,
Abominable, a loathing; but though dead
Shall they have honour and such funereal flame
As strews men's ashes in their enemies' face
And blinds their eyes who hate them: lest men say,
1735   "Lo how they lie, and living had great kin,
And none of these hath pity of them, and none
Regards them lying, and none is wrung at heart,
None moved in spirit for them, naked and slain,
Abhorred, abased, and no tears comfort them:"
1740   And in the dark this grieve Eurythemis,
Hearing how these her sons come down to her
Unburied, unavenged, as kinless men,
And had a queen their sister. That were shame
Worse than this grief. Yet how to atone at all
1745   I know not; seeing the love of my born son,
A new-made mother's new-born love, that grows
From the soft child to the strong man, now soft
Now strong as either, and still one sole same love,
Strives with me, no light thing to strive withal;
1750   This love is deep, and natural to man's blood,
And ineffaceable with many tears.

1740. *Eurythemis:* See note to line 299.

Yet shall not these rebuke me though I die,
Nor she in that waste world with all her dead,
My mother, among the pale flocks fallen as leaves,
Folds of dead people, and alien from the sun;   1755
Nor lack some bitter comfort, some poor praise,
Being queen, to have borne her daughter like a queen,
Righteous; and though mine own fire burn me too,
She shall have honour and these her sons, though dead.
But all the gods will, all they do, and we   1760
Not all we would, yet somewhat; and one choice
We have, to live and do just deeds and die.

CHORUS

Terrible words she communes with, and turns
Swift fiery eyes in doubt against herself,
And murmurs as who talks in dreams with death.   1765

ALTHÆA

For the unjust also dieth, and him all men
Hate, and himself abhors the unrighteousness,
And seeth his own dishonour intolerable.
But I being just, doing right upon myself,
Slay mine own soul, and no man born shames me.   1770
For none constrains nor shall rebuke, being done,
What none compelled me doing; thus these things fare.
Ah, ah, that such things should so fare; ah me,
That I am found to do them and endure,
Chosen and constrained to choose, and bear myself   1775
Mine own wound through mine own flesh to the heart
Violently stricken, a spoiler and a spoil,
A ruin ruinous, fallen on mine own son.
Ah, ah, for me too as for these; alas,
For that is done that shall be, and mine hand   1780
Full of the deed, and full of blood mine eyes,
That shall see never nor touch anything
Save blood unstanched and fire unquenchable.

CHORUS

What wilt thou do? what ails thee? for the house
1785   Shakes ruinously; wilt thou bring fire for it?

ALTHÆA

Fire in the roofs, and on the lintels fire.
Lo ye, who stand and weave, between the doors,
There; and blood drips from hand and thread, and stains
Threshold and raiment and me passing in
1790   Flecked with the sudden sanguine drops of death.

CHORUS

Alas that time is stronger than strong men,
Fate than all gods: and these are fallen on us.

ALTHÆA

A little since and I was glad; and now
I never shall be glad or sad again.

CHORUS

1795   Between two joys a grief grows unaware.

ALTHÆA

A little while and I shall laugh; and then
I shall weep never and laugh not any more.

CHORUS

What shall be said? for words are thorns to grief.
Withhold thyself a little and fear the gods.

ALTHÆA

1800   Fear died when these were slain; and I am as dead,
And fear is of the living; these fear none.

CHORUS

Have pity upon all people for their sake.

ALTHÆA

It is done now; shall I put back my day?

CHORUS

An end is come, an end; this is of God.

ALTHÆA

I am fire, and burn myself; keep clear of fire.   1805

CHORUS

The house is broken, is broken; it shall not stand.

ALTHÆA

Woe, woe for him that breaketh; and a rod
Smote it of old, and now the axe is here.

[*Exit to the palace.*]

CHORUS

Not as with sundering of the earth
   Nor as with cleaving of the sea   1810
Nor fierce foreshadowings of a birth
   Nor flying dreams of death to be
Nor loosening of the large world's girth
And quickening of the body of night,
   And sound of thunder in men's ears   1815
And fire of lightning in men's sight,
   Fate, mother of desires and fears,

1806. *The house is broken:* The royal house of Calydon was eventually
wiped out, except for Deineira, who married Heracles.

Bore unto men the law of tears;
But sudden, an unfathered flame,
1820   And broken out of night, she shone,
She, without body, without name,
In days forgotten and forgone;
And heaven rang round her as she came
Like smitten cymbals, and lay bare;
1825   Clouds and great stars, thunders and snows,
The blue sad fields and folds of air,
The life that breathes, the life that grows,
All wind, all fire, that burns or blows,
Even all these knew her: for she is great;
1830   The daughter of doom, the mother of death,
The sister of sorrow; a lifelong weight
That no man's finger lighteneth,
Nor any god can lighten fate;
A landmark seen across the way
1835   Where one race treads as the other trod;
An evil sceptre, an evil stay,
Wrought for a staff, wrought for a rod,
The bitter jealously of God.

For death is deep as the sea,
1840   And fate as the waves thereof.
Shall the waves take pity on thee
Or the southwind offer thee love?
Wilt thou take the night for thy day
Or the darkness for light on thy way,
1845   Till thou say in thine heart Enough?
Behold, thou art over fair, thou art over wise;
The sweetness of spring in thine hair, and the light in thine
        eyes.
The light of the spring in thine eyes, and the sound in thine
        ears;
Yet thine heart shall wax heavy with sighs and thine eyelids
        with tears.
1850   Wilt thou cover thine hair with gold, and with silver thy
        feet?

Hast thou taken the purple to fold thee, and made thy mouth
    sweet?
Behold, when thy face is made bare, he that loved thee shall
    hate;
Thy face shall be no more fair at the fall of thy fate.
For thy life shall fall as a leaf and be shed as the rain;
And the veil of thine head shall be grief; and the crown shall   1855
    be pain.

[*Enter Althaea.*]

ALTHÆA

Ho, ye that wail, and ye that sing, make way
Till I be come among you.   Hide your tears,
Ye little weepers, and your laughing lips,
Ye laughers for a little; lo mine eyes
That outweep heaven at rainiest, and my mouth   1860
That laughs as gods laugh at us.   Fate's are we,
Yet fate is ours a breathing-space; yea, mine,
Fate is made mine for ever; he is my son,
My bedfellow, my brother.   You strong gods,
Give place unto me; I am as any of you,   1865
To give life and to take life.   Thou, old earth,
That has made man and unmade; thou whose mouth
Looks red from the eaten fruits of thine own womb;
Behold me with what lips upon what food
I feed and fill my body; even with flesh   1870
Made of my body.   Lo, the fire I lit
I burn with fire to quench it; yea, with flame
I burn up even the dust and ash thereof.

CHORUS

Woman, what fire is this thou burnest with?

ALTHÆA

Yea to the bone, yea to the blood and all.   1875

CHORUS

For this thy face and hair are as one fire.

ALTHÆA

A tongue that licks and beats upon the dust.

CHORUS

And in thine eyes are hollow light and heat.

ALTHÆA

Of flame not fed with hand or frankincense.

CHORUS

1880   I fear thee for the trembling of thine eyes.

ALTHÆA

Neither with love they tremble nor for fear.

CHORUS

And thy mouth shuddering like a shot bird.

ALTHÆA

Not as the bride's mouth when man kisses it.

CHORUS

Nay, but what thing is this thing thou hast done?

ALTHÆA

1885   Look, I am silent, speak your eyes for me.

CHORUS

I see a faint fire lightening from the hall.

ALTHÆA

Gaze, stretch your eyes, strain till the lids drop off.

CHORUS

Flushed pillars down the flickering vestibule.

ALTHÆA

Stretch with your necks like birds: cry, chirp as they.

CHORUS

And a long brand that blackens: and white dust.   1890

ALTHÆA

O children, what is this ye see? your eyes
Are blinder than night's face at fall of moon.
That is my son, my flesh, my fruit of life,
My travail, and the year's weight of my womb,
Meleager, a fire enkindled of mine hands   1895
And of mine hands extinguished; this is he.

CHORUS

O gods, what word has flown out at thy mouth?

ALTHÆA

I did this and I say this and I die.

CHORUS

Death stands upon the doorway of thy lips,
And in thy mouth has death set up his house.   1900

ALTHÆA

O death, a little, a little while, sweet death,
Until I see the brand burnt down and die.

CHORUS

She reels as any reed under the wind,
And cleaves unto the ground with staggering feet.

ALTHÆA

1905   Girls, one thing will I say and hold my peace.
        I that did this will weep not nor cry out,
        Cry ye and weep: I will not call on gods,
        Call ye on them; I will not pity man,
        Shew ye your pity.   I know not if I live;
1910   Save that I feel the fire upon my face
        And on my cheek the burning of a brand.
        Yea the smoke bites me, yea I drink the steam
        With nostril and with eyelid and with lip
        Insatiate and intolerant; and mine hands
1915   Burn, and fire feeds upon mine eyes; I reel
        As one made drunk with living, whence he draws
        Drunken delight; yet I, though mad for joy,
        Loathe my long living and am waxen red
        As with the shadow of shed blood; behold,
1920   I am kindled with the flames that fade in him,
        I am swollen with subsiding of his veins,
        I am flooded with his ebbing; my lit eyes
        Flame with the falling fire that leaves his lids
        Bloodless; my cheek is luminous with blood
1925   Because his face is ashen.   Yet, O child,
        Son, first-born, fairest—O sweet mouth, sweet eyes,
        That drew my life out through my suckling breast,
        That shone and clove mine heart through—O soft knees
        Clinging, O tender treadings of soft feet,
1930   Cheeks warm with little kissing—O child, child,
        What have we made each other?   Lo, I felt
        Thy weight cleave to me, a burden of beauty, O son,
        Thy cradled brows and loveliest loving lips,
        The floral hair, the little lightening eyes,
1935   And all thy goodly glory; with mine hands

Delicately I fed thee, with my tongue
Tenderly spake, saying, Verily in God's time,
For all the little likeness of thy limbs,
Son, I shall make thee a kingly man to fight,
A lordly leader; and hear before I die,   1940
"She bore the goodliest sword of all the world."
Oh! oh! For all my life turns round on me;
I am severed from myself, my name is gone,
My name that was a healing, it is changed,
My name is a consuming. From this time,   1945
Though mine eyes reach to the end of all these things,
My lips shall not unfasten till I die.

SEMICHORUS

She has filled with sighing the city,
   And the ways thereof with tears;
She arose, she girdled her sides,   1950
She set her face as a bride's;
She wept, and she had no pity;
   Trembled, and felt no fears.

SEMICHORUS

Her eyes were clear as the sun,
   Her brows were fresh as the day;   1955
She girdled herself with gold,
Her robes were manifold;
But the days of her worship are done,
   Her praise is taken away.

SEMICHORUS

For she set her hand to the fire,   1960
   With her mouth she kindled the same;
As the mouth of a flute-player,
So was the mouth of her;

1944. *My name:* Althaea refers to the Greek word for "heal," *althaiei.*

With the might of her strong desire
1965   She blew the breath of the flame.

SEMICHORUS

She set her hand to the wood,
    She took the fire in her hand;
As one who is nigh to death,
She panted with strange breath;
1970   She opened her lips unto blood,
    She breathed and kindled the brand.

SEMICHORUS

As a wood-dove newly shot,
    She sobbed and lifted her breast;
She sighed and covered her eyes,
1975   Filling her lips with sighs;
She sighed, she withdrew herself not,
    She refrained not, taking not rest;

SEMICHORUS

But as the wind which is drouth,
    And as the air which is death,
1980   As storm that severeth ships,
Her breath severing her lips,
The breath came forth of her mouth
    And the fire came forth of her breath.

[*Enter Second Messenger.*]

SECOND MESSENGER

Queen, and you maidens, there is come on us
1985   A thing more deadly than the face of death;
Meleager the good lord is as one slain.

SEMICHORUS

Without sword, without sword is he stricken;
Slain, and slain without hand.

SECOND MESSENGER

For as keen ice divided of the sun
His limbs divide, and as thawed snow the flesh   1990
Thaws from off all his body to the hair.

SEMICHORUS

He wastes as the embers quicken;
With the brand he fades as a brand.

SECOND MESSENGER

Even while they sang and all drew hither and he
Lifted both hands to crown the Arcadian's hair   1995
And fix the looser leaves, both hands fell down.

SEMICHORUS

With rending of cheek and of hair
Lament ye, mourn for him, weep.

SECOND MESSENGER

Straightway the crown slid off and smote on earth,
First fallen; and he, grasping his own hair, groaned   2000
And cast his raiment round his face and fell.

SEMICHORUS

Alas for visions that were,
And soothsayings spoken in sleep.

SECOND MESSENGER

But the king twitched his reins in and leapt down
2005 And caught him, crying out twice "O child" and thrice,
So that men's eyelids thickened with their tears.

SEMICHORUS

Lament with a long lamentation,
Cry, for an end is at hand.

SECOND MESSENGER

O son, he said, son, lift thine eyes, draw breath,
2010 Pity me; but Meleager with sharp lips
Gasped, and his face waxed like as sunburnt grass.

SEMICHORUS

Cry aloud, O thou kingdom, O nation,
O stricken, a ruinous land.

SECOND MESSENGER

Whereat king Œneus, straightening feeble knees,
2015 With feeble hands heaved up a lessening weight,
And laid him sadly in strange hands, and wept.

SEMICHORUS

Thou art smitten, her lord, her desire,
Thy dear blood wasted as rain.

SECOND MESSENGER

And they with tears and rendings of the beard
2020 Bear hither a breathing body, wept upon
And lightening at each footfall, sick to death.

SEMICHORUS

Thou madest thy sword as a fire,
  With fire for a sword thou art slain.

SECOND MESSENGER

And lo, the feast turned funeral, and the crowns
Fallen; and the huntress and the hunter trapped;   2025
And weeping and changed faces and veiled hair.

[*Enter Oeneus, Atlanta, and huntsmen carrying*
Meleager.]

MELEAGER

Let your hands meet
  Round the weight of my head;
Lift ye my feet
  As the feet of the dead;   2030
For the flesh of my body is molten, the limbs of it molten
  as lead.

CHORUS

O thy luminous face,
  Thine imperious eyes!
O the grief, O the grace,
  As of day when it dies!   2035
Who is this bending over thee, lord, with tears and suppres-
  sion of sighs?

MELEAGER

Is a bride so fair?
  Is a maid so meek?
With unchapleted hair,
  With unfilleted cheek,   2040
Atalanta, the pure among women, whose name is as blessing
  to speak.

ATALANTA

I would that with feet
Unsandalled, unshod,
Overbold, overfleet,
2045   I had swum not nor trod
From Arcadia to Calydon northward, a blast of the envy of
God.

MELEAGER

Unto each man his fate;
Unto each as he saith
In whose fingers the weight
2050   Of the world is as breath;
Yet I would that in clamour of battle mine hands had laid
upon death.

CHORUS

Not with cleaving of shields
And their clash in thine ear,
When the lord of fought fields
2055   Breaketh spearshaft from spear,
Thou art broken, our lord, thou art broken, with travail and
labour and fear.

MELEAGER

Would God he had found me
Beneath fresh boughs!
Would God he had bound me
2060   Unawares in mine house,
With light in mine eyes, and songs in my lips, and a crown
on my brows!

CHORUS

Whence art thou sent from us?
Whither thy goal?

How art thou rent from us,
Thou that wert whole,   2065
As with severing of eyelids and eyes, as with sundering of
body and soul!

MELEAGER

My heart is within me
As an ash in the fire;
Whosoever hath seen me,
Without lute, without lyre,   2070
Shall sing of me grievous things, even things that were ill to
desire.

CHORUS

Who shall raise thee
From the house of the dead?
Or what man praise thee
That thy praise may be said?   2075
Alas thy beauty! alas thy body! alas thine head!

MELEAGER

But thou, O mother,
The dreamer of dreams,
Wilt thou bring forth another
To feel the sun's beams   2080
When I move among shadows a shadow, and wail by impas-
sable streams?

ŒNEUS

What thing wilt thou leave me
Now this thing is done?
A man wilt thou give me,
A son for my son,   2085
For the light of mine eyes, the desire of my life, the desir-
able one?

CHORUS

Thou wert glad above others,
Yea, fair beyond word;
Thou wert glad among mothers;
For each man that heard
Of thee, praise there was added unto thee, as wings to the
feet of a bird.

ŒNEUS

Who shall give back
Thy face of old years
With travail made black,
Grown grey among fears,
Mother of sorrow, mother of cursing, mother of tears?

MELEAGER

Though thou art as fire
Fed with fuel in vain,
My delight, my desire,
Is more chaste than the rain,
More pure than the dewfall, more holy than stars are that
live without stain.

ATALANTA

I would that as water
My life's blood had thawn,
Or as winter's wan daughter
Leaves lowland and lawn
Spring-stricken, or ever mine eyes had beheld thee made dark
in thy dawn.

CHORUS

When thou dravest the men
Of the chosen of Thrace,
None turned him again

Nor endured he thy face 2110
Clothed round with the blush of the battle, with light from a
    terrible place.

CENEUS

Thou shouldst die as he dies
    For whom none sheddeth tears;
Filling thine eyes
    And fulfilling thine ears 2115
With the brilliance of battle, the bloom and the beauty, the
    splendour of spears.

CHORUS

In the ears of the world
    It is sung, it is told,
And the light thereof hurled
    And the noise thereof rolled 2120
From the Acroceraunian snow to the ford of the fleece of
    gold.

MELEAGER

Would God ye could carry me
    Forth of all these;
Heap sand and bury me
    By the Chersonese 2125
Where the thundering Bosphorus answers the thunder of
    Pontic seas.

2121. *Acroceraunian:* Mountains on the west shore of Epirus. *ford of the fleece of gold:* The Hellespont. When Phrixos and Helle were threatened with sacrificial death by their stepmother Ino, their mother, Nephele, a cloud-nymph, brought them a ram with a fleece of gold on which they fled Greece. Crossing from Europe to Asia, Helle fell into the straits and was drowned; but Phrixos reached Colchis safely (see lines 565–601).

2125–2126. *Chersonese:* Swinburne is inexact. The Chersonese is the European peninsula flanking the Hellespont at the south end of the Sea of Marmora (or Propontis) between Thrace and Phrygia. The Bosphorus is at the north end, opening from the Black Sea, or Euxine.

ŒNEUS

Dost thou mock at our praise
And the singing begun
And the men of strange days
2130   Praising my son
In the folds of the hills of home, high places of Calydon?

MELEAGER

For the dead man no home is;
Ah, better to be
What the flower of the foam is
2135   In fields of the sea,
That the sea-waves might be as my raiment, the gulf-stream
a garment for me.

CHORUS

Who shall seek thee and bring
And restore thee thy day,
When the dove dipt her wing
2140   And the oars won their way
Where the narrowing Symplegades whitened the straits of
Propontis with spray?

MELEAGER

Will ye crown me my tomb
Or exalt me my name,
Now my spirits consume,
2145   Now my flesh is a flame?
Let the sea slake it once, and men speak of me sleeping to
praise me or shame.

CHORUS

Turn back now, turn thee,
As who turns him to wake;

2141. *Symplegades:* See lines 597–599.   *Propontis:* Sea of Marmora, between the Hellespont and the Bosphous.

Though the life in thee burn thee,
Couldst thou bathe it and slake 2150
Where the sea-ridge of Helle hangs heavier, and east upon
west waters break?

MELEAGER

Would the winds blow me back
Or the waves hurl me home?
Ah, to touch in the track
Where the pine learnt to roam 2155
Cold girdles and crowns of the sea-gods, cool blossoms of
water and foam!

CHORUS

The gods may release
That they made fast;
Thy soul shall have ease
In thy limbs at the last; 2160
But what shall they give thee for life, sweet life that is over-
past?

MELEAGER

Not the life of men's veins,
Not of flesh that conceives;
But the grace that remains,
The fair beauty that cleaves 2165
To the life of the rains in the grasses, the life of the dews on
the leaves.

CHORUS

Thou wert helmsman and chief;
Wilt thou turn in an hour,
Thy limbs to the leaf,

2151. *Helle:* See note to line 2121.
2155. *the pine learnt to roam:* Ship masts were made of tall pine trees.

2170   Thy face to the flower,
                    Thy blood to the water, thy soul to the gods who divide and
                         devour?

                                       MELEAGER

                                    The years are hungry,
                                        They wail all their days;
                                    The gods wax angry
2175   And weary of praise;
                    And who shall bridle their lips? and who shall straiten their
                         ways?

                                        CHORUS

                                    The gods guard over us
                                        With sword and with rod;
                                    Weaving shadow to cover us,
2180   Heaping the sod,
                    That law may fulfil herself wholly, to darken man's face be-
                         fore God.

                                       MELEAGER

                    O holy head of Œneus, lo thy son
                    Guiltless, yet red from alien guilt, yet foul
                    With kinship of contaminated lives,
2185   Lo, for their blood I die; and mine own blood
                    For bloodshedding of mine is mixed therewith,
                    That death may not discern me from my kin.
                    Yet with clean heart I die and faultless hand,
                    Not shamefully; thou therefore of thy love
2190   Salute me, and bid fare among the dead
                    Well, as the dead fare; for the best man dead
                    Fares sadly; nathless I now faring well
                    Pass without fear where nothing is to fear
                    Having thy love about me and thy goodwill,
2195   O father, among dark places and men dead.

ŒNEUS

Child, I salute thee with sad heart and tears,
And bid thee comfort, being a perfect man
In fight, and honourable in the house of peace.
The gods give thee fair wage and dues of death,
And me brief days and ways to come at thee.   2200

MELEAGER

Pray thou thy days be long before thy death,
And full of ease and kingdom; seeing in death
There is no comfort and none aftergrowth,
Nor shall one thence look up and see day's dawn
Nor light upon the land whither I go.   2205
Live thou and take thy fill of days and die
When thy day comes; and make not much of death
Lest ere thy day thou reap an evil thing.
Thou too, the bitter mother and mother-plague
Of this my weary body—thou too, queen,   2210
The source and end, the sower and the scythe,
The rain that ripens and the drought that slays,
The sand that swallows and the spring that feeds,
To make me and unmake me—thou, I say,
Althæa, since my father's ploughshare, drawn   2215
Through fatal seedland of a female field,
Furrowed thy body, whence a wheaten ear
Strong from the sun and fragrant from the rains
I sprang and cleft the closure of thy womb,
Mother, I dying with unforgetful tongue   2220
Hail thee as holy and worship thee as just
Who art unjust and unholy; and with my knees
Would worship, but thy fire and subtlety,
Dissundering them, devour me; for these limbs
Are as light dust and crumblings from mine urn   2225
Before the fire has touched them; and my face
As a dead leaf or dead foot's mark on snow,
And all this body a broken barren tree

That was so strong, and all this flower of life
2230   Disbranched and desecrated miserably,
And minished all that god-like muscle and might
And lesser than a man's: for all my veins
Fail me, and all mine ashen life burns down.
I would thou hadst let me live; but gods averse,
2235   But fortune, and the fiery feet of change,
And time, these would not, these tread out my life,
These and not thou; me too thou hast loved, and I
Thee; but this death was mixed with all my life,
Mine end with my beginning: and this law,
2240   This only, slays me, and not my mother at all.
And let no brother or sister grieve too sore,
Nor melt their hearts out on me with their tears,
Since extreme love and sorrowing overmuch
Vex the great gods, and overloving men
2245   Slay and are slain for love's sake; and this house
Shall bear much better children; why should these
Weep? but in patience let them live their lives
And mine pass by forgotten: thou alone,
Mother, thou sole and only, thou not these,
2250   Keep me in mind a little when I die
Because I was thy first-born; let thy soul
Pity me, pity even me gone hence and dead,
Though thou wert wroth, and though thou bear again
Much happier sons, and all men later born
2255   Exceedingly excel me; yet do thou
Forget not, nor think shame; I was thy son.
Time was I did not shame thee; and time was
I thought to live and make thee honourable
With deeds as great as these men's; but they live,
2260   These, and I die; and what thing should have been
Surely I know not; yet I charge thee, seeing
I am dead already, love me not the less,
Me, O my mother; I charge thee by these gods,
My father's, and that holier breast of thine,
2265   By these that see me dying, and that which nursed,

Love me not less, thy first-born: though grief come,
Grief only, of me, and of all these great joy,
And shall come always to thee; for thou knowest,
O mother, O breasts that bare me, for ye know,
O sweet head of my mother, sacred eyes,   2270
Ye know my soul albeit I sinned, ye know
Albeit I kneel not neither touch thy knees,
But with my lips I kneel, and with my heart
I fall about thy feet and worship thee.
And ye farewell now, all my friends; and ye,   2275
Kinsmen, much younger and glorious more than I,
Sons of my mother's sister; and all farewell
That were in Colchis with me, and bare down
The waves and wars that met us: and though times
Change, and though now I be not anything,   2280
Forget not me among you, what I did
In my good time; for even by all those days,
Those days and this, and your own living souls,
And by the light and luck of you that live,
And by this miserable spoil, and me   2285
Dying, I beseech you, let my name not die.
But thou, dear, touch me with thy rose-like hands,
And fasten up mine eyelids with thy mouth,
A bitter kiss; and grasp me with thine arms,
Printing with heavy lips my light waste flesh,   2290
Made light and thin by heavy-handed fate,
And with thine holy maiden eyes drop dew,
Drop tears for dew upon me who am dead,
Me who have loved thee; seeing without sin done
I am gone down to the empty weary house   2295
Where no flesh is nor beauty nor swift eyes
Nor sound of mouth nor might of hands and feet.
But thou, dear, hide my body with thy veil,
And with thy raiment cover foot and head,

2277. *Kinsmen:* Castor and Pollux (see note to line 299).
2278. *all . . . That were in Colchis:* The Argonauts who came to the Calydonian hunt (see lines 565–601).

2300   And stretch thyself upon me and touch hands
        With hands and lips with lips: be pitiful
        As thou art maiden perfect; let no man
        Defile me to despise me, saying, This man
        Died woman-wise, a woman's offering, slain
2305   Through female fingers in his woof of life,
        Dishonourable; for thou hast honoured me.
        And now for God's sake kiss me once and twice
        And let me go; for the night gathers me,
        And in the night shall no man gather fruit.

                        ATALANTA

2310   Hail thou: but I with heavy face and feet
        Turn homeward and am gone out of thine eyes.

                                        [*Exit.*]

                        CHORUS

        Who shall contend with his lords
            Or cross them or do them wrong?
        Who shall bind them as with cords?
2315   Who shall tame them as with song?
        Who shall smite them as with swords?
            For the hands of their kingdom are strong.

APPENDICES

Cleopatra

'*Her beauty might outface the jealous hours,*
Turn shame to love and pain to a tender sleep,
And the strong nerve of hate to sloth and tears;
Make spring rebellious in the sides of frost,
Thrust out lank water with hot August growths,
Compel sweet blood into the husks of death,
And from strange beasts enforce harsh courtesy.'
T. HAYMAN, Fall of Antony, 1655.

I

HER mouth is fragrant as a vine,
  A vine with birds in all its boughs;
Serpent and scarab for a sign
  Between the beauty of her brows
And the amorous deep lids divine.

II

Her great curled hair makes luminous
  Her cheeks, her lifted throat and chin.
Shall she not have the hearts of us
  To shatter, and the loves therein
To shred between her fingers thus?

III

Small ruined broken strays of light,
  Pearl after pearl she shreds them through

First published in *The Cornhill Magazine*, September, 1866 (pp. 331–333) and not included in a collected edition until 1912, after Swinburne's death, this poem is printed here because it may be considered as the last of the studies of eroticism to which *Poems and Ballads* was principally devoted.

Her long sweet sleepy fingers, white
   As any pearl's heart veined with blue,
And soft as dew on a soft night.

IV

As if the very eyes of love
   Shone through her shutting lids, and stole
The slow looks of a snake or dove;
   As if her lips absorbed the whole
Of love, her soul the soul thereof.

V

Lost, all the lordly pearls that were
   Wrung from the sea's heart, from the green
Coasts of the Indian gulf-river;
   Lost, all the loves of the world—so keen
Towards this queen for love of her.

VI

You see against her throat the small
   Sharp glittering shadows of them shake;
And through her hair the imperial
   Curled likeness of the river snake,
Whose bite shall make an end of all.

VII

Through the scales sheathing him like wings,
   Through hieroglyphs of gold and gem,
The strong sense of her beauty stings,
   Like a keen pulse of love in them,
A running flame through all his rings.

VIII

Under those low large lids of hers
   She hath the histories of all time;

The fruit of foliage-stricken years;
   The old seasons with their heavy chime
That leaves its rhyme in the world's ears.

IX

She sees the hand of death made bare,
   The ravelled riddle of the skies,
The faces faded that were fair,
   The mouths made speechless that were wise,
The hollow eyes and dusty hair;

X

The shape and shadow of mystic things,
   Things that fate fashions or forbids;
The staff of time-forgotten Kings
   Whose name fall off the Pyramids,
Their coffin-lids and grave-clothings;

XI

Dank dregs, the scum of pool or clod,
   God-spawn of lizard-footed clans,
And those dog-headed hulks that trod
   Swart necks of the old Egyptians,
Raw draughts of man's beginning God;

XII

The poised hawk, quivering ere he smote,
   With plume-like gems on breast and back;
The asps and water-worms afloat
   Between the rush-flowers moist and slack;
The cat's warm black bright rising throat.

XIII

The purple days of drouth expand
   Like a scroll opened out again;

The molten heaven drier than sand,
    The hot red heaven without rain,
Sheds iron pain on the empty land.

XIV

All Egypt aches in the sun's sight;
    The lips of men are harsh for drouth,
The fierce air leaves their cheeks burnt white,
    Charred by the bitter blowing south,
Whose dusty mouth is sharp to bite.

XV

All this she dreams of, and her eyes
    Are wrought after the sense hereof.
There is no heart in her for sighs;
    The face of her is more than love—
A name above the Ptolemies.

XVI

Her great grave beauty covers her
    As that sleek spoil beneath her feet
Clothed once the anointed soothsayer;
    The hallowing is gone forth from it
Now, made unmeet for priests to wear.

XVII

She treads on gods and god-like things,
    On fate and fear and life and death,
On hate that cleaves and love that clings,
    All that is brought forth of man's breath
And perisheth with what it brings.

XVIII

She holds her future close, her lips
    Hold fast the face of things to be;

Actium, and sound of war that dips
   Down the blown valleys of the sea,
Far sails that flee, and storms of ships;

XIX

The laughing red sweet mouth of wine
   At ending of life's festival;
That spice of cerecloths, and the fine
   White bitter dust funereal
Sprinkled on all things for a sign;

XX

His face, who was and was not he,
   In whom, alive, her life abode;
The end, when she gained heart to see
   Those ways of death wherein she trod,
Goddess by god, with Antony.

Swinburne's Publications Through 1867

1857

"William Congreve," *The Imperial Dictionary of Universal Biography*, p. 1107.

"The Early English Dramatists. No. I" [Christopher Marlowe and John Webster], *Undergraduate Papers*, No. I (Dec. 1857), pp. 7–15.

Queen Yseult. Canto I. *Undergraduate Papers*, No. I (Dec. 1857), pp. 41–50.

1858

"The Monomaniac's Tragedy, and Other Poems. (By Ernest Wheldrake, author of 'Eve, a Mystery.' London, 1858.)," *Undergraduate Papers*, No. II, March 1858, pp. 97–102. [A parodic review of an imaginary author.]

"Church Imperialism," *Undergraduate Papers*, No. III, April 1858, pp. 134–137.

1860

The Queen-Mother. Rosamond. Two Plays. [Published by Basil Montagu Pickering in December 1860, and immediately withdrawn and at once re-issued by Edward Moxon & Co.]

1862

"The Fratricide," *Once a Week*, Feb. 1862, pp. 215–216. [Reprinted in *Poems and Ballads* as "The Bloody Son."]

"Victor Hugo's New Novel" [*Les Misérables*], *The Spectator*, April 12, 1862, pp. 215–216.

"A Song in Time of Order," *The Spectator*, April 26, 1862, p. 466. [Reprinted in *Poems and Ballads.*]

"Before Parting," *The Spectator*, May 17, 1862, p. 550. [Reprinted in *Poems and Ballads.*]

"After Death," *The Spectator*, May 24, 1862, pp. 578–579. [Reprinted in *Poems and Ballads.*]

"Faustine," *The Spectator*, May 31, 1862, pp. 606–607. [Reprinted in *Poems and Ballads.*]

"*Les Misérables*. Part II and III," *The Spectator*, June 21, 1862, pp. 694–695.

"A Song in Time of Revolution, 1860," *The Spectator*, June 28, 1862, p. 718. [Reprinted in *Poems and Ballads.*]

"The Sundew," *The Spectator*, July 26, 1862, p. 830. [Reprinted, revised, in *Poems and Ballads.*]

"*Les Misérables*. Part IV," *The Spectator*, August 16, 1862, pp. 831–832.

"*Les Misérables*. Part V," *The Spectator*, August 16, 1862, pp. 915–916.

"August," *The Spectator*, Sept. 6, 1862, p. 997. [Reprinted in *Poems and Ballads.*]

Charles Baudelaire: *Les Fleurs du Mal*," *The Spectator*, Sept. 6, 1862, pp. 998–1000.

"Dead Love," *Once a Week*, Oct. 1862, pp. 432–434.

"Victor Hugo's Philosophy," *The Spectator*, Oct. 25, 1862, pp. 1193–1195.

1864

"A Pilgrimage of Pleasure," in *The Children of the Chapel*, 1864. (A verse play included in a story by his cousin, Mary Gordon. Published anonymously, until the third edition, 1912).

1865

Atalanta in Calydon. A Tragedy, London: Edward Moxon & Co. [Published in March 1865. Further editions in 1865, 1866, 1868, 1875].

Chastelard: A Tragedy, London, Edward Moxon & Co. [Published Nov. 1865.]

"Gentle Spring," *The Royal Academy Catalogue,* 1865.

"The Little White Girl," *The Royal Academy Catalogue,* 1865. [Reprinted in *Poems and Ballads.*]

1866

"Prefatory Essay," *A Selection from the Works of Lord Byron.* Edited and prefaced by Algernon Charles Swinburne, London, Edward Moxon & Co., 1866. [Published Feb. 1866.]

Poems and Ballads, London, Edward Moxon & Co. [Published about July 16, 1866 by Moxon, withdrawn by August 10, and republished in September by John Camden Hotten.]

"Cleopatra," *The Cornhill Magazine,* September 1866, pp. 331–333.

Notes on Poems and Reviews, London, John Camden Hotten, 1866. [Published late October, 1866.]

1867

"Child's Song in Winter," *The Fortnightly Review,* January 1867, pp. 19–20. [Reprinted in *Poems and Ballads, Second Series,* 1878.]

"Ode on the Insurrection in Candia," *The Fortnightly Review,* March 1867, pp. 284–289. [Reprinted in *Songs before Sunrise,* 1871.]

"Morris's *Life and Death of Jason,*" *The Fortnightly Review,* July 1867, pp. 19–28.

"Regret," *The Fortnightly Review,* September 1867, p. 271. [Reprinted, revised, in *Poems and Ballads, Second Series,* 1878.]

"Matthew Arnold's *New Poems,*" *The Fortnightly Review,* October 1867, pp. 414–415.

"The Halt Before Rome, September 1867," *The Fortnightly Review*, September 1867. [Reprinted in *Songs before Sunrise*, 1871.]

"An Appeal to England," *The Morning Star*, November 22, 1867. [Reprinted in *Songs before Sunrise*, 1871.]

"A Lost Vigil," *The Fortnightly Review*, December 1867, pp. 671–672. [Reprinted as "A Wasted Vigil," *Poems and Ballads, Second Series*, 1878.]

William Blake: A Critical Essay, London, John Camden Hotten, 1868. [Published December 1867.]

Poems Omitted From the Present Edition of Poems and Ballads

This is the list in Swinburne's letter to Andrew Chatto of his publishing firm Chatto & Windus. *The Swinburne Letters*, ed. Cecil Y. Lang, New Haven, 1860, III, 199–200.

The Leper

Rondel

Song in Time of Order

Song in Time of Revolution

Before Parting

The Sundew

At Eleusis

August

A Christmas Carol

The Masque of Queen Bersabe

St. Dorothy

The Two Dreams

Aholibah

After Death

May Janet

The Sea-Swallows

The Year of Love

Appendix 4

Dates of Composition of Poems in This Edition

Listed are only those poems for which there is some certainty about the date.

1862

A Ballad of Life, A Ballad of Death, Laus Veneris, Hymn to Proserpine, Ilicet, A Match, Faustine, A Cameo, Stage Love, A Ballad of Burdens

1863

The Triumph of Time, Anactoria, Hermaphroditus

Autumn 1863–September 1864

Atalanta in Calydon

1864

Itylus, Rococo, In Memory of W. S. Landor

1865

Before the Mirror, To Victor Hugo, Dolores, Hesperia, Félise, Hendecasyllabics, Dedication

Charles Baudelaire*

IT is now some time since France has turned out any new poet of very high note or importance; the graceful, slight, and somewhat thin-spun classical work of M. Théodore de Banville hardly carries weight enough to tell across the Channel; indeed, the best of this writer's books, in spite of exquisite humorous character and a most flexible and brilliant style, is too thoroughly Parisian to bear transplanting at all. French poetry of the present date, taken at its highest, is not less effectually hampered by tradition and the taste of the greater number of readers than our own is. A French poet is expected to believe in philanthropy, and break off on occasion in the middle of his proper work to lend a shove forward to some theory of progress. The critical students there, as well as here, judging by the books they praise and the advice they proffer, seem to have pretty well forgotten that a poet's business is presumably to write good verses, and by no means to redeem the age and remould society. No other form of art is so pestered with this impotent appetite for meddling in quite extraneous matters; but the mass of readers seem actually to think that a poem is the better for containing a moral lesson or assisting in a tangible and material good work. The courage and sense of a man who at such a time ventures to profess and act on the conviction that the art of poetry has absolutely nothing to do with didactic matter at all, are proof enough of the wise and serious manner in which he is likely to handle the materials of

---

* *Les Fleurs du Mal*, par Charles Baudelaire. Édition augmentée de beaucoup de poèmes, et diminuée de six pièces. 1861.

From *The Spectator*, September 6, 1862. The text is taken from the Bonchurch edition.

his art. From a critic who has put forward the just and sane view of this matter with a consistent eloquence, one may well expect to get as perfect and careful poetry as he can give.

To some English readers the name of M. Baudelaire may be known rather through his admirable translations, and the criticisms on American and English writers appended to these, and framing them in fit and sufficient commentary, than by his volume of poems, which, perhaps, has hardly yet had time to make its way among us. That it will in the long run fail of its meed of admiration, whether here or in France, we do not believe. Impeded at starting by a foolish and shameless prosecution, the first edition was, it appears, withdrawn before anything like a fair hearing had been obtained for it. The book now comes before us with a few of the original poems cancelled, but with important additions. Such as it now is, to sum up the merit and meaning of it is not easy to do in a few sentences. Like all good books, and all work of any original savour and strength, it will be long a debated point of argument, vehemently impugned and eagerly upheld.

We believe that M. Baudelaire's first publications were his essays on the contemporary art of France, written now many years since. In these early writings there is already such admirable judgment, vigour of thought and style, and appreciative devotion to the subject, that the worth of his own future work in art might have been foretold even then. He has more delicate power of verse than almost any man living, after Victor Hugo, Browning, and (in his lyrics) Tennyson. The sound of his metres suggests colour and perfume. His perfect workmanship makes every subject admirable and respectable. Throughout the chief part of this book he has chosen to dwell mainly upon sad and strange things—the weariness of pain and the bitterness of pleasure—the perverse happiness and wayward sorrows of exceptional people. It has the languid, lurid beauty of close and threatening weather—a heavy, heated temperature, with dangerous hothouse scents in it; thick shadow of cloud about it, and fire of molten light. It is quite clear of all whining and windy lamentation; there is nothing of the bubbling and shrieking style long since exploded. The writer delights in problems, and has a natural leaning to obscure and sorrowful things. Failure and sorrow, next to physical beauty and perfection of sound or scent, seem to have an infinite attraction for him. In some points he resembles Keats, or still more his chosen favourite among modern poets, Edgar Poe; at times, too, his manner of thought has a relish of Marlowe, and even the sincerer side of Byron. From Théophile Gautier, to whom the book is dedicated, he has caught the habit of a faultless and studious simplicity; but, indeed, it seems merely natural to him always to use the right word and the right rhyme. How supremely musical and flexible a perfect artist in writing can make the French language, any chance page of the book is enough to prove; every description, the slightest and shortest even, has a special mark on it of the writer's keen and peculiar power. The style is sensuous and weighty; the sights seen are steeped most often in sad light and sullen colour.

As instances of M. Baudelaire's strength and beauty of manner, one might take especially the poems headed *Le Masque, Parfum Exotique, La Chevelure, Les Sept Vieillards, Les Petites Vieilles, Brumes et Pluies*; of his perfect mastery in description, and sharp individual drawing of character and form, the following stray verses plucked out at random may stand for a specimen:—

> Sur ta chevelure profonde
> Aux âcres parfums,
> Mer odorante et vagabonde
> Aux flots bleus et bruns,
>
> Comme un navire qui s'éveille
> Au vent du matin,
> Mon âme rêveuse appareille
> Pour un ciel lointain.
>
> Tes yeux où rien ne se révèle
> De doux ni d'amer,
> Sont deux bijoux froids où se mêle
> L'or avec le fer.

.   .   .   .   .

> Et ton corps se penche et s'allonge
> Comme un fin vaisseau
> Qui roule bord sur bord et plonge
> Ses vergues dans l'eau.[1]

The whole poem is worth study for its vigorous beauty and the careful facility of its expression. Perhaps, though, the sonnet headed _Causerie_ is a still completer specimen of the author's power. The way in which the sound and sense are suddenly broken off and shifted, four lines from the end, is wonderful for effect and success. M. Baudelaire's mastery of the sonnet-form is worth remarking as a test of his natural bias towards such forms of verse as are most nearly capable of perfection. In a book of this sort, such a leaning of the writer's mind is almost necessary. The matters treated of will bear no rough or hasty handling. Only supreme excellence of words will suffice to grapple with and fitly render the effects of such material. Not the luxuries of pleasure in their simple first form, but the sharp and cruel enjoyments of pain, the acrid relish of suffering felt or inflicted, the sides on which nature looks unnatural, go to make up the stuff and substance of this poetry. Very good material they make, too; but evidently such things are unfit for rapid or careless treatment. The main charm of the book is, upon the whole, that nothing is wrongly given, nothing capable of being re-written or improved on its own ground. Concede the starting point, and you cannot have a better runner.

Thus, even of the loathsomest bodily putrescence and decay he can make some noble use; pluck out its meaning and secret, even its beauty, in a certain way, from actual carrion; as here, of the flies bred in a carcase:—

> Tout cela descendait, montait comme une vague,
> Ou s'élançait en pétillant;

[1] "_Le Serpent qui danse_," "The Dancing Serpent": On your deep hair, with its sharp perfumes, an odorous and vagabond sea of blue and dark waves, like a vessel which awakes to the wind of the morning, my dreaming soul readies itself for a distant sky. Your eyes in which nothing either sweet or bitter is revealed are two cold jewels in which gold and iron mix themselves. . . . And your body bends and stretches like a slender ship that rolls from side to side and plunges its yards into the water.

On eût dit que le corps, enflé d'un souffle vague,
Vivait en se multipliant.

Et ce monde rendait une étrange musique,
Comme l'eau courante et le vent,
Ou le grain qu'un vanneur d'un mouvement rhythmique
Agite et tourne dans son van.[2]

Another of this poet's noblest sonnets is that *A une Passante*, comparable with a similar one of Keats, *Time's sea hath been five years at its slow ebb*, but superior for directness of point and forcible reality. Here for once the beauty of a poem is rather passionate than sensuous. Compare the delicate emblematic manner in which Keats winds up his sonnet with this sharp perfect finale:—

Fugitive beauté
Dont le regard m'a fait soudainement renaître,
Ne te varrai-je plus que dans l'éternité?
Ailleurs, bien loin d'ici, trop tard! *jamais* peut-être!
Car j'ignore où tu fuis, tu ne sais où je vais,
O toi que j'eusse aimée, ô toi qui le savais![3]

There is noticeable also in M. Baudelaire's work a quality of *drawing* which recalls the exquisite power in the same way of great French artists now living. His studies are admirable for truth and grace; his figure-painting has the ease and strength, the trained skill, the beautiful gentle justice of manner, which come out in such pictures as *La Source* of Ingres, or that other splendid study of Flandrin, of a curled-up naked figure under full soft hot light, now exhibiting here. These verses of Baudelaire's are as perfect and good as either:—

[2] From "Un Charogne," "A Rotting Corpse": "They [the flies] all descended and rose like a wave, or rushed out, buzzing; one might have said that the body, swollen with a vague breath, lived on by multiplying itself. And that world sent forth a strange music, like running water and the wind, or the grain which a winnower shakes and tosses in his basket with a rhythmic movement."

[3] From "A Une Passante," "A Passer-by": "Fugitive beauty, whose glance has made me suddenly be reborn, shall I see you again only in eternity? Elsewhere, very far from here, too late! Perhaps never! I am ignorant of where you will slip away to, you do not know where I am going, O you whom I might have loved, O you who knew it!" Keats' poem ends, "Thou dost eclipse / Every delight with sweet remembering, / And grief unto my darling joys dost bring."

Tes sourcils méchants
Te donnent un air étrange,
Qui n'est pas celui d'un ange,
Sorcière aux yeux alléchants.

.   .   .   .

Sur ta chair le parfum rôde
Comme autour d'un encensoir;
Tu charmes comme le soir,
Nymphe ténébreuse et chaude.

.   .   .   .

Le désert et la forêt
Embaument tes tresses rudes;
Ta tête a les attitudes
De l'énigme et du secret;

Tes hanches sont amoureuses
De ton dos et de tes seins,
Et tu ravis les coussins
Par tes poses langoureuses.[4]

Nothing can beat that as a piece of beautiful drawing.

It may be worth while to say something of the moral and meaning of many among these poems. Certain critics, who will insist on
going into this matter, each man as deep as his small leaden plum-
met will reach, have discovered what they call a paganism on the
spiritual side of the author's tone of thought. Stripped of its coat-
ing of jargon, this may mean that the poet spoken of endeavours to
look at most things with the eye of an old-world poet; that he aims
at regaining the clear and simple view of writers content to believe
in the beauty of material subjects. To us, if this were the meaning of
these people, we must say it seems a foolish one; for there is not one
of these poems that could have been written in a time when it was

---

[4] From "Chanson d'après-midi," "Afternoon Song": "[Although] your evil
eyebrows give you a strange air, which is not that of an angel, witch of seductive eyes, . . . About your flesh perfume roams as around a censer. You charm
like the evening, dusky and warm nymph. . . . The desert and the forest scent
your rough hair; your head has the postures of enigma and secrecy; . . . Your
hips are desirous of your back and your breasts, and you ravish the cushions
with your langorous poses."

not the fashion to dig for moral motives and conscious reasons. Poe, for example, has written poems without any moral meaning at all; there is not one poem of the *Fleurs du Mal* which has not a distinct and vivid background of morality to it. Only, this moral side of the book is not thrust forward in the foolish and repulsive manner of a half-taught artist; the background, as we called it, is not out of drawing.

If any reader could extract from any poem a positive spiritual medicine—if he could swallow a sonnet like a moral prescription— then clearly the poet supplying these intellectual drugs would be a bad artist; indeed, no real artist, but a huckster and vendor of miscellaneous wares. But those who will look for them may find moralities in plenty behind every poem of M. Baudelaire's; such poems especially as *Une Martyre*. Like a mediæval preacher, when he has drawn the heathen love, he puts sin on its right hand, and death on its left. It is not his or any artist's business to warn against evil; but certainly he does not exhort to it, knowing well enough that the one fault is as great as the other.

But into all this we do not advise any one to enter who can possibly keep out of it. When a book has been so violently debated over, so hauled this way and that by contentious critics, the one intent on finding that it means something mischievous, and the other intent on finding that it means something useful, those who are in search neither of a poisonous compound nor of a cathartic drug had better leave the disputants alone, or take only such notice of them as he absolutely must take. Allegory is the dullest game and the most profitless taskwork imaginable: but if so minded a reader might extract most elaborate meanings between the Muse of the writer and that strange figure of a beautiful body with the head severed, laid apart

Sur la table de nuit comme une renoncule.[5]

The heavy 'mass of dark mane and heaps of precious jewels' might mean the glorious style and decorative language clothing this

[5] From "Une Martyre, Dessin d'un Mâitre Inconnu," "A Martyress, Drawing by an Unknown Master": "[The head, with the mass of dark hair and its precious jewels, rests] on the night-table, like a ranunculus."

poetry of strange disease and sin; the hideous violence wrought by a shameless and senseless love might stand as an emblem of that analysis of things monstrous and sorrowful, which stamps the whole book with its special character. Then again, the divorce between all aspiration and its results might be here once more given in type; the old question re-handled—

> What hand and brain went ever paired?
> What heart alike conceived and dared?—

and the sorrowful final divorce of will from deed accomplished at last by force; and the whole thing summed up in that noble last stanza:—

> Ton époux court le monde, et ta forme immortelle
> Veille près de lui quand il dort;
> Autant que toi sans doute il te sera fidèle,
> Et constant jusques à la mort.[6]

All this and more might be worked out if the reader cared to try; but we hope he would not. The poem is quite beautiful and valuable enough as merely the 'design of an unknown master.' In the same way one might use up half the poems in the book; for instance, those three beautiful studies of cats (fitly placed in a book that has altogether a feline style of beauty—subtle, luxurious, with sheathed claws) ; or such carefully tender sketches as *Le Beau Navire*; or that Latin hymn 'Franciscæ meæ laudes':—

> Novis te cantabo chordis,
> O novelletum quod ludis
> In solitudine cordis.
>
> Esto sertis implicata,
> O fœmina delicata
> Per quam solvuntur peccata![7]

---

[6] From "Une Martyre": Your spouse roams the world, and your immortal form keeps watch near him while he sleeps; as much as you, no doubt, he will be faithful, and constant till death.

[7] "Praises of my Frances": "I sing to you on new strings, O newly-planted garden, because you play in the solitude of the heart. You should be bound with garlands, O delicate woman, by whom sins are forgiven."

Some few indeed, as that *ex-voto* poem *À une Madone,* appeal at once to the reader as to an interpreter; they are distinctly of a mystical moral turn, and in that rich symbolic manner almost unsurpassable for beauty:—

Avec mes Vers polis, treillis d'un pur métal
Savamment constellé de rimes de cristal,
Je ferai pour ta tête une énorme Couronne;
Et dans ma Jalousie, ô mortelle Madone,
Je saurai te tailler un Manteau, de façon
Barbare, roide et lourd, et doublé de soupçon,
Qui comme une guérite enfermera tes charmes;
Non de Perles brodé, mais de toutes mes Larmes!
Ta Robe, ce sera mon Désir, frémissant,
Onduleux, mon Désir qui monte et qui descend,
Aux pointes se balance, aux vallons se repose,
Et revêt d'un baiser tout ton corps blanc et rose.[8]

Before passing on to the last poem we wish to indicate for especial remark, we may note a few others in which this singular strength of finished writing is most evident. Such are, for instance, *Le Cygne, Le Poison, Tristesses de la Lune, Remords Posthume, Le Flacon, Ciel Brouillé, Une Mendiante Rousse* (a simpler study than usual, of great beauty in all ways, noticeable for its revival of the old fashion of unmixed masculine rhymes), *Le Balcon, Allégorie, L'Amour et le Crâne,* and the two splendid sonnets marked xxvii. and xlii. We cite these headings in no sort of order, merely as they catch one's eye in revising the list of contents and recall the poems classed there. Each of them we regard as worth a separate study, but the *Litanies de Satan,* as in a way the keynote to this whole complicated tune of poems, we had set aside for the last, much as (to judge by its place in the book) the author himself seems to have done.

[8] "To a Madonna, Ex-voto in the Spanish Style": "With my polished verse, a lattice of pure metal learnedly studded with crystal rhymes, I shall make for your head an enormous Crown; and in my Jealousy, O mortal Madonna, I shall know how to cut out a Mantle, of barbarous fashion, rigid and heavy, lined with suspicion, which like a sentry-box will lock in your charms; not embroidered with Pearls but with all my tears. Your Robe, that will be my desire, shuddering, undulating, my Desire which rises and which falls, balances itself on peaks, reposes in valleys, and clothes with a kiss your whole body, white and rose.

Here it seems as if all failure and sorrow on earth, and all the cast-out things of the world—ruined bodies and souls diseased— made their appeal, in default of help, to Him in whom all sorrow and all failure were incarnate. As a poem, it is one of the noblest lyrics ever written; the sound of it between wailing and triumph, as it were the blast blown by the trumpets of a brave army in irretrievable retreat:—

> O toi qui de la Mort, ta vieille et forte amante,
> Engendras l'Espérance—une folle charmante!
> O Satan, prends pitié de ma longue misère!
>
> Toi qui fais au proscrit ce regard calme et haut
> Qui damne tout un peuple autour d'un échafaud,
> O Satan, prends pitié de ma longue misère!
>
> .   .   .   .
>
> Toi qui, magiquement, assouplis les vieux os
> De l'ivrogne attardé foulé par les chevaux,
> O Satan, prends pitié de ma longue misère!
> Toi qui, pour consoler l'homme frêle qui souffre,
> Nous appris à mêler le salpêtre et le soufre,
> O Satan, prends pitié de ma longue misère![9]

These lines are not given as more finished than the rest; every verse has the vibration in it of naturally sound and pure metal. It is a study of metrical cadence throughout, of wonderful force and variety. Perhaps it may be best, without further attempts to praise or to explain the book, here to leave off, with its stately and passionate music fresh in our ears. We know that in time it must make its way; and to know when or how concerns us as little as it probably concerns the author, who can very well afford to wait without much impatience.

[9] "O you who with Death, your old and strong mistress, gives birth to Hope —a charming madwoman! O Satan, take pity on my long misery! You who give to the condemned that calm and disdainful look which damns a whole people around a scaffold, O Satan, take pity on my long misery! . . . You who magically supple the old bones of a hesitating drunkard half-crushed among the horses, O Satan, take pity on my long misery! You who, to console frail suffering man, taught us to mix saltpeter and sulphur, O Satan, take pity on my long misery."

Appendix 6

from *William Blake*[1]

WE must here be allowed space to interpolate a word of the briefest possible comment on the practical side of Blake's character. No man ever lived and laboured in hotter earnest; and the native energy in him had the property of making all his atmosphere of work intense and keen as fire—too sharp and rare in quality of heat to be a good working element for any more temperate intellect. Into every conceivable channel or by way of work he contrived to divert and infuse this overflowing fervour of mind; the least bit of engraving, the poorest scrap or scratch of drawing or writing traceable to his hands, has on it the mark of passionate labour and enjoyment; but of all this devotion of laborious life, the only upshot visible to most of us consists in a heap of tumbled and tangled relics, verse and prose mainly inexplicable, paintings and engravings mainly unacceptable if not unendurable. And if certain popular theories of the just aims of life, duties of an earnest-minded man, and meritorious nature of practical deeds and material services only, are absolutely correct—in that case the work of this man's life is certainly a sample of deplorable waste and failure. A religion which has for Walhalla some factory of the Titans, some prison fitted with moral cranks and divine treadmills of all the virtues, can have no place among its heroes for the most energetic of mere artists. To him, as to others of his kind, all faith, all virtue, all moral duty or religious necessity, was not so much abrogated or superseded as summed up, included and involved, by the one matter of art. To him, as to other such workmen, it seemed better to do this well and let all the rest drift than to do incomparably well in all other things and dispense with this one. For this was the thing he had to do;

---

[1] First published 1868. From Chapter II, "Lyrical Poems." The text is from the Bonchurch edition.

and this once well done, he had the assurance of a certain faith that other things could not be wrong with him. As long as two such parties exist among men who think and act, it must always be some pleasure to deal with a man of either party who has no faith or hope in compromise. These middle-men, with some admirable self-sufficient theory of reconciliation between two directly opposite aims and forces, are fit for no great work on either side. If it be in the interest of facts really desirable that 'the poor Fine Arts should take themselves away,' let it be fairly avowed and preached in a distinct manner. That thesis, so delivered, is comprehensible, and deserves respect. One may add that if art can be destroyed it by all means ought to be. If, for example, the art of verse is not indispensable and indestructible, the sooner it is put out of the way the better. If anything can be done instead better worth doing than painting or poetry, let that preferable thing be done with all the might and haste that may be attainable. And if to live well be really better than to write or paint well, and a noble action more valuable than the greatest poem or most perfect picture, let us have done at once with the meaner things that stand in the way of the higher. For we cannot on any terms have everything; and assuredly no chief artist or poet has ever been fit to hold rank among the world's supreme benefactors in the way of doctrine, philanthropy, reform, guidance, or example: what is called the artistic faculty not being by any means the same thing as a general capacity for doing good work, diverted into this one strait or shallow in default of a better outlet. Even were this true, for example, of a man so imperfect as Burns, it would remain false of a man so perfect as Keats. The great men, on whichever side one finds them, are never found trying to take truce or patch up terms. Savonarola burnt Boccaccio; Cromwell proscribed Shakespeare. The early Christians were not great at verse or sculpture. Men of immense capacity and energy who do seem to think or assert it possible to serve both masters—a Dante, a Shelley, a Hugo—poets whose work is mixed with and coloured by personal action or suffering for some cause moral or political— these even are no real exceptions. It is not as artists that they do or seem to do this. The work done may be, and in such high cases often must be, of supreme value to art, but not the moral implied. Strip the sentiments and re-clothe them in bad verse, what residue will be left of the slightest importance to art? Invert them, retaining the manner or form (supposing this feasible, which it might be), and art has lost nothing. Save the shape, and art will take care of the soul for you:* unless that is all right, she will refuse to run or start at all; but the shape or style of workmanship each artist is bound to look to, whether or no he may choose to trouble himself about the moral or other bearings of his work. This principle, which makes the manner of doing a thing the essence of the thing done, the purpose or result of it the accident, thus reversing the principle of moral or material duty, must inevitably expose art to the condemnation of the other party—the party of those who (as aforesaid) regard what certain of their leaders call an earnest life or a great acted poem (that is, material virtue or the mere doing and saying of good or instructive deeds and words) as infinitely preferable to any possible feat of art. Opinion is free, and the choice always open; but if any man leaning on crutches of theory chooses to halt between the two camps, it shall be at his own peril—imminent peril of conviction as one unfit for service on either side. For Puritanism is in this one one thing absolutely right about art; they cannot live and work together, or the one under the other. All ages which were great enough to have space for both, to hold room for a fair fighting-field between them, have always accepted and acted upon this evident fact. Take the Renaissance age for one example; you must have Knox or Ronsard, Scotch or French; not both at once; there is no place under reformers for the singing of a 'Pléiade.' Take the mediæval period in its broadest sense; not to speak of the notably heretical and immoral Albigeois with their exquisite school of heathenish verse, or of that other rebellious gathering under the great emperor Frederick II., a poet and pagan, when eastern arts and ideas began to look up westward at one man's bidding and open out Saracenic prospects in the very face and teeth of the Church—look at home into familiar things, and see by such poems as Chaucer's 'Court of

---

* Of course, there can be no question here of bad art: which indeed is a nonentity or contradiction in terms, as to speak of good art is to run into tautology. It is assumed, to begin with, that the artist has something to say or do worth doing or saying in an artistic form.

Love,' absolutely one in tone and handling as it is with the old
Albigensian 'Aucassin' and all its paganism,* how the poets of the
time, with their eager nascent worship of beautiful form and external nature, dealt with established opinion and the incarnate
moralities of church or household. It is easy to see why the Church
on its own principle found it (as in the Albigensian case) a matter
of the gravest necessity to have such schools of art and thought cut
down or burnt out. Priest and poet, all those times through, were
proverbially on terms of reciprocal biting and striking. That magnificent invention of making 'Art the handmaid of Religion' had not
been stumbled upon in the darkness of those days. Neither minstrel
nor monk would have caught up the idea with any rapture. As in-

---

* Observe especially in Chaucer's most beautiful of young poems that ap-
palling passage, where, turning the favourite edgetool of religious menace
back with point inverted upon those who forged it, the poet represents men
and women of religious habit or life as punished in the next world, beholding afar off with jealous regret the salvation and happiness of Venus and all
her servants (converse of the Hörsel legend, which shows the religious or
anti-Satanic view of the matter; though there too there is some pity or sympathy implied for the pagan side of things, revealing in the tradition the presence and touch of some poet) : expressly punished, these monks and nuns,
for their continence and holiness of life, and compelled after death to an eternity of fruitless repentance for having wilfully missed of pleasure and made
light of indulgence in this world; which is perfect Albigeois. Compare the
famous speech in 'Aucassin et Nicolette,' where the typical hero weighs in a
judicial manner the respective attractions of heaven and hell; deciding of
course dead against the former on account of the deplorably bad company
kept there; priests, hermits, saints, and such-like, in lieu of knights and
ladies, painters and poets. One may remark also, the minute this pagan revival
begins to get breathing-room, how there breaks at once into flower a most
passionate and tender worship of nature, whether as shown in the bodily beauty
of man and woman or in the outside loveliness of leaf and grass; both
Chaucer and his anonymous southern colleague being throughout careful to
decorate their work with the most delicate and splendid studies of colour
and form. Either of the two choice morsels of doctrinal morality cited above
would have exquisitely suited the palate of Blake. He in his time, one need
not doubt, was considerably worried and gibbered at by 'monkeys in houses of
brick,' moral theorists, and 'panto-pragmatic' men of all sorts; what can we
suppose he would have said or done in an epoch given over to preachers (lay,
clerical, and mixed) who assert without fear or shame that you may demand,
nay, are bound to demand, of a picture or poem what message it has for you,
what may be its moral utility or material worth? 'Poetry must conform itself
to,' etc.; 'art must have a mission and meaning appreciable by earnest men
in an age of work,' and so forth. These be thy gods, O Philistia.

deed they would have been unwise to do; for the thing is impossible.
Art is not like fire or water, a good servant and bad master; rather
the reverse. She will help in nothing, of her own knowledge or free-
will: upon terms of service you will get worse than nothing out of
her. Handmaid of religion, exponent of duty, servant of fact, pio-
neer of morality, she cannot in any way become; she would be none
of these things though you were to bray her in a mortar. All the
battering in the world will never hammer her into fitness for such an
office as that. It is at her peril, if she tries to do good: one might say,
borrowing terms from the other party, 'she shall not try that under
penalty of death and damnation.' Her business is not to do good on
other grounds, but to be good on her own: all is well with her while
she sticks fast to that. To ask help or furtherance from her in any
extraneous good work is exactly as rational as to expect lyrical
beauty of form and flow in a logical treatise. The contingent result
of having good art about you and living in a time of noble writing
or painting may no doubt be this: that the spirit and mind of men
then living will receive on some points a certain exaltation and insight caught from the influence of such forms and colours of verse
or painting; will become for one thing incapable of tolerating bad
work, and capable therefore of reasonably relishing the best; which
of course implies and draws with it many other advantages of a
sort you may call moral or spiritual. But if the artist does his work
with an eye to such results or for the sake of bringing about such
improvements, he will too probably fail even of them. Art for art's
sake first of all, and afterwards we may suppose all the rest shall be
added to her (or if not she need hardly be overmuch concerned);
but from the man who falls to artistic work with a moral purpose
shall be taken away even that which he has—whatever of capacity
for doing well in either way he may have at starting. A living critic*

* I will not resist the temptation to write a brief word of comment on this
passage. While my words of inadequate and now of joyless praise were in
course of printing, I heard that a mortal illness had indeed stricken the illus-
trious poet, the faultless critic, the fearless artist; that no more of fervent
yet of perfect verse, no more of subtle yet of sensitive comment, will be granted
us at the hands of Charles Baudelaire: that now for ever we must fall back
upon what is left us. It is precious enough. We may see again as various a
power as was his, may feel again as fiery a sympathy, may hear again as
strange a murmur of revelation, as sad a whisper of knowledge, as mysterious a

of incomparably delicate insight and subtly good sense, himself
'impeccable' as an artist, calls this 'the heresy of instruction'
(*l'hérésie de l'enseignement*) : one might call it, for the sake of a
shorter and more summary name, the great moral heresy. Nothing
can be imagined more futile; nothing so ruinous. Once let art hum-
ble herself, plead excuses, try at any compromise with the Puritan
principle of doing good, and she is worse than dead. Once let her
turn apologetic, and promise or imply that she really will now be
'loyal to fact' and useful to men in general (say, by furthering their
moral work or improving their moral nature), she is no longer of
any human use or value. The one fact for her which is worth taking
account of is simply mere excellence of verse or colour, which in-
volves all manner of truth and loyalty necessary to her well-being.
That is the important thing; to have her work supremely well done,
and to disregard all contingent consequences. You may extract out
of Titian's work or Shakespeare's any moral or immoral inference
you please; it is none of their business to see after that. Good
painting or writing, on any terms, is a thing quite sufficiently in
accordance with fact and reality for them. Supplant art by all means
if you can; root it out and try to plant in its place something useful
or at least safe, which at all events will not impede the noble moral
labour and trammel the noble moral life of Puritanism. But in the
name of sense and fact itself let us have done with all abject and
ludicrous pretence of coupling the two in harness or grafting the
one on the other's stock : let us hear no more of the moral mission
of earnest art; let us no longer be pestered with the frantic and
flatulent assumptions of quasi-secular clericalism willing to think
the best of all sides, and ready even, with consecrating hand, to lend

---

music of emotion; we shall never find so keen, so delicate, so deep an unison
of sense and spirit. What verse he could make, how he loved all fair and felt
all strange things, with what infallible taste he knew at once the limit and the
licence of his art, all may see at a glance. He could give beauty to the form, expression to the feeling, most horrible and most obscure to the senses or souls
of lesser men. The chances of things parted us once again; the admiration of
some years, at last in part expressed, brought me near him by way of written
or transmitted word; let it be an excuse for the insertion of this note, and for a
desire, if so it must be, to repeat for once the immortal words which too often
return upon our lips:
'Ergo in perpetuum, frater, ave atque vale!'

meritorious art and poetry a timely pat or shove. Philistia had far better (always providing it be possible) crush art at once, hang or burn it out of the way, than think of plucking out its eyes and setting it to grind moral corn in the Philistine mills; which it is certain not to do at all well. Once and again the time has been that there was no art worth speaking of afloat anywhere in the world; but there never has been or can have been a time when art, or any kind of art worth having, took active service under Puritanism, or indulged for its part in the deleterious appetite of saving souls or helping humanity in general along the way of labour and progress.*

Let no artist or poet listen to the bland bark of those porter dogs of the Puritan kingdom even when they fawn and flirt with tongue or tail. *Cave canem.* That Cerberus of the portals of Philistia will swallow your honey-cake to no purpose; if he does not turn and rend you, his slaver as he licks your hand will leave it impotent and palsied for all good work.

* There are exceptions, we are told from the first, to all rules; and the sole exception to this one is great enough to do all but establish a rival rule. But, as I have tried already to say, the work—all the work—of Victor Hugo is in its essence artistic, in its accident alone philanthropic or moral. I call this the sole exception, not being aware that the written work of Dante or Shelley did ever tend to alter the material face of things; though they may have desired that it should, and though their unwritten work may have done so. Accidentally of course a poet's work may tend towards some moral or actual result; that is beside the question.

Notes on Poems and Reviews

It is by no wish of my own that I accept the task now proposed to me. To vindicate or defend myself from the assault or the charge of men whom, but for their attacks, I might never have heard of, is an office which I, or any writer who respects his work, cannot without reluctance stoop to undertake. As long as the attacks on my books —I have seen a few, I am told there are many—were confined within the usual limits of the anonymous press, I let them pass without the notice to which they appeared to aspire. Sincere or insincere, insolent or respectful, I let my assailants say out their say unheeded.

I have now undertaken to write a few words on this affair, not by way of apology or vindication, of answer or appeal. I have none such to offer. Much of the criticism I have seen is as usual, in the words of Shakespeare's greatest follower,

> As if a man should spit against the wind;
> The filth returns in 's face.

In recognition of his fair dealing with me in this matter, I am bound by my own sense of right to accede to the wish of my present publisher, and to the wishes of friends whose advice I value, that on his account, if not on mine, I should make some reply to the charges brought against me— as far as I understand them. The work is not fruitful of pleasure, of honour, or of profit; but, like other such tasks, it may be none the less useful and necessary. I am aware that it cannot be accomplished without some show of egotism; and I am perforce prepared to incur the consequent charge of arrogance. The office of commentator of my own works has been forced upon

This is Swinburne's defense of *Poems and Ballads*, published in pamphlet form by John Camden Hotten in October, 1966.

me by circumstances connected with the issue and re-issue of my
last book. I am compelled to look sharply into it, and inquire what
passage, what allusion, or what phrase can have drawn down such
sudden thunder from the serene heavens of public virtue. A mere
libeller I have no wish to encounter; I leave it to saints to fight with
beasts at Ephesus or nearer. 'For in these strifes, and on such persons, it were as wretched to affect a victory, as it is unhappy to be
committed with them.'

Certain poems of mine, it appears, have been impugned by
judges, with or without a name, as indecent or as blasphemous. To
me, as I have intimated, their verdict is a matter of infinite indiffer-
ence: it is of equally small moment to me whether in such eyes as
theirs I appear moral or immoral, Christian or pagan. But, remembering that science must not scorn to investigate animalcules and
infusoria, I am ready for once to play the anatomist.

With regard to any opinion implied or expressed throughout
my book, I desire that one thing should be remembered: the book
is dramatic, many-faced, multifarious; and no utterance of enjoyment or despair, belief or unbelief, can properly be assumed as the
assertion of its author's personal feeling or faith. Were each poem
to be accepted as the deliberate outcome and result of the writer's
conviction, not mine alone but most other men's verses would leave
nothing behind them but a sense of cloudy chaos and suicidal contradiction. Byron and Shelley, speaking in their own persons, and
with what sublime effect we know, openly and insultingly mocked
and reviled what the English of their day held most sacred. I have
not done this. I do not say that, if I chose, I would not do so to the
best of my power; I do say that hitherto I have seen fit to do nothing of the kind.

It remains then to inquire what in that book can be reasonably
offensive to the English reader. In order to resolve this problem, I
will not fish up any of the ephemeral scurrilities born only to sting
if they can, and sink as they must. I will take the one article that lies
before me; the work (I admit) of an enemy, but the work (I ac-
knowledge) of a gentleman. I cannot accept it as accurate; but I
readily and gladly allow that it neither contains nor suggests anything false or filthy. To him therefore, rather than to another, I

address my reclamation. Two among my poems, it appears, are in his opinion 'especially horrible.' Good. Though the phrase be somewhat 'inexpressive,' I am content to meet him on this ground. It is something—nay, it is much—to find an antagonist who has sufficient sense of honesty and honour to mark out the lists in which he, the challenger, is desirous to encounter the challenged.

The first, it appears, of these especially horrible poems is 'Anactoria.' I am informed, and have not cared to verify the assertion, that this poem has excited, among the chaste and candid critics of the day or hour or minute, a more vehement reprobation, a more virtuous horror, a more passionate appeal, than any other of my writing. Proud and glad as I must be of this distinction, I must yet, however reluctantly, inquire what merit or demerit has incurred such unexpected honour. I was not ambitious of it; I am not ashamed of it; but I am overcome by it. I have never lusted after the praise of reviewers; I have never feared their abuse; but I would fain know why the vultures should gather here of all places; what congenial carrion they smell, who can discern such (it is alleged) in any rosebed. And after a little reflection I do know, or conjecture. Virtue, as she appears incarnate in British journalism and voluble through that unsavoury organ, is something of a compound creature:

> A lump neither alive nor dead,
> Dog-headed, bosom-eyed, and bird-footed;

nor have any dragon's jaws been known to emit or occasion stronger and stranger sounds and odours. But having, not without astonishment and disgust, inhaled these odours, I find myself at last able to analyse their component parts. What my poem means, if any reader should want that explained, I am ready to explain, though perplexed by the hint that explanation may be required. What certain reviewers have imagined it to imply, I am incompetent to explain, and unwilling to imagine. I am evidently not virtuous enough to understand them. I thank Heaven that I am not. *Ma corruption rougirait de leur pudeur.* I have not studied in those schools whence that full-fledged phœnix, the 'virtue' of professional pressmen, rises chuckling and crowing from the dunghill, its birthplace and its deathbed. But there are birds of alien feather, if not of higher flight; and these I would now recall into no hencoop or preserve of mine, but into the open and general field where all may find pasture and sunshine and fresh air; into places whither the prurient prudery and the virulent virtue of pressmen and prostitutes cannot follow; into an atmosphere where calumny cannot speak, and fatuity cannot breathe; in a word, where backbiters and imbeciles become impossible. I neither hope nor wish to change the unchangeable, to purify the impure. To conciliate them, to vindicate myself in their eyes, is a task which I should not condescend to attempt, even were I sure to accomplish.

In this poem I have simply expressed, or tried to express, that violence of affection between one and another which hardens into rage and deepens into despair. The keynote which I have here touched was struck long since by Sappho. We in England are taught, are compelled under penalties to learn, to construe, and to repeat, as schoolboys, the imperishable and incomparable verses of that supreme poet; and I at least am grateful for the training. I have wished, and I have even ventured to hope, that I might be in time competent to translate into a baser and later language the divine words which even as a boy I could not but recognise as divine. That hope, if indeed I dared ever entertain such a hope, I soon found fallacious. To translate the two odes and the remaining fragments of Sappho is the one impossible task; and as witness of this I will call up one of the greatest among poets. Catullus 'translated'—or as his countrymen would now say 'traduced'—the 'Ode to Anactoria'—a more beautiful translation there never was and will never be; but compared with the Greek, it is colourless and bloodless, puffed out by additions and enfeebled by alterations. Let any one set against each other the two first stanzas, Latin and Greek, and pronounce. (This would be too much to ask of all of my critics; but some among the journalists of England may be capable of achieving the not exorbitant task.) Where Catullus failed I could not hope to succeed; I tried instead to reproduce in a diluted and dilated form the spirit of a poem which could not be reproduced in the body.

Now the 'Ode to Anactoria' (as it is named by tradition)—the poem which English boys have to get by heart—the poem (and this is more important) which has in the whole world of verse no companion and no rival but the 'Ode to Aphrodite,' has been twice at least translated or 'traduced.' I am not aware that Mr. Ambrose Phillips, or M. Nicolas Boileau-Despréaux, was ever impeached before any jury of moralists for his sufficiently grievous offence. By any jury of poets both would assuredly have been convicted. Now, what they did I have not done. To the best (and bad is the best) of their ability, they have 'done into' bad French and bad English the very words of Sappho. Feeling that although I might do it better I could not do it well, I abandoned the idea of translation.

I tried, then, to write some paraphrase of the fragment which the Fates and the Christians have spared us. I have not said, as Boileau and Phillips have, that the speaker sweats and swoons at sight of her favourite by the side of a man. I have abstained from touching on such details, for this reason: that I felt myself incompetent to give adequate expression in English to the literal and absolute words of Sappho; and would not debase and degrade them into a viler form. No one can feel more deeply than I do the inadequacy of my work. 'That is not Sappho,' a friend said once to me. I could only reply, 'It is as near as I can come; and no man can come close to her.' Her remaining verses are the supreme success, the final achievement, of the poetic art.

But this, it may be, is not to the point. I will try to draw thither; though the descent is immeasurable from Sappho's verse to mine, or to any man's. I have striven to cast my spirit into the mould of hers, to express and represent not the poem but the poet. I did not think it requisite to disfigure the page with a footnote wherever I had fallen back upon the original text. Here and there, I need not say, I have rendered into English the very words of Sappho. I have tried also to work into words of my own some expression of their effect: to bear witness how, more than any other's, her verses strike and sting the memory in lonely places, or at sea, among all loftier sights and sounds—how they seem akin to fire and air, being themselves 'all air and fire'; other element there is none in them. As to the angry appeal against the supreme mystery of oppressive heaven, which I have ventured to put into her mouth at that point only where pleasure culminates in pain, affection in anger, and desire in despair—as to the 'blasphemies'* against God or Gods of which here and elsewhere I stand accused—they are to be taken as the first outcome or outburst of foiled and fruitless passion recoiling on itself. After this, the spirit finds time to breathe and repose above all vexed senses of the weary body, all bitter labours of the revolted soul; the poet's pride of place is resumed, the lofty conscience of invincible immortality in the memories and the mouths of men.

What is there now of horrible in this? the expressions of fierce fondness, the ardours of passionate despair? Are these so unnatural as to affright or disgust? Where is there an unclean detail? where an obscene allusion? A writer as impure as my critics might of course have written, on this or on any subject, an impure poem; I have not. And if to translate or paraphrase Sappho be an offence, indict the heavier offenders who have handled and rehandled this matter in their wretched versions of the ode. Is my poem more passionate in detail, more unmistakable in subject? I affirm that it is less; and what I affirm I have proved.

Next on the list of accusation stands the poem of Dolores. The gist and bearing of this I should have thought evident enough, viewed by the light of others which precede and follow it. I have striven here to express that transient state of spirit through which a man may be supposed to pass, foiled in love and weary of loving, but not yet in sight of rest; seeking refuge in those 'violent delights' which 'have violent ends,' in fierce and frank sensualities which at

* As I shall not return to this charge of 'blasphemy,' I will here cite a notable instance of what does seem permissible in that line to the English reader. (I need not say that I do not question the right, which hypocrisy and servility would deny, of author and publisher to express and produce what they please. I do not deprecate, but demand for all men freedom to speak and freedom to hear. It is the line of demarcation which admits, if offence there be, the greater offender and rejects the less—it is this that I do not understand.) After many alternate curses and denials of God, a great poet talks of Christ 'veiling his horrible Godhead,' of his 'malignant soul,' his 'godlike malice.' Shelley outlived all this and much more; but Shelley wrote all this and much more. Will no Society for the Suppression of Common Sense, no Committee for the Propagation of Cant, see to it a little? or have they not already tried their hands at it and broken down? For the poem which contains the words above quoted continues at this day to bring credit to its publishers, Messrs. Moxon and Co.

least profess to be no more than they are. This poem, like *Faustine*, is so distinctly symbolic and fanciful that it cannot justly be amenable to judgment as a study in the school of realism. The spirit, bowed and discoloured by suffering and by passion (which are indeed the same thing and the same word), plays for awhile with its pleasures and its pains, mixes and distorts them with a sense half-humorous and half-mournful, exults in bitter and doubtful emotions:

> Moods of fantastic sadness, nothing worth.

It sports with sorrow, and jests against itself; cries out for freedom and confesses the chain; decorates with the name of goddess, crowns anew as the mystical Cotytto, some woman, real or ideal, in whom the pride of life with its companion lusts is incarnate. In her lover's half-shut eyes, her fierce unchaste beauty is transfigured, her cruel sensual eyes have a meaning and a message; there are memories and secrets in the kisses of her lips. She is the darker Venus, fed with burnt-offering and blood-sacrifice; the veiled image of that pleasure which men impelled by satiety and perverted by power have sought through ways as strange as Nero's before and since his time; the daughter of lust and death, and holding of both her parents; Our Lady of Pain, antagonist alike of trivial sins and virtues: no Virgin, and unblessed of men; no mother of the Gods or God; no Cybele, served by sexless priests or monks, adored of Origen or Atys; no likeness of her in Dindymus or Loreto.

The next act in this lyrical monodrama of passion represents a new stage and scene. The worship of desire has ceased; the mad commotion of sense has stormed itself out; the spirit, clear of the old regret that drove it upon such violent ways for a respite, healed of the fever that wasted it in the search for relief among fierce fancies and tempestuous pleasures, dreams now of truth discovered and repose attained. Not the martyr's ardour of selfless love, an unprofitable flame that burnt out and did no service—not the rapid rage of pleasure that seemed for a little to make the flesh divine, to clothe the naked senses with the fiery raiment of faith; but a stingless love, an innocuous desire. 'Hesperia,' the tenderest type of woman or of dream, born in the westward 'islands of the blest,' where the shadows of all happy and holy things live beyond the sunset a sacred and a sleepless life, dawns upon his eyes a western dawn, risen as the fiery day of passion goes down, and risen where it sank. Here, between moonrise and sunset, lives the love that is gentle and faithful, neither giving too much nor asking—a bride rather than a mistress, a sister rather than a bride. But not at once, or not for ever, can the past be killed and buried; hither also the huntress follows her flying prey, wounded and weakened, still fresh from the fangs of passion; the cruel hands, the amorous eyes, still glitter and allure. *Qui a bu boira*: the feet are drawn back towards the ancient ways. Only by lifelong flight, side by side with the goddess that redeems, shall her slave of old escape from the goddess that consumes: if even thus one may be saved, even thus distance the bloodhounds.

This is the myth or fable of my poem; and it is not without design that I have slipped in, between the first and the second part, the verses called *The Garden of Proserpine*, expressive, as I meant they should be, of that brief total pause of passion and of thought, when the spirit, without fear or hope of good things or evil, hungers and thirsts only after the perfect sleep. Now, what there is in all this unfit to be written—what there is here indecent in manner or repulsive in matter—I at least do not yet see; and before I can see it, my eyes must be purged with the euphrasy and rue which keep clear the purer eyes of professional virtue. The insight into evil of chaste and critical pressmen, their sharp scent for possible or impossible impurities, their delicate ear for a sound or a whisper of wrong—all this knowledge 'is too wonderful and excellent for me; I cannot attain unto it.' In one thing, indeed, it seems I have erred: I have forgotten to prefix to my work the timely warning of a great poet and humorist:

> J'en préviens les mères des familles,
> Ce que j'écries n'est pas pour les petites filles
> Dont on coupe le pain en tartines; mes vers
> Sont des vers de jeune homme.[1]

---

[1] The quotation is from *Albertus* by Théophile Gautier, published in Paris, 1832. The following is a translation of the entire section XCVIII, from which the quoted lines (in italics) are taken: "But I, who am no prude, and have no

I have overlooked the evidence which every day makes clearer, that our time has room only for such as are content to write for children and girls. But this oversight is the sum of my offence.

It would seem indeed as though to publish a book were equivalent to thrusting it with violence into the hands of every mother and nurse in the kingdom as fit and necessary food for female infancy. Happily there is no fear that the supply of milk for babes will fall short of the demand for some time yet. There are moral milkmen enough, in all conscience, crying their ware about the streets and byways; fresh or stale, sour or sweet, the requisite fluid runs from a sufficiently copious issue. In due time, perhaps, the critical doctors may prescribe a stronger diet for their hypochondriac patient, the reading world; or the gigantic *malade imaginaire* called the public may rebel against the weekly draught or the daily drug of MM. Purgon and Diafoirus. We, meanwhile, who profess to deal neither in poison nor in pap, may not unwillingly stand aside. Let those read who will, and let those who will abstain from reading. *Caveat emptor.* No one wishes to force men's food down the throats of babes and sucklings. The verses last analysed were assuredly written with no moral or immoral design; but the upshot seems to me moral rather than immoral, if it must needs be one or the other, and if (which I cannot be sure of) I construe aright those somewhat misty and changeable terms.

These poems thus disposed of are (I am told) those which have given most offence and scandal to the venal virtue of journalism. As I have not to review my reviewers, I need not be at pains to refute at length every wilful error or unconscious lie which a workman that way inclined might drag into light. To me, as to all others who may read what I write, the whole matter must continue to

---

gauze or vine-life on my sentence to stick, not one thing shall I omit.—The ladies who this moral tale may read I beg will be indulgent to a few warm details; the wisest of them, I trow, will note them without a blush; the others will scream. Besides—and *mothers of families will please take notice,—what I am writing is not intended for maidens young whose bread and butter is cut in slices for them. My lines are a young man's lines, and not a catechism.* Emasculate them I will not; in their decent cynicism they go on, straight or crooked." Translated by S. C. de Sumichrast, *The Complete Works of Théophile Gautier* (London, 1902) XII, 267.

seem too pitiable and trivial to waste a word or thought on it which
we can help wasting. But having begun this task, I will add yet a
word or two of annotation. I have heard that even the little poem
of 'Faustine' has been to some readers a thing to make the scalp
creep and the blood freeze. It was issued with no such intent. Nor
do I remember that any man's voice or heel was lifted against it
when it first appeared, a new-born and virgin poem, in the *Spectator*
newspaper for 1862. Virtue, it would seem, has shot up surprisingly
in the space of four years or less—a rank and rapid growth, barren
of blossom and rotten at root. 'Faustine' is the reverie of a man gazing on the bitter and vicious loveliness of a face as common and as
cheap as the morality of reviewers, and dreaming of past lives in
which this fair face may have held a nobler or fitter station; the
imperial profile may have been Faustina's, the thirsty lips a
Mænad's, when first she learnt to drink blood or wine, to waste the
loves and ruin the lives of men; through Greece and again through
Rome she may have passed with the same face which now comes
before us dishonoured and discrowned. Whatever of merit or demerit there may be in the verses, the idea that gives them such life
as they have is simple enough; the transmigration of a single soul,
doomed as though by accident from the first to all evil and no good,
through many ages and forms, but clad always in the same type of
fleshly beauty. The chance which suggested to me this poem was one
which may happen any day to any man—the sudden sight of a living face which recalled the well-known likeness of another dead for
centuries: in this instance, the noble and faultless type of the elder
Faustina, as seen in coin and bust. Out of that casual glimpse and
sudden recollection these verses sprang and grew.

Of the poem in which I have attempted once more to embody the
legend of Venus and her knight, I need say only that my first aim
was to rehandle the old story in a new fashion. To me it seemed that
the tragedy began with the knight's return to Venus—began at the
point where hitherto it had seemed to leave off. The immortal agony
of a man lost after all repentance—cast down from fearful hope into
fearless despair—believing in Christ and bound to Venus—desirous
of penitential pain, and damned to joyless pleasure—this, in my
eyes, was the kernel and nucleus of a myth comparable only to that

of the foolish virgins and bearing the same burden. The tragic touch of the story is this: that the knight who has renounced Christ believes in him; the lover who has embraced Venus disbelieves in her. Vainly and in despair would he make the best of that which is the worst—vainly remonstrate with God, and argue on the side he would fain desert. Once accept or admit the least admixture of pagan worship, or of modern thought, and the whole story collapses into froth and smoke. It was not till my poem was completed that I received from the hands of its author the admirable pamphlet of Charles Baudelaire on Wagner's *Tannhäuser*. If any one desires to see, expressed in better words than I can command, the conception of the mediæval Venus which it was my aim to put into verse, let him turn to the magnificent passage in which M. Baudelaire describes the fallen goddess, grown diabolic among ages that would not accept her as divine. In another point, as I then found, I concur with the great musician and his great panegyrist. I have made Venus the one love of her knight's whole life, as Mary Stuart of Chastelard's; I have sent him, poet and soldier, fresh to her fierce embrace. Thus only both legend and symbol appear to me noble and significant. Light loves and harmless errors must not touch the elect of heaven or of hell. The queen of evil, the lady of lust, will endure no rival but God; and when the vicar of God rejects him, to her only can he return to abide the day of judgment in weariness and sorrow and fear.

These poems do not seem to me condemnable, unless it be on the ground of bad verse; and to any charge of that kind I should of course be as unable as reluctant to reply. But I certainly was even less prepared to hear the batteries of virtue open fire in another quarter. Sculpture I knew was a dead art; buried centuries deep out of sight, with no angel keeping watch over the sepulchre; its very grave-clothes divided by wrangling and impotent sectaries, and no chance anywhere visible of a resurrection. I knew that belief in the body was the secret of sculpture, and that a past age of ascetics could no more attempt or attain it than the present age of hypocrites; I knew that modern moralities and recent religions were, if possible, more averse and alien to this purely physical and pagan art than to the others; but how far averse I did not know.

There is nothing lovelier, as there is nothing more famous, in later
Hellenic art, than the statue of Hermaphroditus. No one would compare it with the greatest works of Greek sculpture. No one would
lift Keats on a level with Shakespeare. But the Fates have allowed
us to possess at once Othello and Hyperion, Theseus and Hermaphroditus. At Paris, at Florence, at Naples, the delicate divinity of this
work has always drawn towards it the eyes of artists and poets.* A
creature at once foul and dull enough to extract from a sight so
lovely, from a thing so noble, the faintest, the most fleeting idea of
impurity, must be, and must remain, below comprehension and
below remark. It is incredible that the meanest of men should derive from it any other than the sense of high and grateful pleasure.
Odour and colour and music are not more tender or more pure.
How favourite and frequent a vision among the Greeks was this
of the union of sexes in one body of perfect beauty, none need be
told. In Plato the legend has fallen into a form coarse, hard, and
absurd. The theory of God splitting in two the double archetype of
man and woman, the original hermaphrodite which had to get itself
bisected into female and male, is repulsive and ridiculous enough.
But the idea thus incarnate, literal or symbolic, is merely beautiful.
I am not the first who has translated into written verse this sculp-
tured poem: another before me, as he says, has more than once
'caressed it with a sculptor's love.' It is, indeed, among statues as a
lyric among tragedies; it stands below the Niobe as Simonides be-

* Witness Shelley's version:

> A sexless thing it was, and in its growth
> It seemed to have developed no defect
> Of either sex, yet all the grace of both;
> In gentleness and strength its limbs were decked
> The bosom lightly swelled with its full youth,
> The countenance was such as might select
> Some artist, that his skill should never die,
> Imaging forth such perfect purity.

                                                   Witch of Atlas, st. xxxvi.

But Shelley had not studied purity in the school of reviewers. It is well for
us that we have teachers able to enlighten our darkness, or Heaven knows into
what error such as he, or such as I, might not fall. We might even, in time,
come to think it possible to enjoy the naked beauty of a statue or a picture
without any virtuous vision behind it of a filthy fancy; which would be
immoral.

low Æschylus, as Correggio beneath Titian. The sad and subtle moral of this myth, which I have desired to indicate in verse, is that perfection once attained on all sides is a thing thenceforward barren of use or fruit; whereas the divided beauty of separate woman and man—a thing inferior and imperfect—can serve all turns of life. Ideal beauty, like ideal genius, dwells apart, as though by compulsion; supremacy is solitude. But leaving this symbolic side of the matter, I cannot see why this statue should not be the text for yet another poem. Treated in the grave and chaste manner as a serious 'thing of beauty,' to be for ever applauded and enjoyed, it can give no offence but to the purblind and the prurient. For neither of these classes have I ever written or will I ever write. 'Loathsome and abominable' and full of 'unspeakable foulnesses' must be that man's mind who could here discern evil; unclean and inhuman the animal which could suck from this mystical rose of ancient liveliness the foul and rancid juices of an obscene fancy. It were a scavenger's office to descend with torch or spade into such depths of mental sewerage, to plunge or peer into subterranean sloughs of mind impossible alike to enlighten or to cleanse.

I have now gone over the poems which, as I hear, have incurred most blame; whether deservedly or not, I have shown. For the terms in which certain critics have clothed their sentiments I bear them no ill-will: they are welcome for me to write unmolested, as long as they keep to simple ribaldry. I hope it gives them amusement; I presume it brings them profit; I know it does not affect me. Absolute falsehood may, if it be worth while, draw down contradiction and disproof; but the mere calling of bad names is a child's trick, for which the small fry of the press should have a child's correction at the hands of able editors; standing as these gentlemen ought to do in a parental or pedagogic relation to their tender charges. They have, by all I see and hear, been sufficiently scurrilous—one or two in particular:

> However, from one crime they are exempt;
> They do not strike a brother, striking *me*.

I will only throw them one crumb of advice in return; I fear the alms will be of no avail, but it shall not be withheld:

Why grudge them lotus-leaf and laurel,
  O toothless mouth or swinish maw,
Who never grudged you bells and coral,
  Who never grudged you troughs and straw?

Lie still in kennel, sleek in stable,
  Good creatures of the stall or sty;
Shove snouts for crumbs below the table;
  Lie still; and rise not up to lie.

To all this, however, there is a grave side. The question at issue is
wider than any between a single writer and his critics, or it might
well be allowed to drop. It is this: whether or not the first and last
requisite of art is to give no offence; whether or not all that cannot
be lisped in the nursery or fingered in the schoolroom is therefore
to be cast out of the library; whether or not the domestic circle is
to be for all men and writers the outer limit and extreme horizon
of their world of work. For to this we have come; and all students
of art must face the matter as it stands. Who has not heard it asked,
in a final and triumphant tone, whether this book or that can be
read aloud by her mother to a young girl? whether such and such
a picture can properly be exposed to the eyes of young persons? If
you reply that this is nothing to the point, you fall at once into the
ranks of the immoral. Never till now, and nowhere but in England,
could so monstrous an absurdity rear for one moment its deformed
and eyeless head. In no past century were artists ever bidden to
work on these terms; nor are they now, except among us. The disease, of course, afflicts the meanest members of the body with most
virulence. Nowhere is cant at once so foul-mouthed and so tight-
laced as in the penny, twopenny, threepenny, or sixpenny press.
Nothing is so favourable to the undergrowth of real indecency as
this overshadowing foliage of fictions, this artificial network of
proprieties. *L'Arioste rit au soleil, l'Arétin ricane à l'ombre.* The
whiter the sepulchre without, the ranker the rottenness within.
Every touch of plaster is a sign of advancing decay. The virtue of
our critical journals is a dowager of somewhat dubious antecedents:
every day that thins and shrivels her cheek thickens and hardens the
paint on it; she consumes more chalk and ceruse than would serve
a whole courtful of crones. 'It is to be presumed,' certainly, that in

her case 'all is not sweet, all is not sound.' The taint on her fly-blown reputation is hard to overcome by patches and perfumery. Literature, to be worthy of men, must be large, liberal, sincere; and cannot be chaste if it be prudish. Purity and prudery cannot keep house together. Where free speech and fair play are interdicted, foul hints and evil suggestions are hatched into fetid life. And if literature indeed is not to deal with the full life of man and the whole nature of things, let it be cast aside with the rods and rattles of childhood. Whether it affect to teach or to amuse, it is equally trivial and contemptible to us; only less so than the charge of immorality. Against how few really great names has not this small and dirt-encrusted pebble been thrown! A reputation seems imperfect without this tribute also: one jewel is wanting to the crown. It is good to be praised by those whom all men should praise; it is better to be reviled by those whom all men should scorn.

Various chances and causes must have combined to produce a state of faith or feeling which would turn all art and literature 'into the line of children.' One among others may be this: where the heaven of invention holds many stars at once, there is no fear that the highest and largest will either efface or draw aside into its orbit all lesser lights. Each of these takes its own way and sheds its proper lustre. But where one alone is dominant in heaven, it is encircled by a pale procession of satellite moons, filled with shallow and stolen radiance. Thus, with English versifiers now, the idyllic form is alone in fashion. The one great and prosperous poet of the time has given out the tune, and the hoarser choir takes it up. His highest lyrical work remains unimitated, being in the main inimitable. But the trick of tone which suits an idyl is easier to assume; and the note has been struck so often that the shrillest songsters can affect to catch it up. We have idyls good and bad, ugly and pretty; idyls of the farm and the mill; idyls of the dining-room and the deanery; idyls of the gutter and the gibbet. If the Muse of the minute will not feast with 'gig-men' and their wives, she must mourn with costermongers and their trulls. I fear the more ancient Muses are guests at neither house of mourning nor house of feasting.

For myself, I begrudge no man his taste or his success; I can enjoy and applaud all good work, and would always, when possible,

have the workman paid in full. There is much excellent and some admirable verse among the poems of the day: to none has it given
more pleasure than to me, and from none, had I been a man of letters to whom the ways were open, would it have won heartier ap-
plause. I have never been able to see what should attract men to
the profession of criticism but the noble pleasure of praising. But I
have no right to claim a place in the silver flock of idyllic swans. I
have never worked for praise or pay, but simply by impulse, and to
please myself; I must therefore, it is to be feared, remain where I
am, shut out from the communion of these. At all events, I shall not
be hounded into emulation of other men's work by the baying of
unleashed beagles. There are those with whom I do not wish to share
the praise of their praisers. I am content to abide a far different
judgment:

> I write as others wrote
> On Sunium's height.

I need not be over-careful to justify my ways in other men's
eyes; it is enough for me that they also work after their kind, and
earn the suffrage, as they labour after the law, of their own people.
The idyllic form is best for domestic and pastoral poetry. It is
naturally on a lower level than that of tragic or lyric verse. Its
gentle and maidenly lips are somewhat narrow for the stream and
somewhat cold for the fire of song. It is very fit for the sole diet of
girls; not very fit for the sole sustenance of men.

When England has again such a school of poetry, so headed and
so followed, as she has had at least twice before, or as France has
now; when all higher forms of the various art are included within
the larger limits of a stronger race; then, if such a day should ever
rise or return upon us, it will be once more remembered that the
office of adult art is neither puerile nor feminine, but virile; that its
purity is not that of the cloister or the harem; that all things are
good in its sight, out of which good work may be produced. Then
the press will be as impotent as the pulpit to dictate the laws and
remove the landmarks of art; and those will be laughed at who demand from one thing the qualities of another—who seek for ser-
mons in sonnets and morality in music. Then all accepted work will

be noble and chaste in the wider masculine sense, not truncated and curtailed, but outspoken and fullgrown; art will be pure by instinct and fruitful by nature, no clipped and forced growth of unhealthy heat and unnatural air; all baseness and all triviality will fall off from it, and be forgotten; and no one will then need to assert, in defence of work done for the work's sake, the simple laws of his art which no one will then be permitted to impugn.

Poems And Fragments of Sappho
(7th Century B.C.)[1]

Immortal Aphrodite of the broidered throne, daughter of Zeus, weaver of wiles, I pray thee break not my spirit with anguish and distress, O Queen. But come hither, if ever before thou didst hear my voice afar, and listen, and leaving thy father's golden house camest with chariot yoked, and fair fleet sparrows drew thee, flapping fast their wings around the dark earth, from heaven through mid sky. Quickly arrived they; and thou, blessed one, smiling with immortal countenance, didst ask, What now is befallen me, and Why now I call, and What in my mad heart I most desire to see. "What Beauty now wouldst thou draw to love thee? Who wrongs thee, Sappho? For even if she flies she shall soon follow, and if she rejects gifts shall yet give, and if she loves not shall soon love, however loth." Come, I pray thee, now too, and release me from cruel cares; and all that my heart desires to accomplish, accomplish thou, and by thyself my ally."

That man seems to me peer of gods, who sits in thy presence, and hears close to him thy sweet speech and lovely laughter; that indeed makes my heart flutter in my bosom. For when I see thee but a little, I have no utterance left, my tongue is broken down, and straightway a subtle fire has run under my skin, with my eyes I have no sight, my ears ring, sweat pours down, and a trembling seizes all my body; I am paler than grass, and seem in my madness little better than one dead. But I must dare all, since one so poor. . . .

---

[1] Since Swinburne's youth a number of fragments, some quite complete, have been recovered; only those which Swinburne probably knew are included here, and only those of sufficient length to be meaningful. These translations of 1885 rather than more modern versions were chosen because the diction is in the style of a period deeply under the Swinburnian influence. Translated by H. T. Wharton, London, 1885.

The stars about the fair moon in their turn hide their bright face when she, at about her full, lights up all earth with silver.

And round about the [breeze] murmurs cool through apple-boughs, and slumber streams from quivering leaves.

Come, goddess of Cyprus, and in gold cups serve nectar delicately mixed with delights.

But for thee will I [lead] to the altar [the offspring] of a white goat . . . and add a libation for thee.

This lot may I win, golden-crowned Aphrodite.

This will I now sing deftly to please my girlfriends.

For they whom I benefit injure me most.

To you, fair maids, my mind changes not.

According to my weeping: it and all care let buffeting winds bear away.

Me just now the golden-sandalled Dawn. . . .

Me thou forgettest.

Or lovest another more than me.

When anger spreads through the breast, guard thy tongue from barking idly.

Hadst thou felt desire for things good or noble, and had not thy tongue framed some evil speech, shame had not filled thine eyes, but thou hadst spoken honestly about it.

Men I think will remember us even hereafter.

I loved thee once, Atthis, long ago.

I know not what to do; my mind is divided.

And I flutter like a child after her mother.

Now Love masters my limbs and shakes me, fatal creature, bitter-sweet.

But to thee, Atthis, the thought of me is hateful; thou flittest to Andromeda.

Now Eros shakes my soul, a wind on the mountain falling on the oaks.

Of Gorgo full weary.

The moon has set, and the Pleiades; it is midnight, the time is going by, and I sleep alone.

The moon rose full, and the women stood as though around an altar.

Thus at time with tender feet the Cretan women dance in measure round the fair altar, trampling the fine soft bloom of the grass.

Sappho, why [celebrate] blissful Aphrodite.

Come now, delicate Graces and fair-haired Muses.

A sweet-voiced maiden.

But thou shalt ever lie dead, nor shall there be any remembrance of thee then or thereafter, for thou hast not of the roses of Pieria; but thou shalt wander obscure even in the house of Hades, flitting among the shadowy dead.

No one maiden I think shall at any time see the sunlight that shall be as wise as thou.

What country girl bewitches thy heart, who knows not how to draw her dress about her ankles?

But charming [maidens] plaited garlands.

Thou and my servant Love.

But if thou lovest us, choose another and a younger bed-fellow; for I will not brook to live with thee, old woman with young man.

Mnasidica is more shapely than the tender Gyrinno.

Scornfuller than thee, Erinna, have I nowhere found.

Do thou, Dica, set garlands round thy lovely hair, twining shoots of dill together with soft hands: for those who have fair flowers may best stand first, even in the favor of Goddesses; who turn their face away from those who lack garlands.

I love delicacy, and for me Love has the sun's splendor and beauty.

Sleep thou in the bosom of thy tender girlfriend.

I have a fair daughter with a form like a golden flower, Cleïs the beloved, above whom I [prize] nor all Lydia nor lovely [Lesbos]....

In a dream I spake with the daughter of Cyprus.

Sweet Mother, I cannot weave my web, broken as I am by longing for a boy, at soft Aphrodite's will.

As the sweet-apple blushes on the end of the bough, the very end of the bough, which the gatherers overlooked, nay overlooked not but could not reach.

As on the hills the shepherds trample the hyacinth under foot, and the flower darkens on the ground.

Evening, thou bringest all that bright morning scattered; thou bringest the sheep, the goat, the child back to her mother.

Well favoured is thy form, and thine eyes . . . honeyed, and love is spread over thy fair face . . . Aphrodite has honoured thee above all.

He who is fair to look upon is [good], and he who is good will soon be fair also.

For there was no other girl, O bridegroom, like her.

A. Maidenhood, maidenhood, whither art thou gone away from me? B. Never again will I come to thee, never again.

Thou burnest us.

Appendix 9

Sources for Atalanta in Calydon

HOMER (?9TH CENTURY B.C.), ILIAD[1]

The Curetes on a time were fighting and the Aetolians staunch in
battle around the city of Calydon, and were slaying one another, the
Aetolians defending lovely Calydon and the Curetes fain to waste it
utterly in war. For upon their folk had Artemis of the throne sent
a plague in wrath that Oeneus offered not to her the first-fruits of
the harvest in his rich orchard land, whereas the other gods feasted
on hecatombs; and it was to the daughter of great Zeus alone that
he offered not, whether haply he forgat, or marked it not; and he
was greatly blinded in heart. Thereat the Archer-goddess, the child
of Zeus, waxed wroth and sent against him a fierce wild boar, white
of tusk, that wrought much evil, wasting the orchard land of
Oeneus; many a tall tree did he uproot and cast upon the ground,
aye, root and apple blossom therewith. But the boar did Meleager,
son of Oeneus,[2] slay, when he had gathered out of many cities
huntsmen and hounds; for not of few men could the boar have been
slain, so huge was he; and many a man set he upon the grievous
pyre. But about his body the goddess brought to pass much clamour
and shouting concerning his head and shaggy hide,[3] between the
Curetes and the great-souled Aetolians. Now so long as Meleager,
dear to Ares, warred, so long went it ill with the Curetes, nor might
they abide without their wall, for all they were very many. But when
wrath entered into Meleager, wrath that maketh the heart to swell
in the breasts also of others, even though they be wise, he, then,

---

[1] Reprinted by permission of the publishers and the Loeb Classical Library
from Homer, *The Iliad* IX. 529–599, A. T. Murray, translator (Cambridge,
Mass.: Harvard University Press, 1924–1939).

[2] See below, *Scholia* 534.

[3] See below, *Scholia* 548.

wroth at heart against his dear mother Althaea, above beside his
wedded wife, the fair Cleopatra, daughter of Marpessa of the fair
ankles, Child of Evenus, and of Idas that was mightiest of men that
were then upon the face of earth; who also took his bow to face
the king Phoebus Apollo for the sake of the fair-ankled maid. Her
of old in their halls had her father and honoured mother called Hal-
cyone by name, for that the mother herself in a plight even as that
of the halcyon-bird of many sorrows, wept because Apollo that
worketh afar had snatched her child away. By her side lay Meleager
nursing his bitter anger, wroth because of his mother's curses; for
she prayed instantly to the gods, being grieved for her brother's
slaying; and furthermore instantly beat with her hands upon the
all-nurturing earth, calling upon Hades and dread Persephone, the
while she knelt and made the folds of her bosom wet with tears, that
they should bring death upon her son; and the Erinys that walketh
in darkness heard her from Erebus, even she of the ungentle heart.
Now anon was the din of the foeman risen about their gates, and
the noise of the battering of walls, and to Meleager the elders of the
Aetolians made prayer, sending to him the best of the priests of
the gods, that he should come forth and succor them, and they
promised him a mighty gift; they bade him, where the plain of
lovely Calydon was fattest, there choose him out a fair tract of
fifty acres, the half of it vineland, and the half clear ploughland, to
be cut from out the plain. And earnestly the old horseman Oeneus besought him, standing upon the threshold of his high-roofed chamber, and shaking the jointed doors, in prayer to his son, and earnestly too did his sisters and his honoured mother beseech him—
but he denied them yet more—and earnestly his companions that
were truest and dearest to him of all; yet not even so could they persuade the heart in his breast, until at the last [his] chamber was
being hotly battered, and the Curetes were mounting upon the
walls and firing the great city. Then verily his fair-girdled wife besought Meleager with wailing, and told him all the woes that come
on men whose city is taken; the men are slain and the city is wasted
by fire, and their children and low-girdled women are led captive of
strangers. Then was his spirit stirred as he heard the evil tale, and
he went his way and did on his body his gleaming armor. Thus did

he ward from the Aetolians the day of evil, yielding to his own spirit; and to him thereafter they paid now the gifts, many and gracious; yet even so did he ward them from evil.

HOMER, ODYSSEY [4]

As for you, / Zeus-loved Menelaus, it is not your fate to die / In horse-pasturing Argos. Instead the immortals will send you / To the Elysian plain at the outermost bounds of the earth, / Where tawny Rhadamanthus lives and where life is most easy / For men. There it never snows, no storm winds blow, / Nor does it rain, but the cool West Wind blows always / Briskly off the stream of Oceanus to refresh men there.

HESIOD (8TH CENTURY B.C.) [5]

But to the others father Zeus the son of Cronos gave a living and an abode apart from men, and made them dwell at the ends of earth. And they live untouched by sorrow in the islands of the blessed along the shore of deep swirling Ocean, happy heroes, for the grain-giving earth bears honey-sweet fruit flourishing thrice a year, far from the deathless gods, and Cronos rules over them; for the father of men and gods released him from his bonds. And these last equally have honor and glory.

PINDAR (522/518-c. 440 B.C.) [6]

But, whosoever, while dwelling in their world, have thrice been courageous in keeping their souls pure from all deeds of wrong, pass by the highway of Zeus unto the tower of Cronus, where the

[4] IV. 561–568, translated by Ennis Rees (New York: Random House, 1960).

[5] Reprinted by permission of the publishers and the Loeb Classical Library from Hesiod, *Works and Days*, Hugh G. Evelyn-White, translator (Cambridge, Mass.: Harvard University Press, 1914).

[6] Reprinted by permission of the publishers and the Loeb Classical Library from Pindar, *Olympian Ode II*, lines 70ff. J. E. Sandys, translator (Cambridge Mass.: Harvard University Press, 1915).

ocean-breezes blow around the Islands of the Blest, and flowers of gold are blazing, some on the shore from radiant trees, while others the water fostereth; and with chaplets thereof they entwine their heads and with crowns, according to the righteous councils of Rhadamanthys, who shareth for evermore the judgment-seat of the mighty father, even the lord of Rhea with her throne exalted beyond all beside.

BACCHYLIDES (505 B.C.–450 B.C.) [7]

Him [Heracles, descending to Hell to fetch Cerberus] answered Meleager, his cheek bedewed with tears: "Hard it is for mortals to bend the resolution of the gods. Else had car-borne Oeneus allayed the ire of high, flower-crowned, white-armed Artemis, supplicating, fond fire, with sacrifices of many goats and many tawny-hided oxen. But unappeasable was the wrath of the goddess. She sent, huntress maiden, a monster boar of undaunted fierceness into the lovely dales of Calydon; where, resistless in its might, it felled orchards with its tusks, slaughtered fleecy flocks, and every mortal it encountered. With it we, picked band of Hellas, waged desperate battle for six days without stay; and when high heaven gave Aetolia victory, we set ourselves to bury those whom the tusked monster had slain in furious onset, Ancaeus and Agelaus, best of my dear brothers born of Althaea in the far-famed halls of Oeneus. But still more warriors were doomed to fall, for the offended huntress daughter of Latona had not yet ceased her wrath, and we joined fierce battle with the valiant Curetes for the boar's tawny hide. There among many others I slew Iphiclus and good Aphareus by mother's gallant brethren. For fierce Ares makes no distinction of friend or foe, but shafts fly blindly at opposing ranks, carrying death wherever fortune wills. The sore-stricken daughter of Thestius remembered not this, and—ah hapless mother—resolved my death—ah passion-governed woman. She dragged from rich-carved casked and kindled the quickly burning brand that at my birth fate doomed to be coeval with my days. At the moment I was stripping of his

[7] *Epode 11*, lines 94–154. Translated by E. Poste (London and New York, 1898).

arms Clymenus, valiant son of Deipylus, a youth of noble build,
whom I had overtaken outside the walls, when the Curetes fled to
the goodly towers of ancient Pleuron. A sudden faintness seized my
soul; I felt my strength decline, alas; and with latest breath wept
to feel life's youthful splendour flitting." Men say the eye of
Amphitryo's fearless son then and never else was moistened by pity
for the ill-starred hero, as thus he answered: "Mortal's best fate is
never to be born nor ever to behold the sun's bright rays. But nought
avails repining: so let my tongue frame words to mould the future.
Remains there in the palace of Oeneus, dear to Ares, any virgin
daughter of features like to thine? Her would I gladly make my
honoured bride." Him answered dauntless Meleager's sprite: "In
her father's house I left the sweet-voiced Deinaira, unacquainted
yet with mortal-charming, golden Aphrodite."

EURIPIDES (480–406 B.C.) [8]

This is the fortunate land of Calydon with its pleasant plains,
across the straits opposite the country of Pelops. Oeneus, son of
Porthaon, rules over this Aetolian land; who wedded Althaea,
daughter of Thestius and sister of Leda—

Oeneus, obtaining an abundant harvest from the land, and sacrificing the first fruits—

Rightly art thou named Unhappy Hunter [Meleager], for thine
is an unhappy hunt.

But this indeed, O mother, is a most fair possession, and better
than wealth; its [wealth's] wing is swift, but noble children, even if
they die, are a fair treasure to their homes, and to those that begot
them are a delight of life, and never does it leave this house.

I have believed, therefore, that a marriage wherein evil is joined
to good will not be fortunate in its children, but that from righteous
parents will come forth righteous offspring.

It is fitting that a good woman should remain within the house;
out of doors she is good for nothing.

[8] Fragments from *Meleager*. Translated by W. R. Rutland (Oxford: Basil
Blackwell, 1931). Reprinted by permission..

If men were to attend to the labour of the loom, and women were to take with pleasure to weapons. . . . For, deprived of their knowledge, they would be worth nothing; nor we either.

The Cyprian is a friend to darkness, for light makes needful chaste self-control.

If I were to wed—may it never come about!—I should bear braver children than they who remain always in their houses; for better are the children of a father and mother who endure strenuous modes of life.

That which is strongest is virtue, even though that which is strongest be a woman; the name makes no difference.

I hate a woman . . . above all thee who, doing evil deeds, yet speakest fair words.

Telamon bore a golden eagle upon his shield as defence against the wild beast, and crowned his head with clusters of grapes in honor of Salamis his fatherland, the country of goodly vines. Arcadian Atalanta, hated of the Cyprian, had her dogs; and her bow, and Ancæus brandished a two-edged axe. The sons of Thestius, having the left foot unbooted but shod with sandals, that they might be nimble of knee, as is the custom of all Ætolians.

. . . to do good to the living; each man, dying, is earth and shadow; the nothing sinks into nothingness.

The world is flooded with light, but the world below is foul darkness.

CALLIMACHUS (BORN C. 310 B.C.) [9]

Further thou didst greatly commend swift-footed Atalanta, the slayer of boars, daughter of Arcadian Iasius, and taught her hunting with dogs and good archery. They that were called to hunt the boar of Calydon find no fault with her; for the tokens of victory came into Arcadia which still holds the tusks of the beast.

[9] Reprinted by permission of the publishers and the Loeb Classical Library from Callimachus, *Hymns and Epigrams*, "To Artemis," lines 215–222. Translated by A. W. Mair (Cambridge, Mass.: Harvard University Press, 1921).

APOLLONIUS RHODIUS (295–215 B.C.) [10]

After them from Calydon came the son of Oeneus, strong Meleagrus, and Laocoon—Laocoon the brother of Oeneus, though not by the same mother, for a serving-woman bare him—him, now growing old, Oeneus sent to guard his son: thus Meleagrus, still a youth, entered the bold band of heroes. No other had come superior to him, I ween, except Heracles, if for one year more he had tarried and been nurtured among the Aetolians. Yea, and his uncle well skilled to fight whether with the javelin or hand to hand, Iphiclus, son of Thestius, bare him company on his way.

?HYGINUS (64 B.C.–A.D. 17) [11]

Oeneus and Mars both slept one night with Althaea, daughter of Thestius. When Meleager was born from then, suddenly in the palace the Fates, Clotho, Lachesis, and Atropos, appeared. They thus sang his fate: Clotho said that he would be noble, Lachesis that he would be brave, but Atropos looked at a brand burning on the hearth and said, "He will live only as long as this brand remains unconsumed.' When Althæa the mother heard this, she leaped from the bed, put out the fatal brand, and buried it in the midst of the palace, so that it shouldn't be destroyed by fire.

Since Oeneus, son of Porthaon, king of Aetolia, had made sacrifices yearly to all the gods, but had omitted Diana, she, in anger, sent a boar of immense size to lay waste the district of Calydon. Then Meleager, son of Oeneus, promised that he would go with chosen leaders to attack it.

Castor and Pollux, sons of Jove. Eurytus of Mercury. . . . Parth. . . . Echion, son of Mercury [from Thebes]. Aesculapius, son of

---

[10] Reprinted by permission of the publishers and the Loeb Classical Library from Apollonius Rhodius, *Argonautica* I. 191–201. R. C. Seaton, translator (Cambridge, Mass.: Harvard University Press, 1912).

[11] *Fabulae* 171, 172, 173, 174, 175. Translated by Mary Grant, *Myths of Hyginus* (Lawrence, Kansas, 1960).

Apollo. Jason, son of Aeson [from Thebes]. Alcon, son of Mars, from Thrace. Euphemus, son of Neptune. Iolaus, son of Iphiclus. Lynceus and Idas, sons of Aphareus. Peleus, son of Aeacus. Telamon, son of Aeacus. Admetus, son of Pheres. Laertes, son of Arcesius. Deucalion, son of Minos. Theseus, son of Aegeus. Plexippus . . . [Ideus Lynceus] sons of Thestius, brothers of Althaea. Hippothous, son of Cercyon. Caeneus, son of Elatus. Mopsus, son of Ampycus. Meleager, son of Oeneus. Hippasus, son of Eurytus. Ancaeus, son of Lycurgus. Phoenix, son of Amyntor. Dryas, son of Iapetus. Enaesimus, Alcon, Leucippus, sons of Hippocoon from Amyclae. Atalanta, daughter of Schoeneus.[12]

Ternerdos, Iolcos, Sparta, Pleurone, Messene, Perrhaebia, Phthia, Magnesia, Salamin, Calydon, Thessalia, Oechalia, Ithaca, Tegea, Crete, Dolopia, Athens, [Magnesia], and Arcadia.[13]

Althaea, daughter of Thestius, bore Meleager to Oeneus. There in the palace a glowing brand is said to have appeared. The Fates came there and foretold the fate of Meleager, that he would live as long as the brand was unharmed. Althaea, putting it in a chest, carefully preserved it. In the meantime the wrath of Diana sent a boar of huge size to lay waste the district of Calydon, because Oeneus had not made yearly offerings to her. Meleager, with the help of chosen youths of Greece, killed it, and gave the hide to the virgin Atalanta because of her valor. Ideus, Plexippus, Lynceus . . . brothers of Althaea, wished to take it from her. When she asked the help of Meleager, he intervened, and putting love before family relationship, killed his uncles. When Althaea, the mother, heard that her son had dared to commit such a crime, remembering the warning of the Parcae, she brought out the brand from the chest and threw it in the fire. Thus, in desiring to avenge the death of her brothers, she killed her son. But his sisters, all except Gorge and Deianira, because of their weeping, were by the will of the gods changed into birds. These are called Meleagrides, "guinea hens." And Alcyone, wife of Meleager, died from grief in mourning for him.

---

[12] The hunters of the boar.
[13] States which sent help to Œneus.

When Agrius, son of Porthaon, saw his brother Oeneus bereft
of children and in need, he drove him out of his kingdom, and took
it over himself.

OVID (43 B.C.-A.D. 18) [14]

Now after Theseus had destroyed in Crete
The dreadful monster, Athens then had ceased
To pay her mournful tribute; and with wreaths
Her people decked the temples of the Gods;
And they inkoved Minerva, Jupiter,
And many other Gods whom they adored,
With sacrifice and precious offerings,
And jars of Frankincense.

                              Quick-flying Fame
Had spread reports of Theseus through the land;
And all the peoples of Achaia, from that day,
When danger threatened would entreat his aid.
So it befell, the land of Calydon,
Through Meleäger and her native hero,
Implored the valiant Theseus to destroy
A raging boar, the ravage of her realm.

Diana in her wrath had sent the boar
To wreak her vengeance; and they say the cause
Was this:—The nation had a fruitful year,
For which the good king Oeneus had decreed
That all should offer the first fruits of corn
To Cerës—and to Bacchus wine of grapes—
And oil of olives to the golden haired
Minerva. Thus, the Gods were all adored,
Beginning with the lowest to the highest,
Except alone Diana, and of all the Gods
Her altars only were neglected. No

---

[14] *Metamorphoses* VIII. 11–273. Translated by Brookes More (Boston,
1941). Reprinted by permission.

Frankincense unto her was given! Neglect
Enrages even Deities.

                    "Am I
To suffer this indignity?" she cried,
"Though I am thus dishonored, I will not
Be unrevenged!"   And so the boar was sent
To ravage the fair land of Calydon.

        And this avenging boar was quite as large
As bulls now feeding on the green Epirus,
And larger than the bulls of Sicily.
A dreadful boar.—His burning, bloodshot eyes
Seemed coals of living fire, and his rough neck
Was knotted with stiff muscles, and thick-set
With bristles like sharp spikes.   A seething froth
Dripped on his shoulders, and his tusks
Were like the spoils of Ind.   Discordant roars
Reverberated from his hideous jaws;
And lightning—belched forth from his horrid throat—
Scorched the green fields.   He trampled the green corn
And doomed the farmer to lament his crops,
In vain the threshing-floor has been prepared,
In vain the barns await the promised yield.
Long branches of the vine and heavy grapes
Are scattered in confusion, and the fruits
And branches of the olive tree, whose leaves
Should never wither, are cast on the ground.

        His spleen was vented on the simple flocks,
Which neither dogs nor shepherd could protect;
And the brave bulls could not defend their herds.
The people fled in all directions from the fields,
For safety to the cities.   Terror reigned.
There seemed no remedy to save the land,
Till Meleäger chose a band of youths,
United for the glory of great deeds.

What heroes shall immortal song proclaim?
Castor and Pollux, twins of Tyndarus;
One famous for his skill in horsemanship,
The other for his boxing.   Jason, too, was there,
The glorious builder of the world's first ship,
And Theseus with his friend Perithoüs,
And Toxeus and Plexippus, fated sons
Of Thestius, and the son of Aphareus,
Lynkeüs with his fleet-foot brother Idas
And Caeneus, first a woman then a man,
The brave Leucippus and the argonaut
Acastus, swift of dart; and warlike Dryas,
Hippothoüs and Phoenix, not then blind,
The son of King Amyntor, and the twain
Who sprung from Actor, Phyleus thither brought
From Elis; Telamon was one of them
And even Peleus, father of the great
Achillës; and the son of Pherës joined,
And Iölas, the swift Eurytiön,
Echiön fleet of foot, Narycian Lelex—
And Panopeus, and Hyleus and Hippasus,
And Nestor (youthful then), and the four sons
Hippocoön from eld Amyclae sent,
The father-in-law of queen Penëlopë,
Ancaeus of Arcadia, and the wise
Soothsayer Mopsus, and the prophet, son
Of Oeclus, victim of a traitor-wife—

And Atalanta, virgin of the groves,
Of Mount Lycaeüs, glory of her sex;
A polished buckle fastened her attire;
Her lustrous hair was fashioned in a knot;
Her weapons rattled in an ivory case,
Swung from her white left shoulder, and she held
A bow in her left hand.   Her face appeared
As maidenly for boy, or boyish for girl.

When Meleäger saw her, he at once
Longed for her beauty, though some God forbade.
The fires of love flamed in him; and he said,
"Happy the husband who shall win this girl!"
Neither the time nor his own modesty
Permitted him to say another word.
But now the dreadful contest with the boar
Engaged this hero's energy and thought.

A wood, umbrageous, not impaired with age,
Slopes from a plain and shadows the wide fields,
And there this band of valiant heroes went—
Eager to slay the dreaded enemy,
Some spread the nets and some let loose the dogs,
Some traced the wide spoor of the monster's hoofs.

There is a deep gorge where the rivulets
That gather from the rain, discharge themselves;
And there the bending willow, the smooth sedge,
The marsh-rush, ozier and tall tangled reed
In wild profusion cover up the marsh.
Aroused from this retreat the startled boar,
As quick as lightning from the clashing clouds
Crashed all the trees that cumbered his mad way.—

The young men raised a shout, leveled their spears,
And brandished their keen weapons; but the boar
Rushed onward through the yelping dogs,
And scattered them with deadly sidelong stroke.

Echïon was the first to hurl his spear,
But slanting in its course it only glanced
A nearby maple tree, and next the spear
Of long-remembered Jason cut the air;
So swiftly hurled it seemed it might transfix
The boar's back, but with over-force it sped
Beyond the monster.   Poising first his dart,

The son of Ampyx, as he cast it, he
Implored Apollo, "Grant my prayer if I
Have truly worshipped you, harken to me
As always I adore you! Let my spear
Unerring strike its aim." Apollo heard,
And guided the swift spear, but as it sped
Diana struck the iron head from the shaft,
And the blunt wood fell harmless from his hide.

Then was the monster's savage anger roused;
As the bright lightning's flash his red eyes flamed;
His breath was hot as fire. As when a stone
Is aimed at walls or strong towers, which protect
Encompassed armies,—launched by the taut rope
It strikes with dreaded impact; so the boar
With fatal onset rushed among this band
Of noble lads, and stretched upon the ground
Eupalamon and Pelagon whose guard
Was on the right; and their companions bore
Their bodies from the field.

Another youth,
The brave son of Hippocoön received
A deadly wound—while turning to escape,
The sinew of his thigh was cut and failed
To bear his tottering steps.—And Nestor might
Have perished then, so long before he fought
The heroes of old Troy, but ever wise,
He vaulted on his long lance from the ground
Into the branches of a sheltering tree;
Where in a safe position, he could look,
Down on his baffled foe. The raging boar
Whetted his gleaming tushes on an oak.

Then with his sharpened tusks he gored the thigh
Of mighty Hippasus. Observed of all,
And mounted on their horses—whiter than

The northern snow—the twins (long afterward
Transformed to constellations) sallied forth,
And brandishing their lances, poised in air,
Determined to destroy the bristling boar.
It thwarted their design by hiding in
A thicket intricate; where neither steed
Nor lance could penetrate.   But Telamon
Pursued undaunted, and in haste tripped up
By tangled roots, fell headlong.—Peleüs stooped
To rescue him.

       While he regained his feet,
The virgin, Atalanta, took her bow
And fitting a sharp arrow to the notch,
Twanged the tight cord.   The feathered shaft
Quivered beneath the monster's ear, the red blood
Stained his hard bristles.

       Flushed with her success
Rejoiced the maid, but not more gladly than
The hero Meleäger.   He it was
Who first observed the blood, and pointed out
The stain to his companions as he cried,
"Give honor to the courage of a maid!"
Unwilling to be worsted by a maid,
The rushing heroes raised a mighty cry
And as they shouted in excitement, hurled
Their weapons in confusion; and so great
The multitude their actions interfered.

      Behold! Ancaeüs wielding his war-axe,
And rushing madly to his fate, exclaimed,
"Witness it!   See the weapons of a man
Excel a woman's!   Ho, make way for my
Achievement!   Let Diana shield the brute!
Despite her utmost effort my right hand
Shall slaughter him!"   So mighty in his boast

He puffed himself; and, lifting with both hands
His double-edgéd axe, he stood erect,
On tiptoe fiercely bold.   The savage boar
Caught him, and ripped his tushes through his groin,
A spot where death is sure.—Ancaeüs fell;
And his torn entrails and his crimson blood
Stained the fair verdure of the spot with death.

Ixiön's doughty son was running straight
Against the monster, shaking his long lance
With nervous vigor in his strong right hand;
But Theseus, standing at a distance called:
"Beware! beware, O, dearest of my friends;
Be valiant at a distance, or the fate
Of rashly-bold Ancaeüs may be yours!"

Even as he spoke he balanced in his hand
His brazen-pointed lance of cornel wood;
With aim so true it seemed the great boar's death
Was certain, but an evergreen oak branch
Shielded the beast.—Then Jason hurled his dart,
Which turned by chance, transfixed a luckless dog
And pinned him yelping, to the sanguine earth.—

So fared those heroes.   Better fortune gave
Success to Meleäger; first he threw
A spear that missed and quivered in the ground;
But next he hurled a spear with certain aim.
It pierced the middle of the monster's back;
And rushing in upon the dreaded beast,
While raging it was whirling round and round,
The fearless prince provoked to greater rage
The wounded adversary.   Bloody froth
Dripped down his champing jaws—his purple blood
Poured from a rankling wound.   Without delay
The mighty Meleäger plunged a spear
Deep in the monster's shoulder.   All his friends

Raised a glad shout, and gathering round him, tried
To grasp his hand.—With wonder they beheld
The monster's bulk stretched out upon the plain;
And fearful still to touch him, they began
To stain their weapons in his spouting blood.

At length the hero Meleäger pressed
His conquering foot upon the monster's head
And said, "O Atalanta, glorious maid,
Of Nonacris, to you is yielded spoil,
My lawful right, and I rejoice to share
The merit of this glorious victory."

And while he spoke, he gave to her the pelt,
Covered with horrid bristles, and the head
Frightful with gory tusks: and she rejoiced
In Meleäger and his royal gift.

But all the others, envious, began
To murmur; and the sons of Thestiüs
Levelled their pointed spears, and shouted out;
"Give up the prize!   Let not the confidence
Of your great beauty be a snare to you!
A woman should not interfering filch
The manly honors of a mighty hunt!
Aside! and let your witless lover yield!"
So threatened they and took from her the prize;
And forcibly despoiled him of his rights.

The warlike prince, indignant and enraged,—
Roused with resentment, shouted out.   "What! Ho!
You spoilers of this honor that is ours,
Brave deeds are different far from craven threats!"
And with his cruel sword he pierced the breast
Of rash Plexippus, taken unawares,
And while his brother, Toxeus, struck with fear,
Stood hesitating whether to avenge

Or run to safety, Meleäger plunged
The hot sword, smoking with a brother's blood,
In his breast also.   And so perished they.

Ere this, Althaeä, mother of the prince,
And sister of the slaughtered twain,—because
Her son had killed the boar, made haste to bear
Rich offerings to the temples of the Gods;
But when she saw her slaughtered brothers borne
In sad procession, she began to shriek,
And filled the city with her wild lament.
Unwilling to abide her festal robes
She dressed in sable.—When she was informed
Her own son Meleäger was the cause,
She banished grief and lamentations,—
Thirsting for vengeance.

She remembered well,
How, when she lay in childbirth round her stood
The three attendant sisters of his fate.
There was a billet in the room, and this
They took and cast upon the wasting flames,
And as they spun and drew the fatal threads
They softly chanted, "Unto you we give,
O child new-born! only the life of this;
The period of this billet is your life."
And having spoken so, they vanished in the smoke.

Althaeä snatched the billet from the fire,
And having quenched it with drawn water, hid
It long and secretly in her own room,
Where, thus preserved, it acted as a charm
To save the life of Meleäger.   This
The mother now brought forth, and fetched a pile
Of seasoned tinder ready for the torch.
She lit the torches and the ready pile,
And as the flames leaped up, four times prepared

To cast the fatal billet in the midst;
And four times hesitated to commit
The dreadful deed,—so long the contest veered
Between the feelings of a mother's breast
And the fierce vengeance of a sister's rage.

Now is the mother's visage pale with fear,
And now the sister's sanguinary rage
Glows in her eyes. Her countenance contorts
With cruel threats and in bewildered ways
Dissolves compassionate: And even when
The heat of anger had dried up her eyes
The conflict of her passion brought new tears.

As when the wind has seized upon a ship
And blows against a tide of equal force,
The vexéd vessel feels repellant powers,
And with unsteady motion sways to both;
So did Althaeä hesitate between
The conflict of her passions: when her rage
Had cooled, her fury was as fast renewed:
But always the unsatisfied desire
Of blood, to ease the disembodied shades
Of her slain brothers, seemed to overcome
The mother-instinct; and intensity
Of conduct proved the utmost test of love.

She took the billet in her arms and stood
Before the leaping flames, and said, "Alas,
Be this the funeral pyre of my own flesh!"
And as she held in her relentless hand
The destiny of him she loved, and stood
Before the flames, in all her wretchedness
She moaned, "You sad Eumenidës attend!
Relentless Gods of punishment,—turn, turn
Your dreadful vision on these baneful rites!
I am avenging and committing crime!

With death must death be justified and crime
Be added unto crime!   Let funerals
Upon succeeding funerals attend!

"Let these accumulating woes destroy
A wicked race. Shall happy Oeneus bask
In the great fame of his victorious son,
And Thestius mourn without slaughtered ones?
'Tis better they should both lament the deed!
Witness the act of my affection, shades
Of my departed brothers! and accept
My funeral offering, given at a cost
Beyond my strength to bear.   Ah wretched me!
Distracted is my reason!   Pity me,
The yearnings of a stricken mother's heart
Withholding me from duty!   Aye, although
His punishment be just, my hands refuse
The office of such vengeance.   What, shall he
Alive, victorious, flushed with his success,
Inherit the broad realms of Calydon,
And you, my slaughtered brothers, unavenged,
Dissolved in ashes, float upon the air,
Unpalpitating phantoms?   How can I
Endure the thought of it?   Oh let the wretch
Forever perish, and with him be lost
The hopes of his sad father, in the wreck
Of his distracted kingdom.   Where are now
The love and feelings of a mother; how
Can I forget the bitter pangs endured
While twice times five the slow moon waxed and waned?

"O had you perished in your infancy
By those first fires, and I had suffered it!
Your life was in my power! and now your death
Is the result of wrongs which you have done—
Take now a just reward for what you did:

Return to me the life I gave and saved,
When from the flames I snatched the fatal brand.
Return that gift or take my wretched life,
That I may hasten to my brothers' tomb.

"What dreadful deed can satisfy the law,
When I for love against my love am forced?
For even as my brothers' wounds appear
In visions dreadful to denounce my son,
The love so nurtured in a mother's breast
Breaks down the resolution!   Wretched me!
Such vengeance for my brothers overcomes
First at your birth I gave it, and again
The yearning of a mother for her son!
Let not my love denounce my vengeance!
My soul may follow with its love the shade
Of him I sacrifice, and following him
My shade and his and yours unite below."

She spoke and as she turned her face away,
She threw the fatal billet on the fire,
And as the flames devoured it, a strange groan
Was heard to issue from the burning wood.

But Meleäger at a distance knows
Of naught to wreck his hour of victory,
Until he feels the flame of burning wood
Scorching with secret fire his forfeit life.
Yet with a mighty will, disdaining pain
He grieves his bloodless and ignoble death.
He calls Ancaeüs happy for the wounds
That caused his death.   With sighs and groans he called
His agéd father's name, and then the names
Of brothers, sisters, and wife—and last,
They say he called upon his mother's name.

His torment always with the fire increased,
Until, as little of the wood remained,—
His pain diminished with the heat's decrease;
And as the flames extinguished, so his life
Slowly ascended in the rising air.

And all the mighty realm of Calydon
Was filled with lamentations—young and old,
The common people and the nobles mourned;
And all the wailing women tore their hair.
His father threw his body on the ground,
And as he covered his white hair and face
With ashy dust, bewailed his agéd days.

Althaeä, maddened in her mother's grief,
Has punished herself with a ruthless hand;
She pierced her heart with iron.—Oh! if some God
Had given a resounding harp, a voice
An hundred-fold more mighty, and a soul
Enlarged with genius, I could never tell
The grief of his unhappy sisters.—They,
Regardless of all shame, beat on their breasts;
Before the body was consumed with fire,
Embraced it, and again embracing it,
Rained kisses on their loved one and the bier.
And when the flames had burnt his shrinking form
They strained his gathered ashes to their breasts,
And prostrate on the tomb kissed his dear name,
Cut only in the stone,—and bathed it with their tears.

Latona's daughter, glutted with the woes
Inflicted on Porthaön's house, now gave
Two of the weeping sisters wide-spread wings,
But Gorgë and the spouse of Hercules
Not so were changed. Latona stretched long wings
Upon their arms, transformed their mouths to beaks,
And sent them winging through the lucent air.

APOLLODORUS (ROMAN EMPIRE) [15]

Thestius had daughters and sons by Eurythemis, daughter of Cleoboea: the daughters were Althaea, Leda, Hypermenestra, and the males were Ipiclus, Evippus, Plexippus, and Euryplus.

Porthaon and Euryte, daughter of Hippodamas, had sons, Oeneus, Agrius, Alcathous, Melas, Leucopeus, and a daughter Sterope, who is said to have been the mother of the Sirens by Achelous.

Reigning over Calydon, Oeneus was the first who received a vine-plant from Dionysus. He married Althaea, daughter of Thestius, and begat Toxeus, whom he slew with his own hand because he leaped over the ditch. And besides Toxeus he had Thryeus and Clymenus, and a daughter Gorge, whom Andraemon married, and another daughter Deianira, who is said to have been begotten on Althaea by Dionysus. This Deianira drove a chariot and practised the art of war, and Hercules wrestled for her hand with Achelous. Althaea had also a son Meleager, by Oeneus, though they say that he was begotten by Ares. It is said that, when he was seven days old, the Fates came and declared that Meleager should die when the brand burning on the hearth was put out. On hearing that, Althaea snatched up the brand and deposited it in a chest. Meleager grew up to an invulnerable and gallant man, but came by his end in the following way. In sacrificing the first fruits of the annual crops of the country to all the gods, Oeneus forgot Artemis alone. But she in her wrath sent a boar of extraordinary size and strength, which prevented the land from being sown and destroyed the cattle, and the people that fell in with it. To attack this boar, Oeneus called together all the noblest men of Greece, and promised that to him who should kill the beast he would give the skin as a prize. Now the men who had assembled to hunt the boar were these:—Meleager son of Oeneus; Dryas son of Ares: these came from Calydon; Idas and Lynceus, sons of Aphareus from Messene; Castor and Pollux sons of Zeus and Leda from Lacedaemon; Theseus son of Aegeus

[15] Reprinted by permission of the publishers and the Loeb Classical Library from Apollodorus, *The Library* I. vii.7-viii.3; ix.8-ix.22. J. G. Frazer, translator (Cambridge, Mass.: Harvard University Press, 1921).

from Athens; Admetus from Arcadia; Jason son of Aeson from
Iolius; Iphicles son of Amphytrion from Thebes; Pirithous son of
Ixion from Larissa; Peleus son of Aeacus from Phthia; Telamon
son of Aeacus from Salamis; Eurytion son of Actor from Phthia;
Atalanta daughter of Schoeneus from Arcadia; Amphiaraus son
of Oicles from Argos. With these came also the sons of Thestius.
And when they were assembled, Oeneus entertained them for nine
days. But on the tenth, when Cepheus and Ancaeus disdained to go
a-hunting with a woman, Meleager compelled them to follow the
chase with her, for he desired to have a child also by Atalanta,
though he had to wife Cleopatra daughter of Idas and Marpessa.
When they surrounded the boar, Hyleus and Ancaeus were killed by
the brute, and Peleus struck Eurytion undesignedly with a javelin.
But Atalanta was the first to shoot the boar in the back with an arrow, and Amphiaraus was the next to shoot it in the eye: but
Meleager killed it by a stab in the flank, and on receiving the skin
gave it to Atalanta. Nevertheless the sons of Thestius, thinking scorn
that a woman should get the prize in the face of men, took the skin
from her alleging that it belonged to them by right of birth if
Meleager did not choose to take it. But Meleager in a rage slew the
sons of Thestius and gave the skin to Atalanta. However, from grief
at the slaughter of her brothers Althaea kindled the brand, and
Meleager immediately expired.

But some say that Meleager did not die in that way, but that
when the sons of Thestius claimed the skin on the ground that
Iphicles had been the first to hit the boar, war broke out between
the Curetes and the Calydonians; and when Meleager had sallied
out and slain some of the sons of Thestius, Althaea cursed him, and
he in a rage remained at home; however, when the enemy approached the walls, and the citizens supplicated him to come to the
rescue, he yielded reluctantly to his wife and sallied forth, and having killed the rest of the sons of Thestius he himself fell fighting.
After the death of Meleager, Althaea and Cleopatra hanged themselves and the women who mourned the dead men were turned
into birds.

Now Tyro, daughter of Salmoneus and Alcidice, was brought up by
Cretheus, brother of Salmoneus, and conceived a passion for the

river Enipeus, and often would she to its running waters and utter her plaint to them. But Poseidon in the likeness of Enipeus lay with her, and she secretly gave birth to twin sons, whom she exposed. As the babes lay forlorn, a mare, belonging to some passing horse-keepers, kicked with its hoof one of the two infants and left a livid mark on its face. The horse-keeper took up both the children and reared them; and the one with the livid mark he called Pelias, and the other Neleus. When they were grown up, they discovered their mother and killed their stepmother Sidero. For knowing that their mother was ill-used by her, they attacked her, but before they could catch her she had taken refuge in the precinct of Hera. However, Pelias cut her down on the very altars, and ever after he continued to treat Hera with contumely.

So he told them [the Argonauts] to let fly a dove between the rocks, and, if they saw it pass safe through, to thread the narrows with an easy mind, but if they saw it perish, then not to force a passage. When they heard that, they put to sea, and on nearing the rocks let fly a dove from the prow, and as she flew the clash of the rocks nipped off the tip of her tail. So, waiting till the rocks had recoiled, with hard rowing and the help of Hera, they passed through, the extremity of the ship's ornamented poop being shorn away right round. Henceforth the Clashing Rocks stood still; for it was fated that, so soon as a ship had made the passage, they should come to rest completely.

PAUSANIAS (2ND CENTURY A.D.) [16]

Besides the exploits shared by the Tegeans with the Arcadians, which include the Trojan war, the Persian wars and the battle at Dipaea with the Lacedaemonians, the Tegeans have, besides the deeds already mentioned, the following claims of their own to fame. Ancaeus the son of Lycurgus, though wounded, stood up to the Caly-donian boar, which Atalanta shot at, being the first to hit the beast. For this feat she received, as a prize for valor, the head and hide of

---

[16] Reprinted by permission of the publishers and the Loeb Classical Library from Pausanius, *Description of Greece* VIII.xlv; X.xxxi. W. H. S. Jones, translator (Cambridge, Mass.: Harvard University Press, 1918).

the boar. . . . The modern temple [of Athena Alea at Tegea] is far superior to all other temples in the Peloponnesus on many grounds, . . . On the front gable is the hunting of the Calydonian boar. The boar stands right in the center. On one side are Atalanta, Meleager, Theseus, Telamon, Peleus, Polydeuces, Iolaus, the partner in most of the labors of Heracles, and also the sons of Thestius, the brothers of Althaea, Prothous and Cometes. On the other side of the boar is Epochus supporting Ancaeus who is now wounded and has dropped his axe; by his side is Castor, with Amphiaraus, the son of Oicles, next to whom is Hippothous, the son of Cercyon, son of Agamedes, son of Symphalus. The last figure is Perithous. . . . The ancient image of Athena Alea, and with it the tusks of the Calydonian boar, were carried away by the Roman emperor Augustus after his defeat of Antonius and his allies, among whom were all the Arcadians except the Mantineans. . . . The image of Athena Alea at Rome is as you enter the Forum made by Augustus. Here then it has been set up, made throughout of ivory, the work of Endoeus. Those in charge of the curiosities say that one of the boar's tusks has broken off; the remaining one is kept in the gardens of the emperor, in a sanctuary of Dionysus, and is about half a fathom long. . . . Of the votive offerings in the temple [of Athena Alea at Tegea] these are the most notable. There is the hide of the Calydonian boar, rotted by age and by now altogether without bristles.

[From the description of the paintings of Polygnotus at Delphi:] Meleager, the son of Oeneus, is higher up in the picture than Ajax, the son of Oileus, and he seems to be looking at Ajax. Palamades has no beard, but the others have. As to the death of Meleager, Homer says that the Fury heard the curses of Althaea, and that this was the cause of Meleager's death. But the poem Eoeae, as it is called, and the Minyad agree in giving a different account. For these poems say that Apollo helped the Curetes against the Aetolians, and that Meleager was killed by Apollo. The story about the brand, how it was given by the Fates to Althaea, how Meleager was not to die before the brand was consumed by fire, and how Althaea burnt it up in a passion—this story was first made the subject of a drama by Phrynichus, the son of Polyphradmon, in his *Pleuronian Women*:

For chill doom
He escaped not, but a swift flame consumed him,
As the brand was destroyed by his terrible mother, contriver of evil.

However, it appears that Phrynichus did not elaborate the story as
a man would his own invention, but only touched on it as one already in the mouths of everybody in Greece.

SCHOLIA ON THE ILIAD (BYZANTINE PERIOD) [17]

[*Oeneus*:] Oeneus, king of Aetolia, sacrificing the first fruits of the
yearly harvests to the gods, neglected Artemis alone. The goddess,
being angered, sent upon the Aetolians a great monster of a boar,
which set about destroying not only the land but its inhabitants. The
people of Calydon and of Pleuron went out against it. Meleager, son
of Oeneus, being the first to hit the mark, and obtaining the first
spoils of the boar as a prize, gave the head and the hide to Atalanta
by reason for his love for her. For she went with them to the hunt.
But the sons of Thestius, brothers of Meleager's mother Althaea,
being angered at this, plotted against Meleager; but he, being fore-
warned, slew some of them, and made preparations for others to be
put to flight. Wherefore the people of Pleuron made war upon the
people of Calydon. Meleager at first being angered against his
mother came not to the help of his country; but when the city was
already being plundered, he was persuaded by Cleopatra his wife,
and, going forth, slew some of them, and pursuing others forced
them in their flight to rush thence over precipices. But Althaea,
being wroth with her son, burnt the brand that was given her by the
Fates: and it was destined that of that burning Meleager himself
should die. And Althaea, repenting her of the destruction of her son,
slew herself.

[*his head and shaggy hide*:] For they were together to be given
as prize to him who first struck the boar. Meleager, obtaining them,
gave them to Atalanta, daughter of Iasius, by race an Arcadian;

---

[17] On Book IX, line 534 and line 548. Translated by W. R. Rutland (see
Bibliography).

the kinsmen of Meleager's mother, laying an ambush for her, took away the gifts from the maiden; whereat, being wroth, Meleager slew them. And Althaea, the mother of Meleager, in grief because of her brothers, burnt the brand that was given her of the Fates, it being that which maintained the life of Meleager, whereby Meleager was destroyed with it. [Translated by W.R. Rutland.]

Appendix 10

Swinburne's Greece

EUXINE SEA
BOSPHORUS
THRACE
PROPONTIS
CHERSONESE
Lampsacus
MT. DINDYMUS
HELLESPONT
Troy
PHRYGIA
MT. IDA
LESBOS
Mitylene
AEGEAN SEA
NAXOS
Halikarnassos
TE
SEA

Index of Proper Names

Index of Titles and First Lines